The experience of human suffering has perplexed minds ever since the fall. For Christians, the question of suffering rises to a new level of importance because of our belief in the sovereignty of our loving and merciful God. In *Suffering and the Sovereignty of God*, John Piper and friends tackle some of the hardest and most significant issues of Christian concern, producing one of the most honest, faithful, and helpful volumes ever made available to thinking Christians. It is filled with pastoral wisdom, theological conviction, biblical insight, and spiritual counsel. This book answers one of the greatest needs of our times—to affirm the sovereignty of God and to ponder the meaning of human suffering. We need this book.

—R. ALBERT MOHLER, JR.
President, The Southern Baptist Theological Seminary
Louisville, Kentucky

For all who don't live a charmed life, for all who have given themselves to the point of exhaustion, for all who have been betrayed by pious back-stabbers, for all who wonder if they can even go on, *Suffering and the Sovereignty of God* will be green pastures and deep, still waters. The wisdom of this book stands forth like a kind friend, pointing us to the Crucified and Triumphant One, who says, "Come to me, all who labor and are heavy laden, and I will give you rest."

—RAYMOND C. ORTLUND, JR.
Senior Pastor, Christ Presbyterian Church
Nashville, Tennessee

With courage and honesty, this book squarely faces some of the toughest challenges for Christians. The writers combine utter faithfulness to Scripture with unassuming authenticity. They write as people whose minds have been shaped by God's Word and whose lives have been formed in the crucible of suffering. This book will challenge you to believe that God is truly sovereign, not just in the safe haven of theological inquiry, but also in the painful messiness of real life. You will be encouraged to live more consistently by God's grace and for his glory.

—MARK D. ROBERTS
Senior Pastor, Irvine Presbyterian Church
Irvine, California

Most Christians readily rationalize away God's role in personal and human suffering. In an effort to protect God's moral nature and his being the source of only that which is good, an understanding of his sovereignty is diminished as well as the glory he derives when we recognize his victory over all that is evil. John Piper and Justin Taylor have collaborated with a number of other writers to communicate a refreshing perspective on *Suffering and the Sovereignty of God*. This is not another theological volume that complicates what appears to be an irreconcilable paradox; it is a book that grows out of practical experience and applies Scripture to a realistic world where we all live.

—JERRY RANKIN
President, Southern Baptist International Mission Board

The Devil may inflict scars.
But only as God allows.

Some scars are self-inflicted

Death leaves a scar

Suffering and the Sovereignty of God

John Piper | Justin Taylor

EDITORS

:: CROSSWAY

WHEATON, ILLINOIS

Library of Congress Cataloging-in-Publication Data
Suffering and the Sovereignty of God / edited by John Piper and
Justin Taylor.
  p. cm.
 Includes index.
 ISBN 13: 978-1-58134-809-5 (tpb)
 ISBN 10: 1-58134-809-6 (tpb)
  1. Suffering—religious aspects—Christianity. 2. Providence and
government of God. 3.God—omnipotence. 4. Theodicy. I. Piper, John,
1946– . II. Taylor, Justin, 1976– .
BT732.7.S835 2006
231'.8—dc22   2006018431

Crossway is a publishing ministry of Good News Publishers.

ML		21	20	19	18	17	16	15	14	13	12	11
17	16	15	14	13	12	11	10	9	8	7		

To
The white-robed army of martyrs
". . . until the number of their fellow servants and
their brothers should be complete."

Contents

Appendices

Contributors

Carl F. Ellis, Jr. President, Project Joseph, Chattanooga, Tennessee

John Piper. Pastor for preaching and vision, Bethlehem Baptist Church, Minneapolis, Minnesota

David Powlison. Counselor and teacher, Christian Counseling and Education Foundation, Glenside, Pennsylvania

Stephen F. Saint. Founder, I-TEC (Indigenous People's Technology and Education Center), Dunnellon, Florida

Dustin Shramek. Cross cultural peacemaker, the Middle East and Minnesota

Joni Eareckson Tada. Founder and chief executive officer, Joni and Friends, Agoura Hills, California

Mark R. Talbot. Associate professor of philosophy, Wheaton College, Wheaton, Illinois

Justin Taylor. ESV Bible project manager and associate publisher, Crossway Books, Wheaton, Illinois

Introduction

JUSTIN TAYLOR

Most of the chapters in this book originated as talks given at the 2005 Desiring God National Conference on "Suffering and the Sovereignty of God." The contributors have graciously agreed to convert their oral presentations into written chapters in order to serve a wider audience.

All of the authors of this volume have addressed, in one way or another, the issue of how God's sovereignty relates to human suffering. But they have done so by addressing different questions such as: In what ways is God sovereign over Satan's work? How can we be free and responsible if God ordains our choices? What is the ultimate reason that suffering exists? How does suffering help to advance the mission of the church? How should we understand the origin of ethnic-based clashes and suffering? How does God's grace enter our sufferings? Why is it good for us to meditate upon the depth and pain of severe suffering? What is the role of hope when things look utterly hopeless?

Though some very deep and difficult truths are imbedded within these pages, this is not an academic book. The authors do not write as mere theoreticians, waxing eloquent about abstract themes. No, this is a book of *applied theology*. Its theology has been forged in the furnace of affliction. Two of the contributors are paralyzed and deal with chronic pain. Two experienced the death of a parent when they were young. Two had children who died in the past few years. Two are currently battling prostate cancer. The point of mentioning this is not to portray them as victims or to elicit your sympathy, but rather to reiterate that they are fellow soldiers in the battle, fellow pilgrims on the journey. Think of them as friends who are taking the time to write to you about what God has taught them concerning his mysterious sovereignty in the midst of pain and suffering.

An Overview of the Book

Part 1 focuses most specifically on the sovereignty of God in and over suffering. In chapter 1 John Piper celebrates the biblical truth that God is sovereign over Satan's work—including Satan's delegated world rule, angels, hand in persecution, life-taking power, hand in natural disasters, sickness-causing power, use of animals and plants, temptations to sin, mind-blinding power, and spiritual bondage. In chapter 2 Mark Talbot takes up the issue of how God's will relates to our wills when we hurt each other and ourselves. If God is sovereign, why doesn't God stop such things? Talbot argues that while God never *does* evil, he does indeed *ordain* evil. He then deals with the question of how we can be free and held responsible for our choices.

Given that God is sovereign over all suffering, Part 2 asks why he allows pain. In chapter 3 John Piper argues that the ultimate biblical explanation for the existence of suffering is so that "Christ might display the greatness of the glory of the grace of God by suffering in himself to overcome our suffering." In chapter 4 Piper suggests six ways that the mission of the church is advanced through suffering: our faith and holiness are deepened, our cup increases, others are made bold, Christ's afflictions are filled up, the missionary command to "go" is enforced, and the supremacy of Christ is manifested.

Steve Saint is often identified with suffering, but he points out in chapter 5 that suffering is relative. While we in the West expend vast resources to avoid suffering, we fail to realize that suffering people want to be ministered to by those who have themselves suffered. Saint recounts two deeply painful chapters of his life: the death of his father and the death of his daughter. He believes that God planned both deaths, and that through this suffering God has worked—and is working— untold blessings and is advancing the fulfillment of the Great Commission.

In chapter 6 Carl Ellis helps us to think through ethnic-based suffering under the sovereignty of God. He argues that the body of Christ needs to be a prophetic voice in our culture, developing a more radical understanding of ethnic-based suffering and modeling the true meaning of ethnicity unto the glory of God. In working toward this end, he covers the origin of suffering; the mystery of suffering; the basis of suffering; God's awareness of suffering; our response to suffering; and the people of God and suffering.

The final major section of this book, Part 3, looks at the grace of God in our suffering. In chapter 7 David Powlison discusses not the general *topic* of God and suffering, but rather how God's grace meets you in *your* sufferings. He suggests thinking of his chapter as a workshop, encouraging you to jot notes and write in the margin, working out the principles. Powlison then walks us through each stanza of the great hymn "How Firm a Foundation," teaching us to listen to God's grace speaking to us through its words.

"Weeping may tarry for the night, but joy comes with the morning" (Ps. 30:5). That's the verse behind chapter 8, written by Dustin Shramek. We can wait for joy that comes in the morning because of faith in our good and sovereign God. But we must not forget that the night is often long and dark, and the weeping is often uncontrollable. Through an examination of Psalm 88—the one psalm that ends without a note of hope—Shramek argues that the Bible presupposes the post-fall normality of deep pain. Minimizing the pain of suffering is a failure to love others and a failure to honor God. Only after we sense the severity of suffering can we truly understand why Paul contrasts "slight momentary affliction" with the "weight of glory beyond all comparison" (2 Cor. 4:17).

Chapter 9, by Joni Eareckson Tada, centers around the themes of meeting suffering and joy on God's terms—not ours. She recalls a famous line from *The Shawshank Redemption* where Andy Dufresne says: "Hope is a good thing, maybe the best of things. And no good thing ever dies." But she acknowledges that hope is often hard to come by, recounting the suffering of her friends and her own pain as a quadriplegic. Though Joni longs for the new heavens and the new earth when she will be able to stand on her resurrected legs next to King Jesus, she also plans to thank him for "the bruising of the blessing of that wheelchair," for without it she would have missed untold blessings in her life—even amidst the pain. She ends with a hope-filled, stirring vision of that Day when we will experience Trinitarian fellowship in all its glory.

At the end of this book we have included two appendices. The first, entitled "Don't Waste Your Cancer," began as a meditation by John Piper on the eve of his prostate surgery. A few weeks later, David

Powlison learned that he too had prostate cancer, and he added his own reflections the morning after his diagnosis. Finally, we have included an interview that I conducted with John Piper at the "Suffering and the Sovereignty of God" conference, where I was able to ask him some questions about his own theological journey as well as some of the more difficult issues surrounding the pain of suffering.

Our Prayer

Our prayer is not that this book would make the bestseller list or receive acclaim and praise. Rather, our prayer is that God would direct the right readers—in accordance with his sovereign purposes—to its pages, and that he would change all of us so that we might experience more grace and hope. Perhaps your suffering has been so severe and relentless that you are on the verge of losing all hope. Or at the other end of the spectrum, perhaps you have a slightly guilty feeling because, though you see suffering all around, you have experienced very little suffering directly. Perhaps you are working through some of the deep theological questions surrounding this issue. Or perhaps you simply need to read that others have suffered too—and survived with their faith intact.

While the contributors to this book are all united in their theology of God's sovereignty over suffering, they each approach the topic from a different angle. To use an analogy, there is one diamond, but it can be viewed from multiple perspectives. You don't need to read this book cover to cover. We encourage you to start with a section that addresses your most pressing questions.

Whatever your situation, we pray that God would use this book to show you a little more of himself and help you to understand more about his sovereignty over and in our suffering.

Part 1:
The Sovereignty of God in Suffering

CHAPTER 1

Suffering and the Sovereignty of God: Ten Aspects of God's Sovereignty Over Suffering and Satan's Hand in It

JOHN PIPER

The impetus for this book comes from the ultimate reality of God as the supreme value in and above the universe. God is absolute and eternal and infinite. Everything else and everybody else is dependent and finite and contingent. God himself is the great supreme value. Everything else that has any value has it by connection to God. God is supreme in all things. He has all authority, all power, all wisdom—and he is all good "to those who wait for him, to the soul who seeks him" (Lam. 3:25). And his name, as Creator and Redeemer and Ruler of all, is Jesus Christ.

In the last few years, 9/11, tsunamis, Katrina, and ten thousand personal losses have helped us discover how little the American church is rooted in this truth. David Wells, in his new book, *Above All Earthly Pow'rs: Christ in a Postmodern World*, says it like this:

> This moment of tragedy and evil [referring to 9/11] shone its own light
> on the Church and what we came to see was not a happy sight. For
> what has become conspicuous by its scarcity, and not least in the evan-
> gelical corner of it, is a spiritual *gravitas*, one which could match the
> depth of horrendous evil and address issues of such seriousness.
> Evangelicalism, now much absorbed by the arts and tricks of market-
> ing, is simply not very serious anymore.[1]

---

[1] David Wells, *Above All Earthly Pow'rs: Christ in a Postmodern World* (Grand Rapids, Mich.: Eerdmans, 2005), 4.

In other words, our vision of God in relation to evil and suffering was shown to be frivolous. The church has not been spending its energy to go deep with the unfathomable God of the Bible. Against the overwhelming weight and seriousness of the Bible, much of the church is choosing, at this very moment, to become more light and shallow and entertainment-oriented, and therefore successful in its irrelevance to massive suffering and evil. The popular God of fun-church is simply too small and too affable to hold a hurricane in his hand. The biblical categories of God's sovereignty lie like land mines in the pages of the Bible waiting for someone to seriously open the book. They don't kill, but they do explode trivial notions of the Almighty.

So my prayer for this book is that God would stand forth and reassert his Creator-rights in our lives, and show us his crucified and risen Son who has all authority in heaven and on earth, and waken in us the strongest faith in the supremacy of Christ, and the deepest comforts in suffering, and the sweetest fellowship with Jesus that we have ever known.

The contributors to this volume have all suffered, some more visibly than others. You don't need to know the details. Suffice it to say that none of them is dealing with a theoretical issue in this book. They live in the world of pain and loss where you live. They are aware that some people reading this book are dying. There are people who love those who are dying; people who live with chronic pain; people who have just lost one of the most precious persons in their life; people who do not believe in the goodness of God—or in God at all—who count this book their one last effort to see if the gospel is real. People who are about to enter a time of suffering in their life for which they are totally unprepared.

These authors are not naïve about life or about who you are. We are glad you are reading this book—all of you. And we pray that you will never be the same again.

The approach I am going to take in this chapter is not to solve any problem directly, but to celebrate the sovereignty of God over Satan and his sovereignty over all the evils that Satan has a hand in. My conviction is that letting God speak his word will awaken worship—like Job's—and worship will shape our hearts to understand whatever measure of God's mystery he wills for us to know. What follows is a celebration of "Ten

Aspects of God's Sovereignty Over Suffering and Satan's Hand in It." And what I mean in this chapter when I say that God is sovereign is not merely that God has the *power and right* to govern all things, but that he *does* govern all things, for his own wise and holy purposes.

1. Let Us Celebrate That God Is Sovereign Over Satan's Delegated World Rule

Satan is sometimes called in the Bible "the ruler of this world" (John 12:31; 14:30; 16:11), or "the god of this world" (2 Cor. 4:4), or "the prince of the power of the air" (Eph. 2:2), or a "cosmic power over this present darkness" (Eph. 6:12). This means that we should probably take him seriously when we read in Luke 4:5-7 that "the devil took [Jesus] up and showed him all the kingdoms of the world in a moment of time, and said to him, 'To you I will give all this authority and their glory, for it has been delivered to me, and I give it to whom I will. If you, then, will worship me, it will all be yours.'"

And of course that is strictly true: if the sovereign of the universe bows in worshipful submission to anyone, that one becomes the sovereign of the universe. But Satan's claim that he can give the authority and glory of world kingdoms to whomever he wills is a half truth. No doubt he does play havoc in the world by maneuvering a Stalin or a Hitler or an Idi Amin or a Bloody Mary or a Saddam Hussein into murderous power. But he does this only at God's permission and within God's appointed limits.

This is made clear over and over again in the Bible. For example, Daniel 2:20-21: "Daniel answered and said: 'Blessed be the name of God forever and ever, to whom belong wisdom and might. He changes times and seasons; he removes kings and sets up kings'"; and Daniel 4:17: "The Most High rules the kingdom of men and gives it to whom he will." When the kings are in their God-appointed place, with or without Satan's agency, they are in the sway of God's sovereign will, as Proverbs 21:1 says: "The king's heart is a stream of water in the hand of the LORD; he turns it wherever he will."

Evil nations rise and set themselves against the Almighty. "The kings of the earth set themselves, and the rulers take counsel together, against the LORD and against his anointed, saying, 'Let us burst their bonds apart and cast away their cords from us.' He who sits in the heavens laughs; the Lord holds them in derision" (Ps. 2:2-4). Do they think that their sin and evil and rebellion against him can thwart the counsel of the Lord? Psalm 33:10-11 answers, "The LORD brings the counsel of the nations to nothing; he frustrates the plans of the peoples. The counsel of the LORD stands forever, the plans of his heart to all generations."

God is sovereign over the nations and over all their rulers and all the satanic power behind them. They do not move without his permission, and they do not move outside his sovereign plan.

2. Let Us Celebrate That God Is Sovereign Over Satan's Angels (Demons, Evil Spirits)

Satan has thousands of cohorts in supernatural evil. They are called "demons" (Matt. 8:31; James 2:19), or "evil spirits" (Luke 7:21), or "unclean spirits" (Matt. 10:1), or "the devil and his angels" (Matt. 25:41). We get a tiny glimpse into demonic warfare in Daniel 10 where the angel who is sent in response to Daniel's prayer says, "The prince of the kingdom of Persia withstood me twenty-one days, but Michael, one of the chief princes, came to help me" (Dan. 10:13). So apparently the demon, or evil spirit, over Persia fought against the angel sent to help Daniel, and a greater angel, Michael, came to his aid.

But the Bible leaves us with no doubt as to who is in charge in all these skirmishes. Martin Luther got it right:

> And though this world, with devils filled,
> Should threaten to undo us,
> We will not fear, for God hath willed
> His truth to triumph through us.
> The prince of darkness grim,
> We tremble not for him;
> His rage we can endure,
> For lo! his doom is sure;
> One little word will fell him.[2]

We see glimpses of those little words at work, for example, when Jesus comes up against thousands of demons in Matthew 8:29-32. They

---

[2] Martin Luther, "A Mighty Fortress Is Our God" (1529).

were possessing a man and making him insane. The demons cry out, "What have you to do with us, O Son of God? Have you come here to torment us before the time?" (They know a time is set for their final destruction.) And Jesus spoke to them *one little word*: "Go," and they came out of the man. There is no question who is sovereign in this battle. The people had seen this before and were amazed and said, "He commands even the unclean spirits, and they obey him" (Mark 1:27). They *obey* him. As for Satan: "We tremble not for him; his rage we can endure." But as for Christ: even though they slay him, they always must obey him! God is sovereign over Satan's angels.

3. Let Us Celebrate That God Is Sovereign Over Satan's Hand in Persecution

The apostle Peter describes the suffering of Christians like this: "Your adversary the devil prowls around like a roaring lion, seeking someone to devour. Resist him, firm in your faith, knowing that the same kinds of suffering are being experienced by your brotherhood throughout the world" (1 Pet. 5:8-9). So the sufferings of persecution are like the jaws of a satanic lion trying to consume and destroy the faith of believers in Christ.

But do these Christians suffer in Satan's jaws of persecution apart from the sovereign will of God? When Satan crushes Christians in the jaws of their own private Calvary, does God not govern those jaws for the good of his precious child? Listen to Peter's answer in 1 Peter 3:17: "It is better to suffer for doing good, *if that should be God's will*, than for doing evil." In other words, if God wills that we suffer for doing good, we will suffer. And if he does not will that we suffer for doing good, we will not. The lion does not have the last say. God does.

The night Jesus was arrested, satanic power was in full force (Luke 22:3, 31). And Jesus spoke into that situation one of his most sovereign words. He said to those who came to arrest him in the dark: "Have you come out as against a robber, with swords and clubs? When I was with you day after day in the temple, you did not lay hands on me. But *this is your hour, and the power of darkness*" (Luke 22:52-53). The jaws of the lion close on me tonight no sooner and no later than my Father planned. "No one takes [my life] from me, but I lay it down of my own accord" (John 10:18). Boast not yourself over the hand that made you, Satan. You have one hour. What you do, do quickly. God is sovereign over Satan's hand in persecution.

4. Let Us Celebrate That God Is Sovereign Over Satan's Life-Taking Power

The Bible does not take lightly or minimize the power of Satan to kill people, including Christians. Jesus said in John 8:44, "You are of your father the devil, and your will is to do your father's desires. He was a murderer from the beginning." John tells us, in fact, that he does indeed take the lives of faithful Christians. Revelation 2:10, "Do not fear what you are about to suffer. Behold, the devil is about to throw some of you into prison, that you may be tested, and for ten days you will have tribulation. *Be faithful unto death*, and I will give you the crown of life."

Is God then not the Lord of life and death? He is. None lives and none dies but by God's sovereign decree. "See now that I, even I, am he, and there is no god beside me; I kill and I make alive; I wound and I heal; and there is none that can deliver out of my hand" (Deut. 32:39). There is no god, no demon, no Satan that can snatch to death any person that God wills to live (see 1 Sam. 2:6).

James, the brother of Jesus, says this in a stunning way in James 4:13-16:

> Come now, you who say, "Today or tomorrow we will go into such and such a town and spend a year there and trade and make a profit"—yet you do not know what tomorrow will bring. What is your life? For you are a mist that appears for a little time and then vanishes. Instead you ought to say, "*If the Lord wills, we will live* and do this or that." As it is, you boast in your arrogance. All such boasting is evil.

If the Lord wills, we will live. And if he doesn't, we will die. God, not Satan, makes the final call. Our lives are ultimately in his hands, not Satan's. God is sovereign over Satan's life-taking power.

5. Let Us Celebrate That God Is Sovereign Over Satan's Hand in Natural Disasters

Hurricanes, tsunamis, tornadoes, earthquakes, blistering heat, deadly cold, drought, flood, famine. When Satan approached God in the first chapter of Job, he challenged God, "Stretch out your hand and touch all that he has, and he will curse you to your face" (v. 11). Then the Lord said to Satan, "Behold, all that he has is in your hand. Only against him do not stretch out your hand" (v. 12).

The result was two human atrocities and two natural disasters. One of the disasters is reported to Job in verse 16: "The fire of God fell from heaven [probably lightning] and burned up the sheep and the servants and consumed them, and I alone have escaped to tell you." And then the worst report of all in verses 18-19, "Your sons and daughters were eating and drinking wine in their oldest brother's house, and behold, a great wind came across the wilderness and struck the four corners of the house, and it fell upon the young people, and they are dead."

Even though God had loosened the leash of Satan to do this, it is not what Job focused on. "Job arose and tore his robe and shaved his head and fell on the ground and worshiped. And he said, 'Naked I came from my mother's womb, and naked shall I return. The LORD gave, and the LORD has taken away; blessed be the name of the LORD'" (Job 1:20-21). And the inspired writer added: "In all this Job did not sin or charge God with wrong."

Job had discovered with many of you that it is small comfort to focus on the freedom of Satan to destroy. In the academic classroom and in the apologetics discussion, the agency of Satan in our suffering may lift a little the burden of God's sovereignty for some; but for others, like Job, there is more security and more relief and more hope and more support and more glorious truth in despising Satan's hateful hand and looking straight past him to God for the cause and for his mercy.

Elihu helped Job see this mercy in Job 37:10-14. He said:

By the breath of God ice is given, and the broad waters are frozen fast. He loads the thick cloud with moisture; the clouds scatter his lightning. They turn around and around by his guidance, to accomplish *all that he commands them* on the face of the habitable world. Whether *for*

correction or *for his land* or *for love*, he causes it to happen. Hear this,
O Job; stop and consider the wondrous works of God.

Job's first impulses in chapter 1 were exactly right. When James
wrote in the New Testament about the purpose of the book of Job, this
is what he said: "You have heard of the steadfastness of Job, and you
have seen the purpose of the Lord, how the Lord is compassionate and
merciful" (James 5:11).

God, not Satan, is the final ruler of wind—and the waves. Jesus
woke from sleep and, with absolute sovereignty, which he had from all
eternity and has this very moment, said, "'Peace! Be still!' And the wind
ceased, and there was a great calm" (Mark 4:39; see Ps. 135:5-7;
148:7). Satan is real and terrible. All his designs are hateful. But he is
not sovereign. God is. And when Satan went out to do Job harm, Job
was right to worship with the words "The LORD gave, and the LORD has
taken away; blessed be the name of the LORD."

> There's not a plant or flower below,
>   But makes Thy glories known;
> And clouds arise, and tempests blow,
>   By order from Thy throne.[3]

6. Let Us Celebrate That God Is Sovereign Over Satan's Sickness-Causing Power

The Bible is vivid with the truth that Satan can cause disease. Acts 10:38
says that Jesus "went about doing good and healing all who were
oppressed by the devil, for God was with him." The devil had oppressed
people with sickness. In Luke 13 Jesus finds a woman who had been bent
over, unable to stand up for eighteen years. He heals her on the Sabbath,
and in response to the criticism of the synagogue ruler he says, "Ought
not this woman, a daughter of Abraham *whom Satan bound for eighteen years*, be loosed from this bond on the Sabbath day?" (v. 16). There
is no doubt that Satan causes much disease.

This is why Christ's healings are a sign of the in-breaking of the
kingdom of God and its final victory over all disease and all the works

---

[3] Isaac Watts, "I Sing the Mighty Power of God" (1715).

of Satan. It is right and good to pray for healing. God has purchased it in the death of his Son, with all the other blessings of grace, for all his children (Isa. 53:5). But he has not promised that we get the whole inheritance in this life. And *he* decides how much. We pray, and we trust his answer. If you ask your Father for bread, he will not give you a stone. If you ask him for a fish, he will not give you a serpent (see Matt. 7:9-10). It may not be bread. And it may not be a fish. But it will be good for you. That is what he promises (Rom. 8:28).

But beware lest anyone say that Satan is sovereign in our diseases. He is not. When Satan went to God a second time in the book of Job, God gave him permission this time to strike Job's body. Then "Satan went out from the presence of the LORD and smote Job with sore boils from the sole of his foot to the crown of his head" (Job 2:7, AT). When Job's wife despaired and said, "Curse God and die" (2:9)," Job responded exactly as he did before. He looked past the finite cause of Satan to the ultimate cause of God and said, "Shall we receive good from God, and shall we not accept evil?" (2:10, AT).

And lest we attribute error or irreverence to Job, the writer closes the book in the last chapter by referring to Job's terrible suffering like this: "Then came to him all his brothers and sisters. . . . and comforted him for all the evil that the LORD had brought upon him" (42:11). Satan is real and full of hate, but he is not sovereign in sickness. God will not give him even that tribute. As he says to Moses at the burning bush, "Who has made man's mouth? Who makes him mute, or deaf, or seeing, or blind? Is it not I, the LORD?" (Ex. 4:11; see also 2 Cor. 12:7-9).

7. Let Us Celebrate That God Is Sovereign Over Satan's Use of Animals and Plants

The imagery of Satan as a lion in 1 Peter 5:8 and as a "great dragon" in Revelation 12:9 and as the "serpent of old" in Genesis 3 simply makes us aware that in his destructive work Satan can, and no doubt does, employ animals and plants—from the lion in the Coliseum, to the black fly that causes river blindness, to the birds that carry the avian flu virus, to the pit bull that attacks a child, to the bacteria in your belly that doctors Barry Marshall and Robin Warren recently discovered cause ulcers (winning for them the Nobel Prize in medicine). If Satan can kill and cause disease, no doubt he has at his disposal many large and micro-scopic plants and animals.

But he cannot make them do what God forbids them to do. From the giant Leviathan that God made to sport in the sea (Ps. 104:26) to the tiny gnats that he summoned over the land of Egypt (Ex. 8:16-17), God commands the world of animals and plants. The most vivid demon-strations of it are in the book of Jonah. "The LORD appointed a great fish to swallow up Jonah" (Jonah 1:17). And it did exactly as it had been appointed. "And the LORD spoke to the fish, and it vomited Jonah out upon the dry land" (Jonah 2:10). "Now the LORD God appointed a plant and made it come up over Jonah" (Jonah 4:6). "But when dawn came up the next day, God appointed a worm that attacked the plant, so that it withered" (Jonah 4:7).

Fish, plant, worm—all appointed, all obedient. Satan can have a hand here, but he is not sovereign. God is.

8. Let Us Celebrate That God Is Sovereign Over Satan's Temptations to Sin

Much of our suffering comes from the sins of others against us and from our own sins. Satan is called in the Bible "the tempter" (Matt. 4:3; 1 Thess. 3:5). This was the origin on earth of all the misery that we know—Satan tempted Eve to sin, and sin brought with it the curse of God on the natural order (Gen. 3:14-19; Rom. 8:21-23). Since that time Satan has been tempting all human beings to do what will hurt them-selves and others.

But the most famous temptations in the Bible do not portray Satan as sovereign in his tempting work. The Bible tells us in Luke 22:3-4 that "Satan entered into Judas called Iscariot. . . . He went away and con-ferred with the chief priests and officers how he might betray him to them." But Luke tells us that the betrayal of Jesus by Judas was the ful-fillment of Scripture: "The Scripture had to be fulfilled, which the Holy Spirit spoke beforehand by the mouth of David concerning Judas" (Acts 1:16). And therefore Peter said that Jesus was "delivered up according to the definite plan and foreknowledge of God" (Acts 2:23). As with Job, the Lord gave, and the Lord has taken away—the life of his Son, Jesus Christ. Satan was not in charge of the crucifixion of Christ. God was.

Even more famous than the temptation of Judas is the temptation of Peter. We usually think of Peter's three denials, not his temptation. But Jesus says something to Peter in Luke 22:31-32 that makes plain Satan is at work here but that he is not sovereign: "Simon, Simon, behold, Satan demanded to have you, that he might sift you like wheat, but I have prayed for you that your faith may not fail. And *when* you have turned again [not: *if* you turn], strengthen your brothers." Again, as with Job, Satan seeks to destroy Peter's faith. God gives Satan leash, but Jesus intercedes for Peter, and says with complete sovereignty, "I have prayed for you. You will fall, but not utterly. When you repent and turn back— not *if* you turn back—strengthen your brothers."

Satan is not sovereign in the temptations of Judas or Peter or you or those you love. God is.

9. Let Us Celebrate That God Is Sovereign Over Satan's Mind-Blinding Power

The worst suffering of all is the everlasting suffering of hell. Satan is doomed to experience that suffering. Revelation 20:10 says, "The devil who had deceived them was thrown into the lake of fire and sulfur where the beast and the false prophet were, and they will be tormented day and night forever and ever." Satan's aim is to take as many there with him as he can. To do that, he must keep people blind to the gospel of Jesus Christ, because the gospel "is the power of God for salvation to everyone who believes" (Rom. 1:16). No one goes to hell who is justified by the blood of Christ. "Since, therefore, we have now been justified by his blood, much more shall we be saved by him from the wrath of God" (Rom. 5:9). Only those who fail to embrace the wrath-absorbing substitutionary work of Christ will suffer the wrath of God.

Therefore, Paul says in 2 Corinthians 4:4, "In their case the god of this world [Satan] has blinded the minds of the unbelievers, to keep them from seeing the light of the gospel of the glory of Christ, who is the image of God." This blinding is the most deadly weapon in the arsenal of Satan. If he succeeds with a person, the suffering will be endless.

But at this most critical point Satan is not sovereign, God is. And oh, how thankful we should be! Two verses later in 2 Corinthians 4:6 Paul describes God's blindness-removing power over against Satan's blinding power. "For God, who said, 'Let light shine out of darkness,' has shone in our hearts to give the light of the knowledge of the glory of God in the face of Jesus Christ." The comparison is between God's creating light at the beginning of the world and God's creating light in the darkened human heart. With total sovereignty God said at the beginning and at your new birth, "Let there be light." And there was light.

We were dead in our trespasses and sins, but in great mercy God made us alive together with Christ (Eph. 2:5). We were blind and spiritually dead. We saw nothing compelling or beautiful in the gospel. It was foolishness to us (1 Cor. 1:18, 23). But God spoke with sovereign Creator authority, and his word created life and spiritual sight, and we saw the glory of Christ in the gospel and believed. Satan is a terrible enemy of the gospel. But he is not sovereign. God is. This is the reason that any of us is saved.

10. Let Us Celebrate That God Is Sovereign Over Satan's Spiritual Bondage

Satan enslaves people in two ways. One way is with the misery and suffering that comes from making us think there is no good God worth trusting. The other way is with pleasure and prosperity, making us think we have all we need so that God is irrelevant. To be freed from this bondage we must repent. We must confess that God is good and trustworthy. We must confess that the pleasures and prosperity of life do not compare to the worth of God. But Satan hates this repentance and does all he can to prevent it. That is his bondage.

But when God chooses to overcome our rebellion and Satan's resistance, nothing can stop him. And when God overcomes him and us, we repent and Satan's power is broken. Here it is in 2 Timothy 2:24-26:

> And the Lord's servant must not be quarrelsome but kind to everyone, able to teach, patiently enduring evil, correcting his opponents with gentleness. God may perhaps *grant them repentance* leading to a knowledge of the truth, and they may *escape from the snare of the devil*, after being captured by him to do his will.

Satan is not sovereign over his captives. God is. When God grants repentance, we are set free from the snare of the devil, and we spend our days celebrating our liberation and spreading it to others.

The One and Only Sovereign

The evil and suffering in this world are greater than any of us can comprehend. But evil and suffering are not ultimate. God is. Satan, the great lover of evil and suffering, is not sovereign. God is.

> He does according to his will among the host of heaven and among the inhabitants of the earth; and none can stay his hand or say to him, "What have you done?" (Dan. 4:35)

> [He declares] the end from the beginning and from ancient times things not yet done, saying, "My counsel shall stand, and I will accomplish all my purpose." (Isa. 46:10)

> Who has spoken and it came to pass, unless the Lord has commanded it? Is it not from the mouth of the Most High that good and bad come? (Lam. 3:37-38; see Amos 3:6)

> Many are the plans in the mind of a man, but it is the purpose of the LORD that will stand. (Prov. 19:21; see 16:9)

> The lot is cast into the lap, but its every decision is from the LORD. (Prov. 16:33)

Therefore, "If God is for us, who can be against us? . . . Who shall separate us from the love of Christ? Shall tribulation, or distress, or persecution, or famine, or nakedness, or danger, or sword? As it is written, 'For your sake we are being killed all the day long; we are regarded as sheep to be slaughtered.' No, in all these things we are more than conquerors through him who loved us" (Rom. 8:31, 35-37).

> God moves in a mysterious way
> His wonders to perform;
> He plants His footsteps in the sea
> And rides upon the storm.

Deep in unfathomable mines
Of never failing skill
He treasures up His bright designs
And works His sovereign will.

Ye fearful saints, fresh courage take;
The clouds ye so much dread
Are big with mercy and shall break
In blessings on your head.

Judge not the Lord by feeble sense,
But trust Him for His grace;
Behind a frowning providence
He hides a smiling face.

His purposes will ripen fast,
Unfolding every hour;
The bud may have a bitter taste,
But sweet will be the flower.

Blind unbelief is sure to err
And scan His work in vain;
God is His own interpreter,
And He will make it plain.[4]

---

[4] William Cowper, "God Moves in a Mysterious Way" (1774).

CHAPTER 2

"All the Good That Is Ours in Christ": Seeing God's Gracious Hand in the Hurts Others Do to Us

MARK R. TALBOT

And we know that God causes all things to work together for good to those who love God, to those who are called according to His purpose.

ROMANS 8:28 (NASB)

In *Night,* his memoir of life in the death camps of Birkenau and Auschwitz, Nobel Peace Prize winner Elie Wiesel struggles to convey the experiences that consumed the devout faith of an earnestly pious Jewish boy in the fires of the incomprehensible horrors of Nazi inhumanity.[1] Starting from the unsuspecting innocence of his early adolescence, Wiesel chronicles the pathway from its sunny security to the spiritual night that provoked him to write words like these:

> [A]s the train stopped, . . . we saw flames rising from a tall chimney into a black sky. . . . We stared at the flames in the darkness. A wretched stench floated in the air. Abruptly, our [cattle car's] doors opened. . . .
> "Everybody out! Leave everything inside. Hurry up!"
> We jumped out. . . . In front of us, those flames. In the air, the

---

[1] A word to my readers about how to approach this piece and others like it: We should never expect to understand important but difficult ideas in one reading. Understanding difficult ideas always requires perseverance and rereading. Good writers help you to ask new questions each time you read a piece that later readings should help you to answer. I have tried to write this piece so that you can understand it without reading the footnotes. So read it without reading them until it starts to make sense, and then go back through it reading the footnotes, too. They are intended to make additional points that fill in and support what I am saying in the body of the text. Above all, don't get too discouraged! You don't have to understand a text like this in a week or a month or even in a year. So keep rereading, remembering these words from Scripture, "Blessed is the one who finds wisdom, and the one who gets understanding, for the gain from her is better than gain from silver and her profit better than gold. She is more precious than jewels, and nothing you desire can compare with her. . . . She is a tree of life to those who lay hold of her; those who hold her fast are called blessed" (Prov. 3:13-15, 18). You *will* understand if you keep on trying.

smell of burning flesh. It must have been around midnight. We had arrived. In Birkenau. . . .

The SS officers gave the order.

"Form ranks of fives!" . . . [We began] to walk until we came to a crossroads. . . . Not far from us, flames, huge flames, were rising from a ditch. Something was being burned there. A truck drew close and unloaded its hold: small children. Babies! Yes, I did see this, with my own eyes . . . children thrown into the flames. . . . A little farther on, there was another, larger pit for adults.

I pinched myself: Was I still alive? Was I awake? How was it possible that men, women, and children were being burned and that the world kept silent? No. All this could not be real. A nightmare perhaps . . . Soon I would wake up with a start, my heart pounding, and find that I was back in the room of my childhood, with my books. . . .

NEVER SHALL I FORGET that night, the first night in camp, that turned my life into one long night seven times sealed.
Never shall I forget that smoke.
Never shall I forget the small faces of the children whose bodies I saw transformed into smoke under a silent sky.
Never shall I forget those flames that consumed my faith forever.
Never shall I forget the nocturnal silence that deprived me for all eternity of the desire to live.
Never shall I forget those moments that murdered my God and my soul and turned my dreams to ashes.
Never shall I forget those things, even were I condemned to live as long as God Himself.
Never.[2]

Language, as Wiesel declares, proves helpless to convey such realities. It became clear as he wrote "that it would be necessary to invent a new language" to convey these horrors adequately. For

how was one to rehabilitate . . . words betrayed and perverted by the enemy? Hunger—thirst—fear—transport—selection—fire—chimney:

---

[2] Elie Wiesel, *Night* (New York: Hill and Wang, 2006; first published in French in 1958), 28-34. In a new preface, Wiesel says of these babies:
    I did not say [in *Night*] that they *were alive*, but that was what I thought. But then I convinced myself: no, they were dead, otherwise I surely would have lost my mind. And yet fellow inmates also saw them; they *were alive* when they were thrown into the flames. Historians . . . confirmed it. (xiv)

these words all have intrinsic meaning, but in those times, they meant something else. Writing in my mother tongue . . . I would pause at every sentence, and start over and over again. . . . All the dictionary had to offer seemed meager, pale, lifeless. Was there a way to describe the last journey in sealed cattle cars, the last voyage toward the unknown? Or the discovery of a demented and glacial universe where to be inhuman was human, where disciplined, educated men in uniform came to kill, and innocent children and wary old men came to die? Or the countless separations on a single fiery night, the tearing apart of entire families, entire communities? . . . How was one to speak [of things like these] without trembling and a heart broken for all eternity?[3]

These unspeakable horrors, piled on each other, disoriented Wiesel and led him to throw off his faith. One incident stands out. Wiesel's *Oberkapo* was a Dutchman with over seven hundred prisoners under his command. He was kind to them all. "In his 'service,'" Wiesel writes,

was a young boy, a *pipel*, as they were called. This one had a delicate and beautiful face—an incredible sight in this camp. . . .

One day the power failed at the central electric plant in Buna. The Gestapo, summoned to inspect the damage, concluded that it was sabotage. They found a trail. It led to the block of the . . . *Oberkapo*. And after a search, they found a significant quantity of weapons.

The *Oberkapo* and his *pipel* were tortured, although they named no names. The *Oberkapo* disappeared, but his *pipel* was condemned to die along with two other inmates who were found with arms.

One day, as we returned from work, we saw three gallows . . . . Roll call. The SS surrounding us, machine guns aimed at us: the usual ritual. Three prisoners in chains—and, among them, the little *pipel* . . . .

The SS seemed more preoccupied, more worried, than usual. To hang a child in front of thousands of onlookers was not a small matter. The head of the camp read the verdict. All eyes were on the child. He was pale, almost calm, but he was biting his lips as he stood in the shadow of the gallows. . . .

The three condemned prisoners together stepped onto the chairs. In unison, the nooses were placed around their necks.

---

[3] Ibid., ix. These words were written in 2006 as the preface to a new translation.

"Long live liberty!" shouted the two men.

But the boy was silent.

"Where is merciful God, where is He?" someone behind me was asking.

At the signal, the three chairs were tipped over. . . .

Then came the march past the victims. The two men were no longer alive. Their tongues were hanging out, swollen and bluish. But the third rope was still moving: the child, too light, was still breathing . . .

And so he remained for more than half an hour, lingering between life and death, writhing before our eyes. And we were forced to look at him at close range. He was still alive when I passed him. His tongue was still red, his eyes not yet extinguished.

Behind me, I heard the same man asking:

"For God's sake, where is God?"

And from within me, I heard a voice answer:

"Where is He? This is where—hanging here from this gallows . . ."[4]

Rosh Hashanah came, and ten thousand gathered in the camp to bless God's name. The officiating inmate's voice rose "powerful yet broken, amid the weeping, the sobbing, the sighing of the entire 'congregation': 'All the earth and universe are God's!' . . . 'And I,'" Wiesel writes,

I, the former mystic, was thinking: Yes, man is stronger, greater than God. . . . [L]ook at these men whom You have betrayed, allowing them to be tortured, slaughtered, gassed, and burned, what do they do? They pray before You! They praise Your name!

"All of creation bears witness to the Greatness of God!"

In days gone by, Rosh Hashanah had dominated my life. I knew that my sins grieved the Almighty and so I pleaded for forgiveness. In those days, I fully believed that the salvation of the world depended on every one of my deeds, on every one of my prayers.

But now, I no longer pleaded for anything. I was no longer able to lament. On the contrary, I felt very strong. I was the accuser, God the accused. My eyes had opened and I was alone, terribly alone in a world without God, without man. Without love or mercy. I was nothing but ashes now, but I felt myself to be stronger than this Almighty to whom my life had been bound for so long. In the midst of these men assembled for prayer, I felt like an observer, a stranger.[5]

4 Ibid., 63-65.
5 Ibid., 67f.

Human brutality to other humans had shattered Wiesel's faith:

> In the beginning there was faith—which was childish; trust—which is vain; and illusion—which is dangerous.
>   We believed in God, trusted in man, and lived with the illusion that every one of us has been entrusted with a sacred spark from the Shekhinah's flame; that every one of us carries in his eyes and in his soul a reflection of God's image.

"That," Wiesel concluded, "was the source if not the cause of all our ordeals."[6]

You and I did not go through the Holocaust. We have, at most, only the dimmest notions of the horrors Wiesel experienced. Yet we may know all too well something about the multitudinous ways in which human beings hurt each other, both intentionally and unintentionally; and we may find this knowledge disorienting and shattering to our own faith. Dennis Rader, the Wichita BTK killer—"BTK" was Rader's acronym for "bind, torture, kill"—was in the news in the summer of 2005, and that fall there was a made-for-television movie of his life and terrible crimes. Why does God allow such things to happen?[7] Most of us know couples where a spouse has been unfaithful, causing immense grief to the other spouse and to their children. We know of situations where drunken drivers have veered into the wrong lanes and killed or maimed innocent people. In any large crowd, there are bound to be some people who were sexually abused as children or who have been raped. Some of us may know someone who was tortured. Indeed, things like these may have happened to us, while we were Christians, and while we were begging God to make them stop. So why didn't he?

Some of you may sometimes consider your childhoods and wish your parents had been more careful to help you to grow up as godly Christians. You are perplexed about why they didn't seem to care more about doing that. Why didn't they talk to you about how much you

---

[6] Ibid., xf. This passage is found in Wiesel's new preface, where he tells us that "these cynical musings" were the way the original Yiddish version of his book opened before his editor cut them.

[7] As we will see, "allow" is a theologically loaded term in these contexts. I shall argue that God does not merely passively *permit* such things by standing by and not stopping them. Rather, he actively wills them by *ordaining* them and then bringing them about, yet without himself thereby becoming the author of sin. As the Reformers insisted, although God is not the author of sin, he is also no mere "idle spectator" to it. (I explain the concept of *God's ordaining something* at the end of my second section.)

would regret doing some of the things you did? Some of you may be
thinking right now about distressing coworkers. Perhaps your supervi-
sor really dislikes you, treats you unfairly, and even lies to his superiors
about you, but you can't stop him. Or perhaps you are part of a
Christian organization that has some employees who teach or live in
clearly unbiblical ways, and this distresses you day after day. In that situation, you may find yourself wondering why God doesn't just move
those people out and make the organization more like what, it seems,
he must want it to be.

Then, again, some of us may be thinking about our own choices.
We may be regretting something we have said or done. And we may realize that if our circumstances had been just a little different, then everything, it seems, would be fine right now—if you hadn't had that porn
site pop up unexpectedly on your computer screen, then you might never
have gotten hooked on Internet porn; or if you hadn't bumped into that
co-worker when you were already so upset, then you wouldn't have said
those things that have now cost you your job; or if you hadn't met that
man, there would have been no chance of your having cheated on your
husband with him. So why did God allow things to go the way they did?
You may not doubt or deny your responsibility and guilt, but it still
seems that God could have kept you from falling into sin.

These are the sorts of situations that I want to consider. As my
examples suggest, we will not just consider the ways that we hurt each
other; we will also consider the ways that we hurt ourselves. How does
God's will relate to our wills when we hurt each other and ourselves?
Where is God when human beings cause themselves and others such
hurt? Why doesn't God stop such things?

Open Theism

There is one answer to these kinds of situations that I want to challenge
right away.

Many of us have heard about "open theism." Open theism was
developed to deal with these very situations. It does so by addressing
how our free wills and our responsibility are related to God's will and
the evils that we suffer and see. Open theists want to take God off the
hook for the kinds of evil that we do. They explain these evils by claim-

ing that God can't prevent them without restricting or destroying our freedom. But, they claim, God doesn't do that because he takes our freedom to be so valuable. He takes our freedom to be so valuable that he is willing to pay the price of there being all sorts of human suffering that is caused by our misuse of it.

Gregory Boyd, pastor of Woodland Hills Church in Saint Paul, Minnesota, is an open theist, and he tells this sad story in his *God of the Possible: A Biblical Introduction to the Open View of God* to drive home why:

> Several years ago after preaching a sermon on how God directs our paths, I was approached by an angry young woman (I'll call her Suzanne). Once I was able to get past the initial raging words—directed more against God than they were against me—Suzanne told me her tragic story.
>
> Suzanne had been raised in a wonderful Christian home and had from a very young age been a passionate, godly disciple of Jesus Christ. Indeed, since her early teen years, her only aspirations in life were to be a missionary to Taiwan and to marry a godly man with a similar vision with whom she could raise a godly, missionary-minded family. She had accepted the common evangelical myth that God had one right man picked out for her and so had committed herself to praying daily for this future husband. She prayed that he would acquire a similar vision to evangelize Taiwan, that he would remain faithful to the Lord and remain pure in heart, and so on.
>
> Suzanne eventually went to a Christian college and, quite miraculously, quickly met a young man who shared her vision for Taiwan. Indeed, the commonalities between them as well as all the "coincidences" that had individually led them to just that college at just that time were truly astounding. For three and a half years they courted one another, prayed together, attended church together, prepared themselves for the mission field, and fell deeply in love with one another. During their senior year, this man proposed to Suzanne; surprisingly, she did not immediately say yes to his proposal. Even though so many pieces had miraculously fallen into place, she needed to have an unequivocal confirmation in her heart that this was the man she was to marry.
>
> For several months, Suzanne and her boyfriend fasted and prayed over the matter. They consulted with their parents, their pastor, and their friends, who agreed to give the matter prayerful attention.

Everyone concluded that this marriage was indeed God's will. Before too long, God gave Suzanne the confirmation she needed. While in prayer, she was overwhelmed by a supernatural sense of joy and peace wrapped up with a very clear confirmation that this marriage was, in fact, God's design for her life.

Shortly after college, the newly married couple went away to a missionary school to prepare for their missionary career. Two years into their training, Suzanne learned to her horror that her husband was involved in an adulterous relationship with a fellow student. Her husband repented, but within several months returned to the affair. Despite intensive Christian counseling, this pattern repeated itself several times over the next three years.

During these three years, Suzanne's husband's spiritual convictions altogether disappeared. . . . He grew increasingly argumentative, hostile, and even verbally and physically abusive. In one argument toward the end of their marriage, he actually fractured Suzanne's cheekbone in a fit of rage. Soon after . . . [he] filed for divorce and moved in with his lover. Two weeks later, Suzanne discovered she was pregnant.

The whole sad ordeal left Suzanne emotionally destroyed and spiritually bankrupt. All of her dreams had crashed down on her. She felt that her life was basically over. The worst part of it, however, was not the pain her husband had inflicted on her. The worst part was how profoundly the ordeal had damaged her previously vibrant relationship with the Lord.

Understandably, Suzanne could not fathom how the Lord could respond to her lifelong prayers by setting her up with a man he *knew* would do this to her and her child. Some Christian friends had suggested that perhaps she hadn't heard God correctly. But if it wasn't God's voice that she and everyone else had heard regarding this marriage, she concluded, then no one could ever be sure they heard God's voice. This was as clear as it could ever get. She had a very good point.

Other friends, reminiscent of Job's friends, suggested that her marriage had indeed been God's will. Knowing its outcome, the Lord had led her into it because he loves her so much and was trying to humble her, build her character, or perhaps punish her for previous sin. If a lesson was the point of it all, Suzanne remarked, then God is a very poor teacher. The ordeal didn't teach her anything; it simply left her bitter.

Initially, I tried to help Suzanne understand that this was her exhusband's fault, not God's, but her reply was more than adequate to invalidate my encouragement: If God *knew* exactly what her husband would do, then he bears all the responsibility for setting her up the way he did. I could not argue against her point, but I could offer an alternative way of understanding the situation.

I suggested to her that God felt as much regret over the confirmation he had given Suzanne as he did about his decision to make Saul king of Israel. . . . Not that it was a bad decision—at the time, her ex-husband was a good man with a godly character. The prospects that he and Suzanne would have a happy marriage and fruitful ministry were, at the time, very good. Indeed, I strongly suspect that he had influenced Suzanne and her ex-husband toward this college with their marriage in mind.

Because her ex-husband was a free agent, however, even the best decisions can have sad results. Over time, and through a series of choices, Suzanne's ex-husband had opened himself up to the enemy's influence and became involved in an immoral relationship. Initially, all was not lost, and God and others tried to restore him, but he chose to resist the promptings of the Spirit, and consequently his heart grew darker. Suzanne's ex-husband had become a very different person from the man God had confirmed to Suzanne to be a good candidate for marriage. This, I assured Suzanne, grieved God's heart at least as deeply as it grieved hers.

By framing the ordeal with the context of an open future [in other words, within the context of human free choices which even God cannot know in advance of our making them], Suzanne was able to understand the tragedy of her life in a new way. She didn't have to abandon all confidence in her ability to hear God and didn't have to accept that somehow God intended this ordeal "for her own good." Her faith in God's character and her love toward God were eventually restored and she was finally able to move on with her life.

Understandably, Taiwan was no longer on her heart, but fortunately, the "God of the possible" always has a plan B and a plan C. He's also wise enough to know how to weave our failed plan A's into these alternative plans so beautifully that looking back, it may look like B or C was his original plan all along. This isn't a testimony to his exhaustive definite foreknowledge; it's a testimony to his unfathomable wisdom.

Without having the open view to offer, I don't know how one could effectively minister to a person in Suzanne's dilemma.[8]

---

[8] Gregory A. Boyd, *God of the Possible: A Biblical Introduction to the Open View of God* (Grand Rapids, Mich.: Baker, 2000), 103-6.

When I first started thinking about the relationship between God and evil many years ago—in fact, very shortly after having had a paralyzing accident when I was seventeen—a fair amount of this way of explaining why we suffer struck me as exactly right.[9] After a couple of years of thinking intensely about this issue, I concluded that God had to put up with all kinds of things that he did not like in order to preserve our freedom. This still strikes me as a natural way to think about this issue because it fits in with our own experience. For sometimes we have to put up with what we don't like in order to leave other people their freedom. So, "*Of course*," we think, "it must be the same for God." What I want to show is why we shouldn't think this way, as natural as it is.

I think it is important to say that I never went as far as Boyd does—and I don't think that most Christians do. It is *not* natural to think that God makes mistakes—and yet that is what Boyd seems to imply when he says that God must regret the way he guided Suzanne, including having influenced her and her future husband to attend the college they did.[10] According to Boyd, God made a good—indeed, the "best"—decision but it had really bad results. God, in Boyd's way of looking at things, can be as mistaken as we may be about what someone will actually choose to do. And so I don't think it is unfair to say that Boyd's God is one who sometimes just rolls the dice. He is better at mopping up any messes afterwards than we would be, but he still can be caught out and be more or less helpless to prevent our doing and suffering bad things.

I hope this part of Boyd's thinking strikes you as badly as it strikes me. For, as I will now try to show, it challenges God's glory, and it threatens our sense of assurance that, when things seem to be going really badly for us, the God who loves us remains fully in control.

---

[9] I wrote about my accident and the theological journey it initiated in "True Freedom: The Liberty that Scripture Portrays as Worth Having," in *Beyond the Bounds: Open Theism and the Undermining of Biblical Christianity*, ed. John Piper, Justin Taylor, and Paul Kjoss Helseth (Wheaton, Ill.: Crossway Books, 2003), 77-109. In that piece, I reflect on a wider range of evils than I do here and I interact more carefully with the specific claims of open theism.

[10] For a relatively forthright acknowledgement by an open theist that God can be and has been mistaken about some things, see John Sanders, *The God Who Risks: A Theology of Providence* (Downers Grove, Ill.: InterVarsity Press, 1998), 132. This case of Suzanne's would clearly fit under one of Sanders's ways of characterizing a mistake. He says that "we might say that God would be mistaken if he believed that X would happen"—think here of God believing that Suzanne and her husband would have a happy marriage and a fruitful ministry—"and, in fact, X does not come about. In this sense," Sanders claims, "the Bible does attribute some mistakes to God."

Scripture's General Perspective on God's Relationship to Evil

What are the issues that we need to address in order to think biblically about this topic?

First, we need to know what Scripture says in general about God's relationship to evil. Scripture declares that the Judge of all the earth will always do what is right (see Gen. 18:25). God is, as Moses sings, "the Rock, his works are perfect, and all his ways are just." He is a "faithful God who does no wrong, upright and just is he" (Deut. 32:4, NIV). God never *does* evil.

Yet this is not to say that God does not *create, send, permit,* or even *move others* to do evil,[11] for Scripture is clear that *nothing* arises, exists, or endures independently of God's will. Thus, when the writer of Hebrews states that Christ "upholds the universe by the word of his power" (1:3), he is claiming that God the Son is providentially governing everything through sustaining all of the universe's objects and events as he carries each of them to its appointed end by his all-powerful word.[12] This follows from the fact that the Greek word for "upholds" is *pherō*, which means to bring or bear or produce or carry. As Wayne Grudem notes, *pherō* "is commonly used in the New Testament for carrying something from one place to another, such as bringing a paralyzed man on a bed to Jesus (Luke 5:18), bringing wine to the steward of the feast (John 2:8), or bringing a cloak and books to Paul (2 Tim. 4:13)." Consequently, in our verse's context it "does not mean simply 'sustain,' but has the sense of active, purposeful control over the thing being carried from one place to another," especially since *pherō* appears in our verse as a present participle, which "indicates that Jesus is '*continually* carrying along all things' in the universe by his word of power."[13] So here is the picture: God the Son holds each and every aspect of creation, including all of its evil aspects, in his "hands"—that is, within his all-

---

[11] To move someone to do evil is not the same as tempting that person to do evil. Scripture tells us that God tempts no one (see James 1:13). For how moving someone to do evil and tempting that person to do evil differ, see the passages from W. G. T. Shedd cited in n. 56, and especially 318-22.

[12] See William L. Lane, *Hebrews 1–8*, Word Biblical Commentary, vol. 47A (Dallas: Word, 1991), *loc. cit.*: "The . . . clause ascribes to the Son the providential government of all created existence, which is the function of God himself. As the pre-creational Wisdom of God, the Son not only embodies God's glory but also reveals this to the universe as he sustains all things and bears them to their appointed end by his omnipotent word."

[13] Wayne Grudem, *Systematic Theology: An Introduction to Biblical Doctrine* (Grand Rapids, Mich.: Zondervan, 1994), 316.

powerful and ever-effectual word—and carries it by that word to where it accomplishes exactly what he wants it to do.

Ephesians 1:11 goes even further by declaring that God in Christ "works all things according to the counsel of his will." Here the Greek word for "works" is *energeō*, which indicates that God not merely carries all of the universe's objects and events to their appointed ends but that he actually *brings about* all things in accordance with his will. In other words, it isn't just that God manages to turn the evil aspects of our world to good for those who love him; it is rather that he himself brings about these evil aspects for his glory (see Ex. 9:13-16; John 9:3) and his people's good (see Heb. 12:3-11; James 1:2-4). This includes—as incredible and as unacceptable as it may currently seem—God's having even brought about the Nazis' brutality at Birkenau and Auschwitz as well as the terrible killings of Dennis Rader and even the sexual abuse of a young child: "The LORD has made everything for its own purpose, even the wicked for the day of evil" (Prov. 16:4, NASB).[14] "When times are good, be happy; but when times are bad, consider: God has made the one as well as the other" (Eccl. 7:14, NIV).

As Thomas Goodwin noted, in this passage from Ephesians Paul wants to assure his Jewish Christian brothers and sisters that God has worked grace in their hearts as the consequence of his having predestined them before all time for salvation in Christ so that they will be confident of their eternal inheritance.[15] So how does Paul proceed? He argues from the general principle to the specific case. God "'works *all things* after the counsel of his own will;' he plotted *every thing* beforehand, therefore certainly this [particular thing].'"[16] In thus arguing from the general to the spe-

---

[14] The Hebrew word for "evil" in this verse is *raʿ*, as is the word for "bad" in Ecclesiastes 7:14. *Raʿ*, as I point out below regarding Isaiah 45:7, is the primary Hebrew term for evil.

[15] Verses 11 and 12 read: "In him we have obtained an inheritance, having been predestined according to the purpose of him who works all things according to the counsel of his will, so that we who were the first to hope in Christ might be to the praise of his glory." Verse 13 then starts with the words, "In him you also, when you heard the word of truth." Goodwin, F. F. Bruce, Gordon Fee, Peter O'Brien, and others argue from the "you also" that verses 11 and 12 are referring to the first Jewish Christians and that verse 13 then brings in the later Gentile Christians. This reading seems to be corroborated by Acts 18:24–19:20.

[16] Thomas Goodwin, *An Exposition of the First Chapter of the Epistle to the Ephesians* in *The Works of Thomas Goodwin*, vol. 1 (Eureka, Calif.: Tanski Publications, 1996), *loc. cit.*; my emphasis. Goodwin lived from 1600–1680. His Ephesians commentary was published the year after his death. Goodwin was one of the greatest of the English Puritans.

Ordinarily, if we were to say that someone did something according to the counsel of his own will, what we would mean is that the person first thought through on his own what he was going to

cific, Paul is arguing from what would be obvious to his biblically literate Jewish brothers and sisters to what would be less obvious for them as relatively new converts to Christ. These Jewish Christians would know that God—the God of the Old Testament whom they now recognized as the Father of Jesus Christ—declares "the end from the beginning" (Isa. 46:10)—and, by implication, knows and has ordered everything in-between, even down to foreseeing and ordering the words we will speak (see Ps. 139:4 with Prov. 16:1).[17] They would know that the One who said, "My counsel shall stand, and I will accomplish all my purpose," is the One who ensures this by bringing everything about, including, in the immediate context of Isaiah's words, "calling a bird of prey from the east, . . . from a far country" (Isa. 46:10f.)—that is, Cyrus the Great, king of Persia from 559–530 B.C., who would conquer Babylon in 539 B.C. and then allow the Jews to return to Jerusalem so that they could rebuild the temple (see Ezra 1:1-4). God here calls the pagan, unbelieving Cyrus "a man to fulfill my purpose" (Isa. 46:11, NIV). From events as small as the fall of the tiniest sparrow (see Matt. 10:29) to the death, at the hands of lawless men, of his own dear Son (see Acts 2:23 with 4:28), God speaks and then brings his word to pass; he purposes and then does what he has planned (see Isa. 46:11). Nothing that exists or occurs falls outside God's ordaining will.[18]

Nothing, including no evil person or thing or event or deed. God's

---

do and then carried out what he had determined to do without having to take account of anything other than what he had determined to do. In other words, what he had determined to do was all that he took account of in acting as he did; he did not have to adjust what he did to anything beyond what he had determined to do. So if we interpret this part of Ephesians 1:11 according to its plain sense, then we will affirm with the Scriptures that "Our God is in the heavens; he does all that he pleases" (Ps. 115:3; see also 135:6; Dan. 4:35; and Isa. 46:10, which is quoted below).

At this point, open theists may seem to have one more move available to them. It seems that they could retort that what God has been pleased to do is to give human beings the sort of freedom that involves our deciding what we will do rather than his determining what we will do. But this move is not really a biblical option, given the fact that God would not then be working all things "after the counsel of *his own* will." For he would then be taking into account not only what he willed but what we will.

[17] In Isaiah 46:9, God declares that he is God "and there is no other; I am God, and there is none like me," which is immediately followed by the words of verse 10: "declaring the end from the beginning and from ancient times things not yet done, saying, 'My counsel shall stand, and I will accomplish all my purpose.'" The fact that verse 10 is preceded by this declaration of God's that there is none like him suggests or implies that God's exhaustive foreknowledge is what theologians call a *differentium*—that is, a distinguishing feature, or something that sets him apart and makes him different from every other being. Here the New Living Translation captures the intent of these two verses nicely: "And do not forget the things I have done throughout history. For I am God—I alone! I am God, and there is no one else like me. Only I can tell you what is going to happen even before it happens. Everything I plan will come to pass, for I do whatever I wish."

[18] It is crucial to recognize, as Goodwin did, that Paul's argument would not work if he could not assume that his fellow Jewish Christians would agree that God works *all* things according to the counsel of his will. If anything whatsoever could fall outside God's will, then why not their eternal

foreordination is the ultimate reason why everything comes about, including the existence of all evil persons and things and the occurrence of any evil acts or events. And so it is not inappropriate to take God to be the creator, the sender, the permitter, and sometimes even the instigator of evil. This is what Scripture explicitly claims. For instance, Isaiah 45:7 reports God to declare: "I form light and create darkness, I make well-being and create calamity, I am the LORD, who does all these things." The word for "create" here is the Hebrew word *bara'*, which is the same word that is used for God's creative work in Genesis 1; and the word for "calamity" is *ra'*, which is the word that is almost always translated "evil" in the Old Testament, as we find in places like Genesis 2–3; 6:5; 13:13; and 50:15, 20.[19] Again, Amos asks rhetorically, "When a trumpet sounds in a city, do not the people tremble? When disaster comes to a city, has not the LORD caused it?" (3:6, NIV).[20] Isaiah also says, "The LORD has mixed within [the leaders of the Egyptian cities of

---

inheritance? *This implies that neither Paul himself nor any of the godly Jews of his day would have considered open theism a biblical possibility.*

Open theists often claim that Scripture includes claims that can be taken to support their position as well as claims that support their opponents' position. They then argue that the passages that seem to support their position ought to be taken to determine how we should interpret the passages that seem to oppose their position. But here we have an argument from Paul that clarifies what he and his Jewish brothers and sisters took to be beyond question: God works *all things* according to the counsel of his will. This establishes that we should *not* take the biblical texts that can be read as supporting open theism as determining our interpretation of the ones that cannot. We must take the biblical texts that contradict open theism as the determinative texts, and then interpret the supposedly "open" passages in their light, if we are to remain true to what God has intended us to understand from his word, given Paul's argument. (In fact, one reason to interpret verses such as Psalm 139:4 and Proverbs 16:1 as I have in this argument, and thus we have reason to reject, e.g., David J. A. Clines's interpretation of such verses in his "Predestination in the Old Testament," in *Grace Unlimited*, ed. Clark H. Pinnock (Minneapolis: Bethany House, 1975), 116f.). It is curious that open theists like Boyd and John Sanders never even acknowledge Ephesians 1:11, much less grapple with Paul's argument.

I explain the concepts of *God's ordaining will* and his *foreordination* (as it is broached in the second sentence of the next paragraph) in the last paragraph of this section. What God *ordains* often differs from what he *commands*. For instance, God commands all human beings to worship his Son (see, e.g., Phil. 2:9-11), but he ordained that certain specific human beings would disobey that command and blaspheme against him instead (see, e.g., 2 Peter 2 and Jude, especially vv. 4, 8, 13-15). Again, he commands that all people everywhere repent (see Acts 17:30) and yet he has ordained that some will not (see 2 Peter 2, especially vv. 9 and 17). In Reformed circles, this distinction between what God ordains and what he commands is often marked as the distinction between his *secret* will—which is never frustrated—and his *revealed* will—which human beings violate regularly. For a nice summary of the distinction, see Grudem, *op. cit.*, 213-16.

[19] God's creative activity in Isaiah 45:7 is stated in terms of his forming or making or creating whole *kinds* or *categories* of things. He is not represented in this verse as creating a *particular* light or a *particular* calamity; he creates light *as such* and evil *as such*. So this verse cuts off the possibility that God sometimes creates evil and sometimes does not.

[20] The New International Version's translation of the second half of this verse seems to me to be preferable over other translations, such as the English Standard Version's (which reads: "Does disaster come to a city, unless the LORD has done it?") because it avoids potentially confusing the reader with the

Zoan and Memphis] a spirit of distortion,"[21] and they have then "led Egypt astray in all that it does" (19:14, NASB).

Nor is maintaining that God never does evil equivalent to claiming that he does not *send* evil. Sometimes he sends evil spirits—one to torment King Saul (see 1 Sam. 16:14-23), another which caused the leaders of Shechem to deal treacherously with King Abimelech (see Judg. 9:23), and a third to lie through King Ahab's prophets and thus entice him to travel to Ramoth-gilead where he would be killed (see 1 Kings 22:13-40). And sometimes he sends delusions, as Paul affirms when he says that, because the perishing refuse "to love the truth and so be saved, . . . God sends them a strong delusion, so that they may believe what is false, in order that all may be condemned who did not believe the truth but had pleasure in unrighteousness" (2 Thess. 2:11f.).

In Genesis 19, God sent angels to destroy Sodom and Gomorrah (see especially v. 13). In Exodus 7–12, he sent the ten plagues. In Numbers 21:6, he sent poisonous snakes to bite the grumbling Israelites. In 2 Samuel 24, he sent a pestilence on Israel that killed seventy thousand men. In 2 Kings 24:2-4, after having vowed earlier that because of Manasseh's sins he would bring upon Jerusalem and Judah "such evil [*ra*] that the ears of every one who hears of it will tingle" (21:12, RSV), God sent marauding bands of foreign peoples against Judah to destroy it because of King Manasseh's sins. All this came upon Judah by God's word (see 24:3).[22] In Isaiah 10, God vows to send Assyria against godless Judah, but then he also vows to "pun-

---

possibility that God *does* evil. As Douglas Stuart notes in *Hosea–Joel*, Word Biblical Commentary, vol. 31 (Waco, Tex.: Word, 1987), 324, the focus of verses 3-6 of chapter 3 is "on certain natural associations of a cause and effect variety"—and so rendering the Hebrew word *'asah* as "cause" rather than the much more common "do" is certainly not inappropriate.

As Grudem points out regarding the interpretation of Isaiah 45:7, while someone could try to restrict the kind of evil that God creates to nothing other than natural disaster, there is no reason why we should take it so restrictedly (see *op. cit.*, 326, n. 7). In fact, the proper interpretation of Amos 3:6 implies that such a restriction is improper. For warning trumpets were blown in ancient cities primarily to signal that those cities were facing or undergoing military attack (see Stuart, *op. cit.*, 325: "Everyone knew the significance of blowing a [trumpet] in a city. It was the means of alarm (cf. Hos. 5:8) and usually warned of enemy attack."). So Amos 3:6 affirms that God is the ultimate cause of even those disasters that can be attributed to human choice.

Grudem's examination of the relationship between God and evil, as found on 322-30 of his book, is among the best.

[21] The translations of "confusion" and "dizziness" for the Hebrew *'av'eh* seem too weak.

[22] In order to avoid confusion with the distinction that I made in footnote 18 between what God ordains and what he commands, it is probably important to note that the phrase usually translated here as "at his command" is more literally translated as "from his mouth." In other words, what this verse is claiming is that all of this came about because it was part of God's all-powerful and ever-effectual word.

ish the speech of the arrogant heart of the king of Assyria" (v. 12) by sending a plague among his warriors (v. 16). When the Lord's angel fulfilled this
vow, 185,000 Assyrian warriors died (see Isa. 37:36).[23]

Scripture also establishes that God *permits others* to do evil, as
when he permitted Satan to destroy all of Job's property and children,
so that it would be clear that even then Job would not curse God (see
Job 1:6-12), and when he allowed foreign nations in Old Testament
times each to walk in its own sinful way (see Acts 14:16). The idea that
no one ever does evil to someone else unless God at least permits or
allows it is suggested by other passages, such as Genesis 31:7, where
Jacob says to his wives that God did not allow their father Laban to do
ra' to him; and Exodus 12:23, where Moses states that God will not
allow the destroyer to enter the Jewish homes and kill their firstborn;
and Luke 22:31, where the use of the Greek *exaiteō* seems to imply that
Satan had to ask God permission before he could sift Simon.[24]

Indeed, some biblical passages, such as Isaiah 19:2, portray God as
moving others to do evil: "I will stir up Egyptians against Egyptians, and
they will fight, each against another and each against his neighbor, city
against city, kingdom against kingdom" (see also 9:11). Second Samuel
24:1 states that "the anger of the LORD was kindled against Israel" and
so "he incited David against them" by inciting David to count the
Israelites.[25] Moreover, reading Job 1:6-12 prompts the conclusion that

---

[23] In 2 Kings 17:23-25 we are told that God sent lions among the foreign peoples that the king of Assyria
had sent to Samaria to replace the Israelites whom he had exiled. Many of us probably put ourselves
in the place of the exiled Israelites instead of the foreigners and so we may not readily recognize that
to the foreigners this was a real evil, even if it was an evil by which God was redressing the evil done
to his people. The same point must be kept in mind when reading about, e.g., God's sending hail against
the Egyptians in the seventh plague (Ex. 9:23-26), which to the Egyptians was a very great evil, as is
clear from the fact that Pharaoh then said, "This time I have sinned; the LORD is in the right, and I and
my people are in the wrong. Plead with the LORD, for there has been enough of God's thunder and
hail" (v. 27f.). This is the only time that the Pharaoh was so affected by one of the plagues that he
admitted that he had sinned. (At Deut. 6:22, Moses says, "And the LORD showed signs and wonders,
great and grievous, against Egypt and against Pharaoh and all his household, before our eyes".)

[24] This is the interpretation of Luke 22:31 in versions such as the NIV and the NASB. This claim can ultimately be expanded into the claim that no evil—whether or not it is perpetrated by another person—
can befall God's people without God's permission. Thus Psalm 16:10 claims that God will not allow
David to see corruption. Similarly, Psalm 55:22 claims that God "will never permit the righteous to be
moved." Psalms 66:9 and 121:3 and 1 Corinthians 10:13 further confirm the claim that God protects
his people and will not allow any ultimate spiritual harm to befall them. In each of these cases the NASB
gives what I think is the more felicitous translation by translating the appropriate terms as "allow"
instead of the English Standard Version's "let." I leave it to my readers to work out from Scripture the
implication that no evil befalls *anyone*—not even the wicked—without God's permitting it.

[25] The parallel passage found at 1 Chronicles 21:1 tells us that it was Satan who incited David to commit this evil, which suggests that God incited David to this evil through permitting Satan to incite him.

when God said to Satan, "Have you considered my servant Job, that there is none like him on the earth, a blameless and upright man, who fears God and turns away from evil?" in verse 8, he was actually putting Job in Satan's gunsights.

I have belabored the Scriptures in order to drive home this point: as one of my students said rather wonderfully in responding to open theism, "Open theists are trying to let God off the hook for evil. But God doesn't want to be let off the hook." The verses that I have cited establish that Scripture repudiates the claim that God *does* evil while at the same time everywhere implying that God *ordains* any evil there is. To say that God "ordains" something is to say that he has planned and purposed and willed it from before the creation of the world—that is, from before time began.[26] And whatever God has eternally planned and purposed and willed—whatever he has in that sense *foreordained*—inevitably takes place; to say that God has ordained (or foreordained) something is to say that he has determined that it will take place.[27] As Isaiah puts it, "The LORD of hosts has sworn, 'As I have planned, so shall it be, and as I have purposed, so shall it stand'. . . . For the LORD of hosts has purposed, and who will annul it?" (14:24, 27). Nothing—no evil thing or person or event or deed—falls outside God's ordaining will. Nothing arises, exists, or endures independently of God's will. So when even the worst of evils befall us, they do not ultimately come from anywhere other than God's hand.

Human Freedom and Responsibility

This is strong meat. It can be very hard for us to digest these truths. Yet even considering these claims raises other issues. For if these claims are true, then what becomes of human freedom? If everything that occurs happens because God has willed it to occur from before time began, then

---

[26] For the general concept of God's ordaining things before time began and then bringing them to pass in history, see (e.g.) 1 Corinthians 2:7 with Ephesians 1:7-10. Even Boyd admits that God has predestined some events from before creation and then brought them about in time, including the incarnation and the crucifixion (see his *God of the Possible*, 45).

[27] This comes out clearly in comparing various translations of Isaiah 37:26. In the NIV it reads like this: "Have you not heard? Long ago I ordained it. In days of old I planned it; now I have brought it to pass, that you [Sennacherib, king of Assyria] have turned fortified cities into piles of stone." In the ESV it reads like this: "Have you not heard that I determined it long ago? I planned from days of old what now I bring to pass, that you should make fortified cities crash into heaps of ruins." The Hebrew word that gets translated here as either "ordained" or "determined" is *'asah*, which means *to make* or *do*.

how can human acts be free? And if we are not free, then what happens to the crucial notion of human responsibility? How could it ever be right either to praise or blame or to reward or punish anyone?

This is the second set of issues that we must address. We need to investigate how Scripture represents the relationship between divine foreordination and human freedom. In other words, we need to think about how what God has willed relates to what we will. And we need to determine what Scripture claims about human responsibility.

Open theists are what philosophers call *free-will libertarians*.[28] Free-will libertarianism involves a claim about what must be true if human beings are to be truly free and thus capable of genuine responsibility. For free-will libertarians, true freedom involves more than just my doing whatever I choose to do. Such *freedom of choice*, Robert Kane argues, is just "surface freedom,"[29] because someone could manipulate me so that I always chose to do what that person wanted me to do.[30] True freedom, Kane and other free-will libertarians hold, requires that a person not only is able to make specific choices but also was able at the time she chose to choose differently than she actually did. So I have only freely chosen to eat chocolate ice cream if, as I chose it over rum raisin ice cream, I could actually have chosen rum raisin instead. Again, you are only free in choosing to remain sitting right now if you can also choose to stand up. But if something would stop you from standing up (let's say that someone is with you who would hold you down if you tried to stand up), then even if (rather than fight that person) you choose to remain sitting, you are not really free. For Kane and other free-will libertarians, all of this means that we must possess what they call *freedom of the will*—that is, freedom to decide what we will want and thus to deter-

---

[28] In order to forestall some potential confusions, it may be important to note that *free-will libertarianism* and *political libertarianism* are very different. Moreover, as I note two paragraphs hence, not all free-will libertarians are open theists.

[29] See Robert Kane, *A Contemporary Introduction to Free Will* (New York and Oxford: Oxford University Press, 2005), 2. As Harry Frankfurt has pointed out, even animals possess some freedom of choice because "an animal may be free to run in whatever direction it wants" ("Freedom of the Will and the Concept of a Person," in Harry G. Frankfurt, *The Importance of What We Care About: Philosophical Essays* [Cambridge and New York: Cambridge University Press, 1988], 20).

[30] E.g., sometimes we see parents luring their children away from doing one thing by offering them something different that they want even more. As Kane points out, Aldous Huxley's *Brave New World* depicts a world where ordinary citizens are left free to choose as they want but where what they want is shaped and controlled by the state (see *op. cit.*, 3f.). Kane's own free-will libertarianism is most fully developed in his *Significance of Free Will* (New York and Oxford: Oxford University Press, 1996).

mine for ourselves who we will be and thus what we will choose—in addition to *freedom of choice*.[31]

Now here is the crucial point: for free-will libertarians, we cannot be held responsible for what we are and do if our wills aren't free in this libertarian sense. If the ultimate explanation for my choosing as I do lies outside me, then I am not really free and I cannot be held responsible for how I choose. And if I cannot be held responsible, then I cannot justly be praised or blamed or rewarded or punished for how I choose. On the level of everyday life, this seems to make sense. We know that virtually all serial killers were sexually abused as children, and so it seems proper to place part of the blame for whom they have become on their abusers and not just on the killers themselves.[32] This is what makes it seem necessary to free-will libertarians that we must have freedom of the will if God is to be just in holding us responsible for what we do. And surely we should grant that in Scripture God *does* hold us responsible for what we do—just read, for example, Romans 1:18–3:20. So free-will libertarians conclude that we must possess freedom of the will, which means that God cannot foreordain what we do.

For open theists, there is an additional rub, given what they think are the requirements for our possessing libertarian freedom. Open theists

---

[31] As Kane puts it, *freedom of choice* is valuable because it allows us to satisfy our desires. When we have freedom of choice, we can choose to get what we want. But

> free will runs deeper than these ordinary freedoms. To see how, suppose we had maximal freedom to make choices of the kinds just noted to satisfy our desires, yet the choices we actually made were in fact manipulated by others, by the powers that be. In such a world we would have a great deal of everyday freedom to do whatever we wanted, yet our freedom of *will* would be severely limited. We would be free to *act* or to choose *what* we willed, but we would not have the ultimate power over what it is that we willed. (*Contemporary Introduction*, 2)

For free-will libertarians like Kane, we are only truly free if our wants and desires—the things we choose either to satisfy or not to satisfy—are "up to us," where the ultimate "sources or origins of our actions would . . . be 'in us' [and not] in something else (such as the decrees of fate, *the foreordaining acts of God*, or antecedent causes and laws of nature) outside us and beyond our control" (6; my emphasis).

[32] See Kane's *Contemporary Introduction*, 4f. For a fuller account of a real-life case where it seems that part of the blame for how a person has turned out needs to be placed on others, see Gary Watson's retelling of the story of Robert Harris in *Perspectives on Moral Responsibility*, ed. John Martin Fischer and Mark Ravizza (Ithaca and London: Cornell, 1993), 131-37.

Only God knows the human heart, and so he alone can fairly assess how much blame each of us deserves for what we have done. Blame will always rest primarily on the actual perpetrators of a specific evil—in other words, serial killers are primarily responsible for their crimes—and therefore the actual perpetrators are primarily blameable and punishable for their own acts (see Deut. 24:16; 2 Kings 14:1-6; Isa. 3:11; Jer. 31:30; Gal. 6:7). This is not to say, however, that the sins of others cannot have a negative effect on us (see Ex. 20:5; Num. 14:18). Indeed, the acts and omissions of others, insofar as they contribute to someone's sin, can make them blameable and punishable, too (see Ezek. 3:16-21; Matt. 18:6f.).

comprise just a subset of free-will theists because they hold, as some free-will theists do not, that if God *knows* what we are going to choose, say, next week, then what we are going to choose must already be determined in some way. They maintain that if God knows right now that I am going to choose chocolate ice cream instead of rum raisin ice cream next week, then that means that the claim, "Mark is going to choose chocolate ice cream instead of rum raisin ice cream next week," is true right now; and this means that my choosing that way next week is already set. When the time comes, it may *seem* as if I am freely choosing to act as I do, but in fact that cannot be. So open theists insist that God cannot foreknow the future, if humans are to be free and responsible beings.[33]

All of this seems like pretty good reasoning, although there are actually all sorts of possible answers to it.[34] Yet I am not interested in arguing philosophically against either free-will libertarianism or open theism right now; I want to see what Scripture says. And what we find in Scripture is this: Scripture holds human beings to be acting responsibly when God *foreknows* what they will choose, and even when it says or implies that God has *predestined* or *foreordained* what they will choose.

In addition to some of the verses that I have already cited in the previous section,[35] I am thinking here in particular about what happened during Peter's sermon on the day of Pentecost. At one point in it he declared, "Men of Israel, hear these words: Jesus of Nazareth, a man attested to you by God with mighty works and wonders and signs that

---

[33] Strictly speaking, what they claim is that God cannot know our future choices, at least not with any certainty. They usually concede that God is pretty good at predicting what we are most likely to do. He could know for certain other truths, as long as his knowledge of those truths did not impinge on our ability to choose freely.

For a particularly clear statement of the main argument of open theists for this position, see Boyd's *God of the Possible*, 121-23.

[34] For those who are willing to get a philosophical workout, see Brian Leftow's *Time and Eternity* (Ithaca and London: Cornell University Press, 1991) and Paul Helm's *Eternal God: A Study of God Without Time* (New York: Oxford University Press, 1988) for these answers.

[35] If we, following Jesus and his apostles, take God to be the primary author of Scripture, then we not only can but must read each part of it in the light of its other parts and seek to make consistent sense of it as a whole. We must, moreover, allow its clearer and more comprehensive affirmations to determine our interpretation of its less clear and less comprehensive affirmations. Hebrews 1:3 and Ephesians 1:11, properly interpreted, are clear and comprehensive affirmations of the fact that nothing that exists or occurs falls outside God's ordaining will. And so on the basis of those two texts I shall assume that God foreknows and foreordains all human acts, including those that are reported in the passages from Acts and Matthew and John that I am about to discuss. Consequently, the only issue that I need to address right now is whether human beings are ever held responsible for such acts in Scripture.

For an excellent summary of what Scripture claims and assumes and implies about itself, see Grudem, *op. cit.*, 47-138.

God did through him in your midst, as you yourselves know—this Jesus, *delivered up according to the definite plan and foreknowledge of God,* you crucified and killed by the hands of lawless"—that is, wicked and yet responsible—"men" (Acts 2:22-23). What, then, was the reaction of the Israelites to Peter's accusation that they had been party to God's will in crucifying the Christ? Did they claim that they were not responsible just because their actions were foreknown by God and a part of his predetermined plan—in other words, because Christ's death, including their own choice to crucify him at the hands of lawless men, was part of God's working all things according to the counsel of his will?[36] Did they claim that they could not be blamed because God knew ahead of time what they would choose to do? No! Luke tells us, a few verses later, that "when they heard [that God had made the Jesus whom they had crucified both Lord and Christ] they were cut to the heart"—in other words, they acknowledged the depth of their wrongdoing regarding God's Christ—"and said to Peter and the rest of the apostles, 'Brothers, what shall we do?' And Peter said to them, 'Repent and be baptized every one of you in the name of Jesus Christ *for the forgiveness of your sins*'" (2:37-38a). We only need to ask forgiveness for what we are responsible for.[37] So divine foreknowledge and human responsibility are taken to be compatible in Scripture.

Next, let us consider our Lord's words at the Last Supper. As his disciples participated with him in his final Passover feast, Jesus told them that one of them would betray him. This made them very sorrowful, and they began to say to him "one after another, 'Is it I, Lord?'" Jesus answered like this: "He who has dipped his hand in the dish with me will betray me. The Son of Man goes *as it is written*"—that is, as it was previously predicted—"*of him, but woe to that man by whom the Son*

---

[36] The phrase "delivered up according to the definite plan and foreknowledge of God"—or, as the NIV translates it, "handed over to you by God's set purpose and foreknowledge"—suggests that Judas's betrayal of Jesus, Caiaphas's willingness to sacrifice Jesus for the sake of the Jewish people (see John 18:14 with 11:45-50), and Pilate's cowardice about standing up to the Jews after they handed Jesus over to him (see John 18:28–19:16) were all specific parts of God's predetermined plan. Many years before, Sennacherib had been an unwitting instrument of God's greater purposes, as we are told in Isaiah 10:6f.: "Against a godless nation I send him, and against the people of my wrath I command him, . . . to tread them down like the mire of the streets. *But he does not so intend, and his heart does not so think*; but it is in his heart to destroy." And so it seems reasonable to conclude, against the kinds of arguments that I cite by open theists in footnotes 38 and 39, that these three men (along with Herod and others) spoke and acted exactly as God had ordained (see, e.g., John 11:51-53).

[37] While I might say, after it has happened, "Sorry!" I don't really need to ask your forgiveness for my tripping and bumping into you unless my tripping was the result of something like my carelessness.

of Man is betrayed! It would have been better for that man if he had not been born" (Matt. 26:22-24). Does this sound as if the disciple who was to betray Jesus was not to be blamed for what he was about to do? Of course not! Acts 1:18 labels Judas's choice to betray Jesus an act of wickedness; and the phrase "it would have been better for that man if he had not been born" is meant to convey that he is going to face very fearful judgment for what he has done. Moreover, we are told at John 6:64 that "Jesus knew from the beginning . . . who it was who would betray him." Yet Judas was responsible for the wickedness he chose to do, as he himself recognized (see Matt. 27:4).[38]

Finally, consider Acts 4:24-28, where the believers are praying after Peter and John had been released from custody after they had been arrested for proclaiming the gospel. You may remember that prayer:

"Sovereign Lord, who made the heaven and the earth and the sea
and everything in them, who through the mouth of our father David,
your servant, said by the Holy Spirit,
   'Why did the Gentiles rage,
   and the peoples plot in vain?

---

[38] Sanders does not comment on these passages from Matthew and John. Boyd provides a fairly lengthy interpretation of John 6:64 and other passages in that gospel in an attempt to show (1) that John 6:64 does not imply that Jesus knew from eternity that Judas would betray him; (2) that John 17:12 does not provide support for the position that "Judas was damned from the beginning of time"; and (3) that, while Judas was the one who fulfilled Scripture by betraying Jesus, he did not have to be the one who fulfilled that role (see 37-39).

If we grant from passages such as Isaiah 46:10-11 that God has exhaustive foreknowledge of all future events, including all future human choices, then there is no reason why we should not read John 6:64 in the traditional way, since it is certainly possible that the incarnate Jesus, as God the Son, could and did know this during his incarnation, just as he predicted in Matthew 26:33-35 that before the cock would crow Peter would deny him three times. Boyd's second and third points will not be granted by those who interpret passages such as Hebrews 1:3 and Ephesians 1:11 as I do.

The implausibility of Boyd's explanation of Jesus' prediction that Peter would deny him three times before the cock would crow in Matthew 26:33-35 shows how weak some of the arguments of the open theists are. Boyd argues that we can explain such a prediction "simply by supposing that the person's character, combined with the Lord's perfect knowledge of all future variables, makes the person's future behavior certain" (35). He then says:

   Contrary to the assumption of many, we do not need to believe that the future is exhaustively settled to explain this prediction. We only need to believe that God the Father knew and revealed to Jesus one very predictable aspect of Peter's character. Anyone who knew Peter's character perfectly could have predicted that under certain highly pressured circumstances (that God could easily orchestrate), he would act just the way he did. (35)

Yet in order for Jesus to risk making a prediction that Peter would deny him three times before dawn (remember: in the Old Testament, a prophet was discredited as God's spokesman if all of his predictions did not come true [see Deut. 18:21f.]), the circumstances that God would have had to orchestrate would have included his ensuring that Peter would be confronted with questions about his relationship with Jesus exactly three times. And how could God ensure this without at least potentially overriding the freedom of the questioners to ensure that result?

The kings of the earth set themselves,
   and the rulers were gathered together,
      against the Lord and against his Anointed'—

for truly in this city there were gathered together against your holy
servant Jesus, whom you anointed, both Herod and Pontius Pilate,
along with the Gentiles and the peoples of Israel, *to do whatever
your hand and your plan had predestined to take place."*

Plotting is something that people choose to do, and *setting oneself*
against someone is another thing that a human being chooses either to
do or not to do. Here Herod and Pontius Pilate and the Gentiles and the
Israelites were all *gathered together* in setting themselves against God
and Christ—and there really is no doubt that they are all being *blamed*
for what they had chosen to do; in other words, they are being held
responsible for the choices they made, even though what they have plotted and set themselves to do is what God's hand and his plan had predestined would take place.[39] Thus it seems that, in Scripture, God's
having foreordained that some human choices will be made is not

---

[39] In general, open theists like Boyd and Sanders make a great effort to show how passages like this
one and the one from Acts 2 can take an "open" interpretation and thus do not support the sorts of
claims that I am making. It is surprising, therefore, how little attention open theists pay to these two
passages. Boyd simply declares that while

> Scripture portrays the crucifixion as a predestined event, *it never suggests that the indi-*
> *viduals who participated in this event were predestined to do so or foreknown as doing*
> *so.* It was certain that Jesus would be crucified, but it was not certain from eternity that
> Pilot [*sic*], Herod, or Caiaphas would play the roles they played in the crucifixion. (*God
> of the Possible*, 45; my emphasis)

These are mere assertions that, moreover, seem not to acknowledge and grapple with the most
natural interpretation of the text. For this claim, "truly in this city there were gathered together against
your holy servant Jesus . . . both Herod and Pontius Pilate, along with the Gentiles and the peoples
of Israel, to do whatever your hand and your plan had predestined to take place," is most naturally
interpreted as involving the sovereign God of the universe using those who were gathered against Jesus
as instruments to carry out his will. This follows both from the fact that the natural subject of the
final "to do" clause is Herod and Pontius Pilate and the Gentiles and Israelites and in the light of passages such as Hebrews 1:3 and Ephesians 1:11.

Sanders also treats these two passages much too briefly, saying that "It was God's definite purpose . . . to deliver the Son into the hands of those who had a long track record of resisting God's work"
(*op. cit.*, 103). By this he seems to acknowledge that God intended to use Herod and Pilate and the
Gentile and Jewish peoples as the instruments for carrying out his will. But he then quotes Luke 7:30—
"the Pharisees and the lawyers rejected the purpose of God for themselves"—as proof that human
beings can resist the divine will. Yet here we may reply that the Pharisees and lawyers were resisting
God's *revealed* will and that neither they nor anyone else can resist his *secret* will. We see this distinction at work in, e.g., 1 Samuel 2:12-25, where Eli's sons were treating God's revealed will regarding
sacrifice with contempt, but when Eli warned them about God's judgment for their evil dealings, we
are told that "they would not listen to the voice of their father"—who was, of course, proclaiming
God's revealed will to them—"for it was the will of the LORD to put them to death" (v. 25).

incompatible with holding those human beings responsible for those choices.

So according to the Scriptures, no matter what free-will libertarians and open theists say, neither God's foreknowledge nor his foreordination of all things, including all human choices and acts, preclude human responsibility.

Choosing and Willing

Scripture emphasizes that we possess what free-will libertarians call freedom of choice. This comes out in the many passages where our choices and their consequences are stressed, passages such as Deuteronomy 30:19, "I call heaven and earth to witness against you today, that I have set before you life and death, blessing and curse. Therefore choose life, that you and your offspring may live"; and Joshua 24:14f., "Now therefore fear the LORD and serve him in sincerity and in faithfulness. Put away the gods that your fathers served beyond the River and in Egypt, and serve the LORD. And if it is evil in your eyes to serve the LORD, choose this day whom you will serve." Then there is Proverbs 1:29, "Because they hated knowledge and did not choose the fear of the LORD, . . . therefore they shall eat the fruit of their way, and have their fill of their own devices"; and Proverbs 3:31, "Do not envy a man of violence and do not choose any of his ways." Again, we have Proverbs 16:16, "How much better to get wisdom than gold! To get understanding is to be chosen rather than silver"; and Isaiah 56:4f.:

> For thus says the LORD:
> "To the eunuchs who keep my Sabbaths,
>   who choose the things that please me
>   and hold fast my covenant,
> I will give in my house and within my walls
>   a monument and a name
>   better than sons and daughters;
> I will give them an everlasting name
>   that shall not be cut off."

Finally, there is Luke 10:41f., "But the Lord answered her, 'Martha, Martha, you are anxious and troubled about many things, but one thing is necessary. Mary has chosen the good portion, which will not be taken away from her.'"

Many other passages do not mention choice explicitly but presuppose our freedom to choose, such as the command at Leviticus 19:4, "Do not turn to idols or make for yourselves any gods of cast metal: I am the LORD your God"; and the four times the Israelites are exhorted in the first chapter of Joshua to be strong and courageous as they cross the river Jordan to take possession of the Promised Land. There are exhortations such as those found in Psalm 85:8, "Let me hear what God the LORD will speak, for he will speak peace to his people, to his saints; but let them not turn back to folly"; and Proverbs 4:20, 22-24, 26f.,

> My son, be attentive to my words;
> incline your ear to my sayings. . . .
> For they are life to those who find them,
> and healing to all their flesh.
> Keep your heart with all vigilance,
> for from it flow the springs of life.
> Put away from you crooked speech,
> and put devious talk far from you. . . .
> Ponder the path of your feet;
> then all your ways will be sure.
> Do not swerve to the right or to the left;
> turn your foot away from evil.

Then there are the counsels and exhortations for Christians to walk in the light (see John 12:35f. and 1 John 1:5-7) and by the Spirit (Gal. 5:16-25; 1 Thess. 2:12; 4:1-7), because this is what Christ has set us free to do (see Gal. 5:1, 13; cf. Eph. 2:10). There are also warnings such as those found at Proverbs 3:7, "Be not wise in your own eyes; fear the LORD, and turn away from evil"; and Proverbs 4:14f.: "Do not enter the path of the wicked, and do not walk in the way of the evil. Avoid it; do not go on it; turn away from it and pass on"; and Ephesians 5:3-21 and Hebrews 2:1-3, 4:11, and 12:25, as well as the combination of warnings and promises found in Ezekiel 3:16-21 and 18:19-32. At Ezekiel 33:11, God pleads with the Israelites to turn back from their evil ways so that they may live. In Acts 14:15-17, Paul and Barnabas plead with the people of Lystra not to perform the blasphemy of offering sacrifice to them. In Acts 26, Paul tells King Agrippa of his conversion and how God has sent him to the Gentiles "to open their eyes, so that they may turn from darkness to light and from the power of Satan to God, that they may receive forgiveness of sins and a place among those who are sanctified by faith in [Christ]" (v. 18). At 2 Timothy 3:5 and Titus 3:9, Paul commands his readers to avoid specific sorts of people and controversies.

So our freedom to choose, along with our responsibility, is affirmed throughout Scripture. In fact, our ability to listen and to choose and to act in the light of instruction and teaching and counseling is part of what differentiates us from the beasts: "I will instruct you and teach you in the way you should go; I will counsel you with my eye upon you. Be not like a horse or a mule, without understanding, which must be curbed with bit and bridle, or it will not stay near you" (Ps. 32:8f.).

But does Scripture corroborate the claim of free-will libertarians that humans are responsible for their choices and their acts because they possess *freedom of the will*? In other words, does Scripture endorse Kane's claim that true freedom—the freedom really worth having, without which (he claims) we are not truly responsible nor truly deserving of praise or blame or reward or punishment—requires us to be free in the sense that we are able to choose not merely *which* of our wants and desires we will satisfy but are also able to choose *what* we will want and desire and thus are the ultimate sources or origins of our actions? Does Scripture represent the final shaping of our lives as right now "up to us" and "in us" rather than up to or in something else?

It does not. Indeed, it emphatically denies that we now possess the freedom to shape ourselves in the most fundamentally important way— that is, with regard to whether we will remain slaves to sin or become bondservants to righteousness (see Rom. 6:16-19; 2 Pet. 2:19). Scripture everywhere asserts or assumes that in this post-fall world each and every one of us is by nature spiritually dead (see Eph. 2:1-3; Col. 2:13) and thus helpless to determine for ourselves at the deepest and most crucial level of our existence who we will be.[40] As Paul says, "the sinful mind"— that is, the mind that is spiritually dead and thus enslaved to sin—"is

---

[40] Peter T. O'Brien says, in commenting on Ephesians 2:1, "here [Paul] employs the adjective 'dead' figuratively to describe the state of being lost or under the dominion of death. . . . It is sometimes called spiritual death and denotes a state of alienation or separation from God" (*The Letter to the Ephesians* [Grand Rapids, Mich.: Eerdmans, 1999]), *loc. cit.*

hostile to God. It does not submit to God's law, *nor can it do so"* (Rom. 8:7, NIV). To be spiritually dead means to lack the power to choose godliness and thus escape the corruption that is in the world because of sinful desire (see 2 Pet. 1:3f.). Yet the spiritually dead are not inactive—indeed, their sinful natures control and even drive them (see Rom. 8:8, NIV), for their minds are set on and enslaved to what that nature desires (see Rom. 8:5, NIV).[41] In this state, as Peter O'Brien observes, we *"cannot* respond to life's decisions neutrally," for we "are deeply affected by *evil, determining influences"* that "may be described in terms of the environment ('the age of this world'), a supernaturally powerful opponent ('the prince of the power of the air, the spirit that is now at work among those who are disobedient' [cf. John 8:44]), and an inner inclination towards evil ('the flesh')."[42]

Scripture—and especially the New Testament—drives home the fact that each and every one of us is either still dominated by sin—as Jesus said, "Truly, truly, I say to you, everyone who commits sin is a slave to sin" (John 8:34)—or has been set free by God to live a life of righteousness—"if the Son sets you free, you will be free indeed" (John 8:36; cf. 2 Cor. 3:17). Either we are for the God who is the Father of Jesus Christ or we are against him (see Mark 9:40); there is no middle state

---

[41] Peter says that they are filled with "the lustful desires of sinful human nature" (2 Pet. 2:18, NIV), which John enumerates as "the cravings of sinful man, the lust of his eyes and the boasting of what he has and does" (1 John 2:16, NIV).

It may seem paradoxical that someone can be both spiritually dead and active, but think of sociopathic killers. Serial killers are not infrequently described by those who deal with them as seeming to have something dead within them and yet they deploy all their energies to do their horrors. Indeed, it is what is dead within them, that allows and even drives them to do what they do. For their consciences are dead, which makes them all the more dangerous because they no longer possess that inner monitor which should stop them from even contemplating doing such horrible deeds. *More* choices open up before them precisely because they feel so little compunction to do only what is right. In fact, Jude gives us a picture of how the spiritually dead can be very active in their wrongdoing when he condemns certain people who had crept into the church, whom he describes as blaspheming what they do not understand and being destroyed "by all that they, like unreasoning animals, understand instinctively" (10). He calls these people "blemishes on your love feasts, as they feast with you *without fear,* looking after themselves; . . . fruitless trees in late autumn, *twice dead,* uprooted; *wild waves* of the sea, casting up the foam of their own shame; *wandering* stars" (12f.). Such people are freer than true Christians to do bad things. Likewise, Isaiah describes Sodom and Gomorrah in a way where it is clear that their inhabitants were dead to any feeling of shame regarding what they were doing (see Isa. 3:9). It is as human beings become spiritually blind, as they become alienated from God's life, as their hearts harden, and as they become callous that they then have nothing to stop them from giving themselves up to all kinds of sensuality and may even become "greedy to practice every kind of impurity" (Eph. 5:17-19).

[42] This is O'Brien's summarizing comment on Paul's claims in Ephesians 2:1-3 (see 163f.). As O'Brien points out, Paul's claims are consistent with what we find elsewhere in the New Testament; see, e.g., James 3:15 and 1 John 2:15-17 and 3:7-10.

(see Tit. 1:15f.), for, to put it somewhat differently, each of us is either a creature of the light or a creature of darkness (see 2 Cor. 6:14; 1 John 1:5f.).[43] Every human being in this post-fall world starts out as a slave to sin (see Rom. 6:17; Eph. 2:3f.; Col. 2:7), for this is our inescapable legacy from Adam (see Rom. 5:12, 19). Adam's disobedience has made us all sons and daughters of disobedience (see Rom. 5:19 with Eph. 2:2). As God himself said when looking down upon human beings after the flood, every inclination of the unredeemed human heart is *ra* from childhood (see Gen. 8:21). So David declares, and Paul reiterates:

> The fool says in his heart, "There is no God."
> They are corrupt, they do abominable deeds,
>   there is none who does good.
> The LORD looks down from heaven on the children of man,
>   to see if there are any who understand,
>   who seek after God.
> They have all turned aside; together they have become corrupt;
>   there is none who does good,
>   not even one. (Ps. 14:1-3; cf. Rom. 3:9-20)

"The wicked"—that is, what each of us is naturally, in our "flesh," as long as we have not been spiritually reborn of God's Spirit (see John 3:1-8 with Jer. 25:30f. and Rom. 7:5 and 8:1-14)—"are estranged from the womb; they go astray from birth, speaking lies" (Ps. 58:3). We are all sinful from the moment we are conceived and then we are birthed as iniquitous; this is the truth that adulterous, murderous King David came to realize in his "inner parts" (Ps. 51:5f., NIV). The whole world lies under the evil one's control (see 1 John 5:19, NIV; cf. 2 Cor. 4:4; Eph. 2:2) and would remain so forever if it were not for the rich—indeed, immeasurable—grace and mercy of God in Christ (see Eph. 2:1-10).

Consequently, it is neither "up to us" nor is it "in us" to choose whether we will remain slaves to sin or become bondservants to righteousness. As it was for the Israelites who were born enslaved under

---

[43] John 12:46, Acts 26:18, Ephesians 5:8, and 1 Peter 2:9 all assume that we are all at first creatures of darkness who, if there is to be any hope for us, must be delivered from that domain and transferred to the kingdom of light (see Col. 1:13). 2 Corinthians 6:14f. assumes that there are only two classes of human beings, variously described as the righteous and the unrighteous or wicked (the Greek word is *anomia*, which means "lawlessness" and hence "unrighteousness" or "wickedness"), or those of the light and those of darkness, or those in Christ and those of Satan.

Pharaoh, divine deliverance is our only hope (see Eph. 2:1-10 and Col. 2:13-15 with Ex. 13:3). As Jesus told Nicodemus, we must be born again of God's Spirit if we are to see his kingdom (see John 3:1-8). But such a birth comes "not of natural descent, *nor of human decision* or a husband's will"; we must be "born of God" (John 1:13, NIV). "No one can come to me," Jesus said to the grumbling Jews, "unless the Father who sent me draws him" (John 6:44); "no one can come to me," he reiterated to his disciples moments later, "unless the Father enables him" (6:65, NIV). God must put his Spirit within us and thus cause us—yes, *cause* us[44]—to walk in his righteousness (see Ezek. 36:27). "By his own choice," James declares to his Christian brothers and sisters, "he gave birth to us by the message of the truth" (James 1:18, New Jerusalem Bible). The Spirit runs along the pathway of God's holy Word (see John 6:63), but our hearts will open to receive him as the supernatural source of spiritual life only if God enables us to hear the word of the gospel with faith (see Gal. 3:2 with Eph. 2:8-10 and Acts 16:14). And so it is with all of us as it was with the Gentiles in Antioch of Pisidia: as we hear the gospel preached, just as many of us as God has ordained to eternal life will believe (see Acts 13:48 with Rom. 10:14-17).[45]

---

[44] In the ESV, Ezekiel 36:27 reads: "And I will put my Spirit within you, and cause you to walk in my statutes and be careful to obey my rules." The Hebrew for "cause" is *'asah*, which, as we have already seen, means *to do* or *make*. Most English versions translate it here as "cause"; the NIV's atypical "move" seems much too weak because someone can move someone else to do something without actually causing the person to act in that way. Rendering *'asah* as "cause" harmonizes with the fact that Scripture always represents us as passive in the process of spiritual rebirth. Regeneration—which is the technical term, when it is used in its theologically narrower sense, for our being born again—is entirely God's work.
[45] The Greek word that is translated as "appointed" in the ESV for Acts 13:48 is *tassō*, which can be translated as *appoint* or *order* or *ordain*. Thus, the RSV reads: "And when the Gentiles heard this, they were glad and glorified the word of God; and as many as were ordained to eternal life believed."
The primacy of God in the entire process of our salvation is emphasized by Scripture's assumption that he chooses those who come to faith. See, e.g., 1 Thessalonians 1:4f.—"we know, brothers loved by God, that *he has chosen you*, because our gospel came to you not only in word, but also in power and in the Holy Spirit and with full conviction"—and 2 Thessalonians 2:13—"But we ought always to give thanks to God for you, brothers beloved by the Lord, *because God chose you* as the firstfruits to be saved, through sanctification by the Spirit and belief in the truth"—as well as Psalm 65:4—"Blessed is the one *you choose* and bring near, to dwell in your courts!"
F. F. Bruce emphasizes God's sovereignty in this process in the way that he translates Ephesians 1:11—"It was in Christ, too, that we were claimed by God as his portion, having been foreordained according to the purpose of him who works all things according to the counsel of his will." He comments:
The verb translated "we were claimed . . . as his portion" has been rendered more freely in a number of recent versions. . . . But we are dealing with a passive form of the verb which means "appoint by lot," "allot," "assign," and the passive sense should be brought out unless there is good reason to the contrary. The reason for the rendering "we were claimed by God as his portion" (rather than "we were assigned our portion") is that it is in keeping with OT precedent [see, e.g., Deut. 32:8f.]. . . . [H]ere, believers in Christ are God's chosen people, claimed by him as his portion or heritage. . . .
The idea of the divine foreordination is repeated from verse 5. There God is said to

True freedom, then, is ours only if God has brought us to spiritual life by birth through his Spirit. It is only then that we are set free in a way that makes us able to choose to be bondservants to righteousness (see Rom. 6; 8:2-8; Gal. 5:13; 1 Pet. 2:16). Perhaps it is not too much to say that it is only after God has regenerated us that we possess true freedom of the will, for it is only after our spiritual rebirth that we are able through the power of God's Spirit living within us to choose anything other than sin. Yet, contrary to what free-will libertarians say, even before this, even while we were still unable to help ourselves and still hapless slaves to sin, we were properly liable to punishment (see Eph. 5:6; Col. 3:5-10).[46] Indeed, as Paul puts it in Ephesians 2:3, as long as we are unregenerate and precisely because we are unregenerate, we are "by nature children of wrath." According to Scripture, then, neither praise nor blame nor reward nor punishment depend on our possessing freedom of the will, as free-will libertarians define it.

Joseph's Story

How can this be? The reasoning of free-will libertarians seems quite plausible: the kind of freedom that we must possess if we are to be held responsible and thus liable to praise or blame and reward or punishment must involve our ability to shape ourselves at the most fundamental level of our personalities—the level of choosing *who* we will be by being able to choose *what* our wants and desires are. For if we possess no more than the ability to choose *which* of our wants and desires we will satisfy, then it seems that the ultimate responsibility for who we are depends on God

---

have foreordained his people "according to the good pleasure of his will"; here this is said to be part of his eternal governance of the universe, for he "works all things according to the counsel of his will." His will may be disobeyed, but his ultimate purpose cannot be frustrated, for he overrules the disobedience of his creatures in such a way that it subserves his purpose. (F. F. Bruce, *The Epistles to the Colossians, to Philemon, and to the Ephesians* [Grand Rapids, Mich.: Eerdmans, 1984], 262-64)

The picture here is that the sovereign Lord of all the universe just points to those whom he wishes to save and says, "I will take those." Of course, Bruce's distinction between God's will and his ultimate purpose is the same distinction that Reformed theology makes between God's revealed and secret wills (see n. 18).

[46] "Properly" because we are in this state subject to God's wrath—and the Judge of all the earth will always do what is just and right (see Gen. 18:25). As O'Brien notes:

The 'wrath' in view [in Eph. 2:3] is God's holy anger against sin and the judgment that results (cf. Eph. 5:6; Col. 3:5-6). It is neither an impersonal process of cause and effect, nor God's vindictive anger, nor unbridled and unrighteous revenge, nor an outburst of passion. Wrath describes neither some autonomous entity alongside God, nor some principle of retribution that is not to be associated closely with his personality. (163)

or fate or physical or psychological necessity or whatever it is that has ultimately determined what are our wants and desires.[47]

In fact, however, the biblical position seems clearly to be both that God has ordained everything that happens in our world of time and space and that it is not now "up to us" nor is it "in us" to choose whether we will remain slaves to sin or become bondservants to righteousness.[48] Those who love evil hate good (see Mic. 3:2; Ps. 52:3; cf. Ps. 45:7; 101). Light can have no fellowship with darkness (see 2 Cor. 6:14). No one can serve two masters; and so we are either inclined to sin or to righteousness (see Matt. 6:19-24). Yet, as we have seen, to which of these two we are inclined is not ultimately "up to us." And yet Scripture maintains that we still choose freely and responsibly and thus remain properly punishable for our own wrongdoing.

Short of the accounts of our Lord's crucifixion in Acts that we examined earlier, Genesis provides us with Scripture's clearest example of this.[49] This is the point of the story of Joseph, who was born as the first of the two sons of Jacob's beloved wife Rachel, who then died while giving birth to her second son, Benjamin. All told, Jacob had twelve sons, six by his less-loved wife, Leah, two by Rachel, two by Rachel's maid-

---

[47] While this reasoning initially seems quite plausible, it is actually wrong. For it assumes that our wants and desires are *all* that we consider in making our choices, in which case it follows that the range of our choices would be restricted by the range of our wants and desires. Consequently, if God or fate or physical or psychological factors (or whatever) determine the range of our wants and desires, then God or fate or physical or psychological factors (or whatever) indirectly yet inevitably determine the range of our choices. Scripture, however, both assumes and asserts that we are to take *more* than our wants and desires into consideration in making our choices—namely, we are to take God and his law into consideration, with the understanding that if his law runs against our wants and desires, then we are to choose to follow his law rather than satisfy our wants and desires. And, according to Scripture, every human being knows this (see, e.g., Rom. 1:18–2:16). We do not need libertarian freedom of the will, then, in order to be responsible. All we need is freedom of choice plus an awareness that sometimes God is commanding us to follow his law rather than satisfy our wants and desires.

[48] In other words, according to Scripture, each one of us possesses a primary inclination either to sin or to righteousness. This primary inclination determines our wants and desires. So there is no such thing as *freedom of the will* at the most fundamental level of human being. As our Lord said, each of us is either for him or against him (see Luke 11:14-28). In the spiritual realm, as should be clear from our examination of Ephesians 2:1-3, neutrality is impossible.

With some careful thinking, we can see why there can be no such thing as freedom of the will at the most fundamental level of human being. Ultimately, even though we *should be* motivated to make our choices in terms of God's law, our *actual* motivation to make a choice between any two possibilities—let's designate them possibility A and possibility B—is that either A or B is more consistent with our primary inclination. (If by God's regenerating grace my primary inclination is to righteousness, then I will in fact be motivated by what should motivate me.) Consequently, if we were to have no primary inclination, then we would not be moved to make any choices. Moreover, it is impossible to choose our primary inclination because we have nothing more primary than it to motivate that choice.

[49] From here through the end of my next section, I am relying somewhat on what I have already said in my earlier piece, "True Freedom," in *Beyond the Bounds*, 88-100. That piece deals explicitly with some of the objections that open theists would make to my interpretation of Joseph's story.

servant, Bilhah, and two by Leah's maidservant, Zilpah. If any family has ever been destined to have family rivalries, it was this one.

Joseph's story really starts in Genesis 37, where we read of him being his father's pet. Jacob foolishly lavished things on Joseph, like a many-colored robe. This led Joseph's brothers to realize that their father loved Joseph more than he loved them and so, we are told, "they hated him and could not speak peacefully to him" (37:4). To make matters worse, when Joseph was seventeen he had two dreams predicting that he would rule over his entire family, and he foolishly told his brothers about them.

These things prompted Joseph's brothers to plot to kill him, but then, just because the opportunity arose, they sold him into slavery instead. He wound up in Egypt. There he went through a series of ups and downs, including being imprisoned for two years on the false charge that he had tried to seduce his master's wife. Yet finally he rose to become Pharaoh's second-in-command. And then Jacob sent Joseph's brothers to Egypt to buy food because there was a famine in Canaan. Of course, Joseph recognized them, but he didn't tell them who he was. Instead, he forced them to return home to fetch his full brother, Benjamin, while he held Simeon in prison until they returned. He then tested them to see how they would react to the idea of his keeping Benjamin as his servant and finally, as he watched their grief-stricken reactions to that possibility, he revealed to them who he was.

And here is the crucial point: when he finally revealed to his brothers who he was, he did not deny that it was their sinful actions of many years before that accounted for his being in Egypt. At Genesis 45:4, we find him saying, "Come near to me, please. . . . I am your brother, Joseph, whom *you sold* into Egypt." Yet he tries to keep them from getting too dismayed or fearful upon seeing him again in these circumstances—where he really is ruling over them, just as he dreamed—by stating that what they did was ultimately God's doing: "And now do not be distressed or angry with yourselves because *you sold* me here, for *God sent* me before you to preserve life" (45:5). God sent Joseph to Egypt through his brothers selling him into slavery. Joseph then reiterates, without again mentioning his brothers' part in it, that God sent him to Egypt: "God sent me ahead of you to preserve for you a remnant on earth and to save your lives by a great deliverance" (45:7, NIV). Then he finally concludes, "So *it was not you* who sent me here, but God" (45:8). Reading the whole story carefully clarifies that Joseph appeals to God's will as the final explanation of everything that happened to him, and ultimately God gets the credit for all the good that resulted.

Of course, this is not to deny Joseph's brothers' part in the whole story, nor the evil of what they did, nor their responsibility, nor their guilt. All of that, it is clear, Scripture considers compatible with the claim that God ordained their choosing to do what they did. Indeed, that very point is made at the very end of the story, in the last few lines of Genesis. After Jacob died, Joseph's brothers, still haunted by what they themselves call "all the evil that we did to him" (50:15), made up a story and sent it by messenger to Joseph, no doubt because they were afraid to show their faces, for fear he would now exact vengeance on them. Their story went: "Dad commanded us right before he died to tell you, 'Please forgive your brothers for their transgression and their sin against you, because they did in fact do evil to you.' So please forgive us for what we've done" (see 50:15-17). So how did Joseph respond when he finally saw them face to face? He said, "Do not fear, for am I in the place of God? As for you, you meant evil against me, but God meant it for good, to bring it about that many people should be kept alive, as they are today" (50:19-20).

Now understanding the construction of this claim—"As for you, you meant evil against me, but God meant it for good"—is absolutely crucial if we are to understand the relationship between God's will and our wills, between God's ordaining that someone will do some evil act and some human being's actually doing it. The word for "evil" here is, once again, the Hebrew word *raᶜ*. *Raᶜ* is in the feminine singular case. In languages like Hebrew and Greek, the case of nouns, pronouns, and adjectives indicates the grammatical relations among various words. And the "it" in this claim—"God meant *it* for good"—is also in the feminine singular. So by the rules of grammar, "it" clearly takes as its antecedent the previous *raᶜ*. In other words, the pronoun "it" refers to the noun "evil," just like "it" would refer to the word "book" if I were to say, "Would you please bring me my book? It is on the table." But, then, Joseph's claim is most accurately and clearly translated (with a little expansion to make it clear what is being talked about) like this: "As for you, my brothers, in selling me into slavery you meant evil against me, but God meant that evil event for good."

In other words, Joseph here referred to just one specific event, namely, his brothers selling him to the Ishmaelites, who then took him to Egypt. Yet he explained the occurrence of that one event in two different ways: his brothers intended to do him harm by selling him into slavery—remember, they hated him and even were plotting to kill him—even as God intended that sale for Joseph's and many others' (including his brothers') good. In the light of what we have concluded thus far, this amounts to God's having ordained Joseph's brothers' evil willing, but as part of a greater good.

Dual explanations like this are scattered throughout the Scriptures. There is one at the very beginning of the book of Job, right after God put Job in Satan's gunsights and then gave Satan permission to do anything other than lay a hand directly on Job himself. So Satan sent the Sabeans to steal Job's oxen and donkeys and kill their herdsmen, and then caused lightning to electrocute Job's sheep and the servants attending them, and then sent the Chaldeans to raid his camels and slaughter their keepers, and then caused a great wind that killed all of his children. When Job learned of all of these evils, he ripped his clothes, shaved his head, "and fell on the ground and worshiped," saying, "Naked came I from my mother's womb, and naked shall I return. The LORD gave, *and the LORD has taken away*; blessed be the name of the LORD" (1:20f.). In other words, Job took God's will to be the ultimate explanation of all of this evil. And the author of the book of Job then makes sure that we understand that this is right, for he adds, "In all this Job did not sin or charge God with wrong" (1:22). In other words, it was not sinful or wrong for Job to claim that God had a sovereign, ordaining hand in these evils. God did not *do* them; Satan did. But the evils that Satan did, he did only with God's permission, which the Scriptures themselves imply amounts to God's foreordination. Satan did these things to harm Job, but God ordained them for his own glory and ultimately for Job's good.

The story of Paul's shipwreck in Acts 27 involves the same sort of dual explanation. In verses 22-25, God promised categorically through Paul that no one on the ship was going to be lost. Yet later when some of the sailors were secretly trying to jump ship, Paul declared to his centurion guard and his soldiers, "Unless these [sailors] stay in the ship, you cannot be saved" (see vv. 30-32). This led the soldiers to act in a way that kept the sailors aboard. And thus everyone was saved, as God had ordained. Since God had previously promised that no one would be lost, we can conclude that the soldiers' acting to keep the sailors on board was among the events that God had foreordained.

Again, in the book of Jonah we are first told that, at his urging, the sailors on Jonah's ship hurled him into the sea (see 1:14f.) and then, when he is in the belly of the great fish, Jonah says to God, "you cast me into the deep" (2:3). In addition, verses like Proverbs 21:1—"The king's heart is a stream of water in the hand of the LORD; he turns it wherever he will"—clarify that, even with kings, whose wills are most sovereign on earth, what they will is what God wills them to will because God governs their hearts. One striking instance of this involves King Saul's suicide, which the Chronicler describes as a matter of God's having put Saul to death for his breach of faith in not obeying God's command to him through Samuel and in Saul's having consulted with a medium at Endor (see 1 Chron. 10:1-14 with 1 Sam. 10:8, 13:7-14, and 28:1-19).[50]

So it seems that we can appropriately conclude, with the great theologian Charles Hodge, that "[w]hat is true of the history of Joseph, is true of all history."[51] All of history is composed of this sort of dual explanation: God foreordains what humans choose. He is never absent or inactive when human beings hurt each other or themselves. In the person of his Son, he is always in our midst, as the one who holds each and every aspect of creation, including all of its evil aspects, in his hands so that he may carry it to where it accomplishes exactly what he wants. Scripture includes verses that, at least on a first reading, and perhaps

---

[50] The Chronicler's account goes like this: Saul had been wounded by the Philistine archers and, fearing that he would be abused by them if he fell into their hands, he asked his armor-bearer to kill him. But his armor-bearer refused. So Saul took his own sword and killed himself by falling on it. So when the Chronicler observes, in verse 14, that "the LORD put [Saul] to death," what he means is that God did this through moving Saul to choose, voluntarily and no doubt responsibly, to end his own life.

We are told that Saul's armor-bearer refused to kill him because "he feared greatly" (1 Chron. 10:4). I think the most plausible interpretation of those words is that Saul's armor-bearer understood that he would be held responsible if he chose to carry out Saul's request. So the whole account seems to be saturated with human choice and responsibility, yet all of it exercised according to God's secret will.

[51] Charles Hodge, *Systematic Theology*, 3 vols. (Grand Rapids, Mich.: Eerdmans, 1986 [first published in 1871]), 1:544.

even on a second or third reading, may seem to imply something else.[52] But as we have already seen, this is the perspective that is central to Scripture's interpretation of our Lord's crucifixion; and it is the perspective of verses like Hebrews 1:3 and Ephesians 1:11, which are clearly intended to cover everything that happens in our world. Of course, our Lord's crucifixion is the supreme instance of how God ordains real evil for his own glory and his children's good: in that case, the most awful act ever done—the crucifixion by wicked yet responsible men of God's only Son, "the Holy and Righteous One" who is the very "Author of life" (Acts 2:23 and 3:14f.)—was and is also the most wonderful event that has ever occurred because it was through Christ's utterly unjust and undeserved crucifixion and death that God was reconciling the world to himself (see 2 Cor. 5:18-21).

God's Will and Our Wills

It is not accidental that very early in Genesis, long before we get to Joseph's story, we are told that "every inclination of [the unredeemed human heart] is evil from childhood" (Gen. 8:21, NIV; cf. 6:5). We now know what that means: it means that each of us enters this post-fall world as a slave to sin. Sin, Paul declares, "came into the world through one man, and death through sin, and so death spread to all men because all sinned" (Rom. 5:12). Sin reigns among all of Adam's descendants because he sinned. By his disobedience, he brought evil into the heart of the human race. Except by God's redeeming grace, it now runs through all of us as our primary inclination. Every son and daughter of Adam and Eve is now naturally dominated by sin. We know, then, what motivated Joseph's brothers. We know what they brought to Joseph's situation. God, as the One who actively sustains all things (see again Heb. 1:3 with Col. 1:17), was the source of their being. But they, as Adam's descendants, were the sole source of their sin. Their sinful inclinations made them the

---

[52] For instance, 1 Timothy 2:4 states that God "desires all people to be saved and to come to the knowledge of the truth"; 2 Peter 3:9 says that he does not wish that any should perish; and Ezekiel 18:32 declares that he has "no pleasure in the death of anyone." Such verses clearly appear to run counter to the claim that our Lord sustains the universe in such a way that everything within it accomplishes exactly what he wants. I cannot address such verses here. For careful exposition of verses like these, see, e.g., Thomas R. Schreiner and Bruce A. Ware, eds., *The Grace of God, the Bondage of the Will: Biblical and Practical Perspectives on Calvinism* (Grand Rapids, Mich.: Baker, 1995), two vols. and David N. Steele, Curtis C. Thomas, and S. Lance Quinn, *The Five Points of Calvinism: Defined, Defended, and Documented* (Phillipsburg, N.J.: P&R, 2004 (second edition)).

authors of their own sin. And, consequently, they did evil while God did not, for while God sustained them in their sin, he was not its source. This is why Scripture states that God creates, sends, permits, and even moves others to do evil while never doing evil himself. He creates and sustains sinful persons without himself being the source of their sin.

God ordains evil by willing that evil persons and things and events and deeds exist and persist. Joseph's brothers would never have existed if God had not willed their being. He formed their inward parts and knitted them together in their mothers' wombs (see Ps. 139:13).[53] They would have had no power to choose or to act if God had not moment-by-moment sustained them. God wrote each of their days in his book before time began (see Ps. 139:16). He hemmed them in, "behind and before" (Ps. 139:5; cf. Job 13:27). Nothing about them or their choices or acts surprised him.[54] God has never fallen prey to a vain trust in the goodness of human beings, as Wiesel did.

Yet, as the guilty reactions of Joseph's brothers suggest (see Gen. 42:21f. with 44:16; 45:3, 5; 50:15-17), we should know that the fact that God has ordained everything, including our free choices, does not remove or lessen our responsibility, our guilt, or our liability to be punished for our sins (see Gal. 6:7).

So what has our examination of the Scriptures yielded? It has yielded this: we find, scattered throughout the Old and New Testaments, cases where human intentions, choices, and actions and God's intention, choice, and action run parallel, cases where both the human intentions, choices, and actions and God's intention, choice, and action are taken as referring to and each as fully explaining the same object or event. These intentions, choices, and actions are referred to under different descriptions—the human intentions, choices, and actions are sometimes wicked or evil, although God's intention, choice, and action is always good, even when he is ordaining an evil event—and the human and divine intentions, choices, and actions are each taken to explain the same reality in different ways. For instance, by their evil act, Joseph's broth-

---

[53] The words of Psalm 139 are David's words, who is one of God's chosen ones, but there is every reason to think that virtually all of those words through verse 16 apply equally well to all human beings.

[54] Sanders claims that God had "no reason to suspect" that Adam and Eve would sin. Their sin surprised God. See *The God Who Risks*, 45-49 and my response in "True Freedom," 94ff.

ers meant to do him harm; but by means of ordaining their evil act, God meant to do Joseph and many others good. But each choice—the one by sinful humans and the other by our perfectly good God—is taken as a full or complete explanation of the same object or event.

So the biblical view is this: God has ordained or willed or planned everything that happens in our world from before creation, from before time began. God is the primary agent—the primary cause, the final and ultimate explanation—of everything that happens, yet the causal relationship between God and his creatures is such that his having foreordained everything is compatible with—and indeed takes nothing away from—their creaturely power and efficacy. Unless we are dealing with a situation in which God has miraculously intervened and thus overridden mere creaturely causality, creaturely activity—as "secondary" or "proximate" causes considered simply on the created level—fully explains whatever happens in this world. And all of this is as true of the relationship between divine and free human agency as it is of the relationship between divine and natural—that is, physical and biological—agency.[55]

---

[55] It is not hard to understand how God's agency relates to natural agency: God makes physical and biological beings and the natural laws that they obey, and then sustains those beings so that they affect each other according to those laws. So when the wind blows, the cradle rocks because the wind is the "secondary" or "proximate" cause of the cradle's rocking, given the physical laws that God has set for our universe. Again, I as a biological being get bruised when the wind blows so hard that a tree limb breaks loose and falls on me, because that is what happens when God sustains both me and that tree limb and the physical and biological laws that govern how falling tree limbs and animal bodies relate to each other. In both of these examples, God is the "primary" cause of what happens because, if he didn't sustain these beings and the laws they obey, then they would have no existence and no power to affect anything. And there doesn't seem to be any problem in claiming that God ordained or willed or planned these beings to interact with each other in these ways from before creation. God's foreordination of these beings and events does not seem to violate in any way their "natural" interactions.

But it is much harder to understand how God can ordain or will or plan our free acts from before time began without his foreordination cancelling the freedom of those acts. In fact, as I argue in the text's next paragraph, we simply cannot fully understand how this can be. And yet we have now seen that Scripture affirms both God's primary agency, which involves the fact that his ordaining will is the final and ultimate explanation for our free acts, and the fact that we still do them freely and responsibly. Either we accept the witness of the Scriptures here or we do not. Footnotes 56 and 58 show that some great theologians have been willing to bite the bullet about this and just accept the fact that divine and free human agency do both exist in the sort of dual-explanation way that I explored in the previous section. Here is a little more from the Westminster Confession of Faith on the same topic:

> God, the great Creator of all things, doth uphold, direct, dispose, and govern all creatures, actions, and things (see Dan. 4:34f.; Ps. 135:6; Acts 17:25-28; Job 38–41), from the greatest even to the least, by his most wise and holy providence (see Prov. 15:3; Ps. 104:24; 145:17), according to his infallible foreknowledge (see Acts 15:17f.), and the free and immutable counsel of his own will (see Ps. 33:10f.), to the praise of the glory of his wisdom, power, justice, goodness and mercy (see Isa. 63:14; Ps. 145:7).

> Although, in relation to the foreknowledge and decree of God, the first cause, all things come to pass immutably and infallibly; yet, by the same providence, he ordereth them to

"But," you ask, "how can this possibly be? How can Joseph's brothers have acted freely and responsibly if what they did was what God had previously ordained? How can Pilate and Herod and Judas and the Jewish people be properly blamed for what God had predestined to take place? How can God govern the choices of human beings without that entailing that those choices are no longer free? How can the same event have two complete explanations?" My answer is this: We *cannot* understand how these things can possibly be. We cannot understand how some human act can be fully explained in terms of God's having freely intended it without that explanation cancelling the freedom and responsibility of its human intenders. We cannot understand how divine and human agency are compatible in a way that allows the exercise of each kind of agency to be fully explanatory of some object or event. And yet—and this is the absolutely crucial point—we *can* understand why we cannot understand it. It is because our attempts to understand this involve our trying to understand the unique relationship between the Creator and his creatures in terms of our understanding of some creature-to-creature relationship. But these attempts, it should be obvious, involve us in a kind of "category mistake" that dooms our attempts from the start. A "category mistake" involves attempting to think about something under the wrong category. How the Creator's agency relates to his creatures' agency is to be categorized quite differently from how any creature's agency relates to any other creature's agency. This should be obvious merely by our remembering that God has created everything *ex nihilo*—out of nothing—while all creaturely creation involves some sort of limited action on some pre-existing "stuff."

When Scripture reveals anything about the relationship between

---

fall out according to the nature of second causes, either necessarily, freely, or contingently (see Gen. 8:22; Ex. 21:12-14 with Deut. 19:4-6; 1 Kings 22:1-38; Isa. 10:5-7). . . .

The almighty power, unsearchable wisdom, and infinite goodness of God, so far manifest themselves in his providence, that it extendeth itself even to the first fall, and all other sins of angels and men (see Rom. 11:32f.; 1 Chron. 10:4-14; 2 Sam. 16:5-11), and that not by a bare permission, but such as hath joined with it a most wise and powerful bounding (see 2 Kings 19:28), and otherwise ordering and governing of them, in a manifold dispensation, to his own holy ends (see Isa. 10:6f.); yet so as the sinfulness thereof proceedeth only from the creature, and not from God; who being most holy and righteous, neither is nor can be the author or approver of sin (see 1 John 2:16; Ps. 50:21). (*Westminster Confession of Faith*, 5.1, 2, 4)

I have included some of the Confession's biblical proofs for these claims, but only those which are the most important of those that I have not discussed elsewhere in this piece. Each one of these proof texts is worth reading.

divine and human agency, it merely affirms what Joseph declared in Genesis 50:20—it affirms both divine and human agency, with both kinds of agency referring to and explaining the same event, but with each kind of agency explaining that event in its own way. Thus Scripture reveals that both human agency and divine agency are to be fully affirmed without attempting to tell us how this can be, because we have no way to understand it, no matter what Scripture would say: all of our analogies concerning different agents or different kinds of agency must be drawn from what holds between and among creatures, and so we necessarily lack the conceptual wherewithal to plumb how God's fore-ordaining agency enables and yet governs our own free agency.[56] As David said, after confessing that God knew his every word even before it was on his own tongue, such knowledge is too wonderful for us; it is, quite literally, too lofty for us to attain (see Ps. 139:4-6).[57]

In summary, this means that we should affirm the age-old Christian doctrine of God's complete providence over all. God has sovereignly ordained, from before the world began, everything that

---

[56] I don't mean this to say that the ways that God governs both the godly and the ungodly are completely dark to us. In his *Dogmatic Theology* (Phillipsburg, N.J.: P&R, 2003; third one-volume edition, ed. Alan Gomes [first published in three volumes in 1888 and 1894]), W. G. T. Shedd makes some very illuminating remarks in his sections on God's efficacious and permissive decrees (318-322) and on election and reprobation (326-44). But both in the cases where we can gain some insight and in those where we cannot, we are to affirm with the Psalmist that God fashions the hearts of *all* human beings (33:15).

Those who want to dismiss this position often label it as "Calvinism," but Fergus Kerr, O. P., has emphasized that it is also the great medieval Catholic Thomas Aquinas's position:

For Thomas, God is the cause that enables all agents to cause what they do. . . . There is no problem. He cites Isaiah 26:12 ["O LORD, . . . you have done for us all our works"] . . . together with John 15:5: 'Without me, you can do nothing'; and Philippians 2:13: 'It is God who worketh in us to will and to accomplish according to his good will'. *For Thomas, evidently, Scripture settles it; there is no need for theoretical explanations of how divine freedom and human freedom do not, or need not be thought to, encroach on each other.* . . . Thomas only excludes certain tempting views: yes, God does everything, God is not a partner in the existence and activities of the world; God does everything, however, in such a way that the autonomy and reality of created agents is respected. Above all: the effect is not attributed to a human agent and to divine agency in such a way that it is partly done by God and partly by the human agent; rather, it is done wholly by both, according to a different way, just as the same effect is wholly attributed to the instrument and also wholly to the principal agent—but now Thomas is referring us to an analogy, and either we see it or we don't. In the end, he excludes certain views and leaves us simply with the mystery of the relationship between divine creativity and human autonomy. . . . Thomas has nothing more basic to offer than these observations. (Fergus Kerr, O.P., *After Aquinas: Versions of Thomism* [Oxford: Blackwell, 2002], 44-46. My thanks to my former student, Michael Ajay Chandra, for bringing this passage to my attention.)

[57] As Justin Taylor has neatly put it to me, if we are biblical about these things, then we know that we will never be held accountable to explain *how* divine and human agency are compatible, but we will be held accountable for believing *that* they are.

happens in our world, but in a way that does no violence to creation's secondary causes and in a way that does not take away from human freedom or responsibility.[58]

Beyond All Doubt

If all of this is true, then what should we be sure of when we are hurt by others or when we hurt others or ourselves? When we are thinking about human suffering and its relationship to God's will and our wills, what should be beyond all doubt?

It should be beyond all doubt that no one suffers anything at anyone else's hand without God having ordained that suffering. During his first hour or so in Birkenau, Elie Wiesel saw the notorious Joseph Mengele, looking "like the typical SS officer: a cruel, though not unintelligent, face, complete with monocle." [59] Mengele was asking the new arrivals a few questions and then, with a conductor's baton, casually directing them either to his left, so that they went immediately to the gas chambers, or to his right to the forced-labor camp. In seeing Mengele, Wiesel was seeing a very evil man whom, nevertheless, God was actively sustaining and governing, nanosecond by nanosecond, through his evil existence. And we can be sure that, from before time began, God had ordained that at that place those moments would be filled with just those persons, doing and suffering exactly as they did. We can be sure, because of what God says in places like Hebrews 1:3 and Ephesians 1:11, that even those persons in those moments did not

---

[58] Here is the way that the Westminster Confession (3:1) makes this section's point. Notice how closely it parallels Aquinas:
> God, from all eternity, did, by the most wise and holy counsel of His own will freely, and unchangeably ordain whatsoever comes to pass (see Eph. 1:11; Rom. 11:33; Heb. 6:17; Rom 9:15, 18): yet so, as thereby neither is God the author of sin (see James 1:13, 17; 1 John 1:5), nor is violence offered to the will of the creatures; nor is the liberty or contingency of second causes taken away, but rather established (see Acts 2:23; Matt. 17:12; Acts 4:27, 28; John 19:11; Prov. 16:33).

[59] *Night*, 31. Mengele was a medical doctor who was nicknamed "The Angel of Death." He carried out unspeakable experiments on some of his prisoners, including injecting chemicals into childrens' eyes in an attempt to change their eye color from brown to the preferred Aryan blue. He would visit the children, acting kindly and bringing them candy and clothing in order to keep them calm and happy, and then transport them in what looked like a Red Cross truck or in his personal vehicle to his laboratory beside the crematoria where he would perform his horrible experiments and then burn their bodies. He specialized in experiments involving identical twins. He was intrigued to see if he could make them differ genetically by, among other horrors, performing sex-change operations on one of them or removing one twin's limbs or organs in macabre surgical procedures that were performed without the use of anesthesia and that had no scientific basis or value.

fall out of God's "hands" but that he actually brought the whole situation about, guiding and governing and carrying it by his all-powerful and ever-effectual word to where it would accomplish exactly what he wanted it to do.

We can also be sure that when we hurt each other, the God who has made us in his image is watching and will call us to account (see Gen. 9:4-6). Even though he ordains all of our free sinful choices, those sinful choices still "count" and we are held responsible for them. Even though he ordained the acts of a Joseph Mengele, God will not allow the blood of his victims to cry out forever. He will bring Mengele and all wrongdoers to justice (see Deut. 32:35, quoted at Rom. 12:19; Ps. 94). He will avenge innocent blood by punishing those who have shed it (Joel 3:17-21).[60]

We can also be sure that, whatever God is accomplishing as he actively carries along all things, it is just and right. As the Scriptures emphatically declare, God is indeed the Rock on which we, in even life's most evil moments, can rest, the one whose works are perfect and all of whose ways are just. In ordaining the evil works of others, he himself does no wrong, "upright and just is he."

Of course, this is not to say that we will always know what God is accomplishing through the evils that we suffer or do. We can be sure, as Scripture confirms, that God has made everything for its purpose, even evil persons like Joseph Mengele or Dennis Rader. We can be sure that God has made our lives' most evil moments as well as their best. Yet why he has ordained that particular evil persons do particular evil things may be as unclear to us as his sufferings were to Job.

Yet if we are Christians, then we can be sure beyond all doubt that God is causing all things—including all of our suffering at the hands of evil persons—to work together for good because he has called us according to his purpose (see Rom. 8:28). We can be sure that even the worst of our suffering will someday be revealed to be an integral part of "all the good that is ours in Christ" (Philem. 6, RSV). For God has promised this. And God's promises are as deeds already done. As the apostle Paul has written:

---

[60] This is true even when Christians have done what is wrong, although our punishment may be wholly borne by Christ's sacrifice.

For those whom he foreknew he also predestined to be conformed to the image of his Son, in order that he might be the firstborn among many brothers. And those whom he predestined he also called, and those whom he called he also justified, and those whom he justified he also glorified. (Rom. 8:29-30)

Our future glorification is so sure that it is viewed by Paul as having already taken place, and so he puts it in the past tense. And out of this assurance comes Paul's great exclamations:

What then shall we say to these things? *If God is for us, who can be against us?* He who did not spare his own Son but gave him up for us all, how will he not also with him graciously give us all things? . . . Who shall separate us from the love of Christ? Shall tribulation, or distress, or persecution, or famine, or nakedness, or danger, or sword? As it is written,

"For your sake we are being killed all the day long;
we are regarded as sheep to be slaughtered."

No! In all these things we are more than conquerors through him who loved us. For I am sure that neither death nor life, nor angels nor rulers, nor things present nor things to come, nor powers, nor height nor depth, *nor anything else in all creation*, will be able to separate us from the love of God in Christ Jesus our Lord.[61]

As the New Living Translation renders verse 37, "No, *despite all these things, overwhelming victory is ours through Christ*," who has loved us with a timeless love and who will therefore be faithful to us forever (see Jer. 31:3).

Yet sometimes these great exclamations certainly don't seem to be true. Sometimes it seems as if what is happening to us or to Christians whom we love or even to Christians, such as Boyd's Suzanne, whom we just heard about—sometimes it seems that what is happening is so bad that it seems impossible that God could be ordaining them for our good.[62]

---

[61] Romans 8:31f., 35-39. I have changed the punctuation at the beginning of verse 37 to make Paul's "No" as emphatic as he means it.

[62] I am specifying Christians here, because God's promise that all things work together for good is for them and not for all human beings. It is through our acceptance by faith of Christ's reconciling work that we are given the right to be called children of God and thus to have the immeasurable comfort of knowing that God is our loving Father who, we are promised, is working out all things for our good.

I myself find it very difficult to understand how this can be with some of the worst things that human beings do, like sexually abusing young children or raping or torturing someone mercilessly. And, of course, something much less horrible than these sorts of things can happen to us and still leave us wondering how God could be ordaining it for our good. I have seen marriages break apart after thirty-five years and felt to some degree the grief and utter discombobulation of the abandoned spouse. I have watched tragedies unfold that seem to remove all chance for any more earthly happiness.

But, of course, none of this is new. In Scripture, there is much sorrow and tragedy, with a great deal of it caused by other people. And, as we read the Scriptures, we can hear the moanings and groanings and roarings of God's people:

> I am weary with my moaning;
>> every night I flood my bed with tears;
>> I drench my couch with my weeping.
> My eye wastes away because of grief;
>> it grows weak because of all my foes. (Ps. 6:6f.)

> My God, my God, why hast thou forsaken me?
>> why art thou so far from helping me,
>> and from the words of my roaring?[63]

And then there are these utterly poignant words of Job, early in his book, after he has lost nearly everything, including his children:

> Why is light given to him who is in misery,
>> and life to the bitter in soul,
> who long for death, but it comes not,
>> and dig for it more than for hidden treasures,
> who rejoice exceedingly
>> and are glad when they find the grave?
> Why is light given to a man whose way is hidden,
>> whom God has hedged in?

---

[63] Psalm 22:1, KJV. This older translation of the Hebrew word *sheagah* as "roaring" is in some ways better than more recent translations like "groaning." The word refers first and foremostly to the roaring of a lion, and so I think we have good reason to believe that David's experience was like the experience of someone in such extremity in an emergency room that he literally roars like a lion in his pain.

For my sighing comes instead of my bread,
  and my [roarings][64] are poured out like water.
For the thing that I fear comes upon me,
  and what I dread befalls me.
I am not at ease, nor am I quiet;
  I have no rest, but trouble comes. (Job 3:20-26)

Could any words be more poignant than these?—Perhaps only those of our Lord as he was forsaken of his Father on the cross.

But it is of these sorts of things that the apostle Paul is writing when he cries, in Romans 8, that nothing in all of creation can separate us from the love of God in Christ Jesus our Lord. Paul was not speaking in the abstract here; he was speaking out of his own experience, as it is clear when he is defending his apostleship:

> Are they servants of Christ? I am a better one—I am talking like a madman!—with far greater labors, far more imprisonments, with countless beatings, and often near death. Five times I received at the hands of the Jews the forty lashes less one. Three times I was beaten with rods. Once I was stoned. Three times I was shipwrecked; a night and a day I was adrift at sea; on frequent journeys, in danger from rivers, danger from robbers, danger from my own people, danger from Gentiles, danger in the city, danger in the wilderness, danger at sea, danger from false brothers; in toil and hardship, through many a sleepless night, in hunger and thirst, often without food, in cold and exposure. And, apart from other things, there is the daily pressure on me of my anxiety for all the churches. Who is weak, and I am not weak? Who is made to fall, and I am not indignant? (2 Cor. 11:23-29)

Paul reports afflictions so severe that he and those with him "despaired of life itself" (2 Cor. 1:8; see vv. 8-11).

Many of us have tasted such grief. I have known afflictions far worse than my paralysis. I have had seasons of perplexity about God's providence that have been so deep that night after night sleep has fled from me. Yet these griefs have been God's gifts. For only by such severe suffering has my loving Father broken me free of some of my deeper

---

[64] The Hebrew word is *sheagah*.

idolatries. In the nights' watches, while others sleep, my wakeful heart must find its rest in him or it will find no rest at all.

"Be gracious to me, O God," David prayed when the Philistines seized him at Gath, "for man tramples on me; all day long an attacker oppresses me; my enemies trample on me all day long, for many attack me proudly. When I am afraid," he states,

> I put my trust in you.
> In God, whose word I praise,
>   in God I trust; I shall not be afraid.
> What can flesh do to me?

"All day long," David continues, "they twist my words";

> all their thoughts are against me for *ra*ᶜ.
> They stir up strife, they lurk;
>   they watch my steps,
>   as they have waited for my life. (Ps. 56:1-6)

But God, David knows, has kept count of his nightly tossings; he has numbered his futile wanderings; he has kept track of all of David's sorrows. He has put David's tears in a bottle and written all of his anguish in his book.[65] And David knows that the God who cares for him that much will never abandon him. "This I know," he declares, "that *God is for me*. In God, whose word I praise, in the LORD, whose word I praise, in God I trust; I shall not be afraid. *What can man do to me?*" (Ps. 56:9b-11). David knows that God *will* keep his feet from sliding so that he may still walk before God "in the light of life" (Ps. 56:13).

I would not pretend to tell someone who has been sexually abused as a child how God means that evil for her good. But I know some men and women who have found their own abuse to be God's gift. I would not tell an angry Suzanne that I can clearly see how God has meant her husband's sin for her good. But I know some who trace God's hand even through such sorrows. It would not be my place to tell Elie Wiesel that the ten thousand who sighed out their prayers of praise to God on that Rosh Hashanah now long ago took the better part than he did as he

---

[65] My previous two sentences compile various renderings of the difficult-to-translate words of Psalm 56:8. I have also preferred the ESV's marginal reading for v. 5a.

stood apart from their faith. But perhaps Corrie ten Boom could witness to him of God's providence and loving goodness, even in such straits.

The mystery of why God has ordained the evils he has is as deep as the mystery of the evils in our hearts. And just as only God can plumb the depths of our hearts, so only God knows how the hurts we do to each other and to ourselves figure into his loving cure of us who shelter ourselves under the blood and righteousness of his Son. It is not always our place to attempt to give an answer to those who are questioning God's goodness because of the evils that others have done to them or that they have done to themselves; sometimes we should just stand silently by their sides. Moreover, we will not always, right now, have these answers for ourselves. But in glory the answers will be clear, when we will see Jesus face to face. Then we will see that God has indeed done all that he pleased and has done it all perfectly, both for his glory and our good, for in the light of Jesus' countenance—in that "light of life"— we will see that through our sufferings our loving Father has been conforming us to the likeness of his Son.

As David said, "Weeping may last for the night, but joy *is* coming in the morning" (Ps. 30:5).[66]

---

[66] Thanks to my students Rose Acquavella, John Higgins, Luke Damoff, Andrew Herther, Megan Ensor, and Jon Searle for helpful comments on an earlier draft.

Part 2:
The Purposes of God in Suffering

"My strength is made perfect in weakness"

Lokumu Hati na mpasi / mpota

Kembo Jesus wearing The scars

CHAPTER 3

The Suffering of Christ and the Sovereignty of God

JOHN PIPER

What I would like to do this chapter is magnify Christ in his suffering. In the process I would like to venture the ultimate biblical explanation for the existence of suffering. And I would like to do it in such a way that you and I would be freed from the paralyzing effects of discouragement and self-pity and fear and pride so that we would spend ourselves—able or disabled—to spreading a passion for the supremacy of God in all things (including suffering) for the joy of all peoples through Jesus Christ.

The Ultimate Biblical Explanation for the Existence of Suffering

I believe the entire universe exists *to display the greatness of the glory of the grace of God.* I might have said more simply that the entire universe exists to display the greatness of the glory of God. That would be true. But the Bible is more specific. The glory of God shines most brightly, most fully, most beautifully in the manifestation of the glory *of his grace.* Therefore, this is the ultimate aim and the final explanation of all things—including suffering.

God decreed from all eternity to display the greatness of the glory of his grace for the enjoyment of his creatures, and he revealed to us that this is the ultimate aim and explanation of why there is sin and why there is suffering, and why there is a great suffering Savior. Jesus Christ, the

Son of God, came in the flesh to suffer and die and by that suffering and death to save undeserving sinners like you and me. This coming to suffer and die is the supreme manifestation of the greatness of the glory of the grace of God. Or to say it a little differently, the death of Christ in supreme suffering is the highest, clearest, surest display of the glory of the grace of God. If that is true, then a stunning truth is revealed, namely, suffering is an essential part of the created universe in which the greatness of the glory of the grace of God can be most fully revealed. Suffering is an essential part of the tapestry of the universe so that the weaving of grace can be seen for what it really is.

Or to put it most simply and starkly: the ultimate reason that suffering exists in the universe is so that Christ might display the greatness of the glory of the grace of God by suffering in himself to overcome our suffering. The suffering of the utterly innocent and infinitely holy Son of God in the place of utterly undeserving sinners to bring us to everlasting joy is the greatest display of the glory of God's grace that ever was, or ever could be.

This was the moment—Good Friday—for which everything in the universe was planned. In conceiving a universe in which to display the glory of his grace, God did not choose plan B. There could be no greater display of the glory of the grace of God than what happened at Calvary. Everything leading to it and everything flowing from it is explained by it, including all the suffering in the world.

The Biblical Pathway That Leads to This Truth

Walk with me now, if you would, on the biblical pathway that has led me to this truth. To this point it just looks like high-sounding theology or philosophy. But it is far more than that. It is what the very words of Scripture clearly teach.

Revelation 13:8

Let's begin with Revelation 13:8. John writes, "All who dwell on earth will worship [the beast], everyone whose name has not been written before the foundation of the world in the book of life of the Lamb that was slain." That is a good, careful, literal translation. This means that before the world was created there was a book called *the book of life of the Lamb that was slain.* The Lamb is Jesus Christ crucified. The book is the book of Jesus Christ crucified. Therefore, before God made the world he had in view Jesus Christ slain, and he had in view a people purchased by his blood written in the book. Therefore, the suffering of Jesus was not an afterthought, as though the work of creation did not go the way God planned. Before the foundation of the world God had a book called *the book of life of the Lamb that was slain.* The slaying of the Lamb was in view *before* the work of creation began.

2 Timothy 1:9

Then consider 2 Timothy 1:9. Paul looks back into eternity before the ages began and says, "[God] saved us and called us to a holy calling, not because of our works but because of his own purpose and grace, which he gave us [that is, he gave us this grace] in Christ Jesus before the ages began." God gave us *grace* [undeserved favor—favor toward sinners, grace!] in Christ Jesus before the ages began. We had not yet been created. We had not yet existed so that we could sin. But God had already decreed that grace—an "in Christ" kind of grace, blood-bought grace, sin-overcoming grace—would come to us in Christ Jesus. All that before the creation of the world.

So there is a *book of life of the Lamb who was slain,* and there is "grace" flowing to undeserving sinners who are not yet created. Don't miss the magnitude of that word "slain" (*esphagmenou*): "the Lamb who was *slain.*" It is used in the New Testament only by the apostle John and means "slaughter." So here we have suffering—the slaughter of the Son of God—in the mind and plan of God before the foundation of the world. The Lamb of God will suffer. He will be slaughtered. That's the plan.

Why? I'll give you the biblical text which tells the answer, but let me state it again: it's because *the aim of creation is the fullest, clearest, surest display of the greatness of the glory of the grace of God. And that display would be the slaughter of the best being in the universe for millions of undeserving sinners.* The suffering and death of the Lamb of God in history is the best possible display of the glory of the grace of God. That is why God planned it before the foundation of the world.

Ephesians 1

Here's the biblical support first from Ephesians 1. In verses four to six Paul says, "[God] chose us *in him* [that is, in Christ] before the foundation of the world, that we should be holy and blameless before him. In love he predestined us for adoption *through Jesus Christ*, according to the purpose of his will, *to the praise of the glory of his grace.*" The goal of the entire history of redemption is to bring about the praise of the glory of the grace of God.

But notice that twice in these verses Paul says that this plan happened "in Christ" or "through Christ" before the foundation of the world. He says that God chose us *in Christ* before the foundation of the world in order *to bring about the praise of the glory of his grace.* And he says in verse 5 that God predestined our adoption *through Christ* before the foundation of the world *to bring about the praise of the glory of his grace.* What does it mean that "in Christ" we were chosen and that our adoption was to happen "through Christ"? We know that, according to Paul, Christ suffered and died as a redeemer so that we might be adopted as children of God (Gal. 4:5). Our adoption could not happen apart from the death of Christ.

Therefore, what Paul means is that to choose us "in Christ" and to plan to adopt us "through Christ" was to plan the suffering and death of his Son before the foundation of the world. And Ephesians 1:6, 12, and 14 make plain that the goal of this plan was to bring about "the praise of the glory of the grace of God." That is what God was aiming at. And that is why he planned the suffering and death of his Son for sinners before the creation of the world.

Revelation 5:9-12

Now consider the second biblical support that the aim of creation is the fullest display of the greatness of the glory of God's grace in the slaughter of his Son. We see it in Revelation 5:9-12. Here the hosts of heaven are worshiping the Lamb precisely because he was slain— killed, slaughtered.

> And they sang a new song, saying, "Worthy are you to take the scroll and to open its seals, *for you were slain*, and by your blood you ransomed people for God from every tribe and language and people and

nation.". . . Then I looked, and I heard around the throne . . . myriads of myriads and thousands of thousands, saying with a loud voice, "Worthy is the Lamb who was slain, to receive power and wealth and wisdom and might and honor and glory and blessing!"

The hosts of heaven focus their worship not simply on the Lamb, but on the "Lamb who was slain." And they are still singing this song in Revelation 15:3. Therefore we can conclude that the centerpiece of worship in heaven for all eternity will be the display of the glory of the grace of God in the slaughtered Lamb. Angels and all the redeemed will sing of the suffering of the Lamb forever and ever. The suffering of the Son of God will never be forgotten. The greatest suffering in history will be at the center of our worship and our wonder forever and ever. This is not an afterthought of God. This is the plan from before the foundation of the world.

Everything else is subordinate to this plan. Everything else is put in place for the sake of this plan: the display of the greatness of the glory of the grace of God in the suffering of the Beloved is the goal of the creation and the goal of all history.

The Mystery of God Ordaining but Not Doing Sin

Do you see what this implies about sin and suffering in the universe? According to this divine plan, God permits sin to enter the world. God ordains that what he hates will come to pass. It is not sin in God to will that there be sin. We do not need to fathom this mystery. We may content ourselves by saying over the sin of Adam and Eve what Joseph said over the sin of his brothers when they sold him into slavery: "As for you, you meant evil against me, but God meant it for good" (Gen. 50:20).

As for you, Adam and Eve, you meant evil against God as you rejected him as your Father and Treasure, but oh what an infinite good he planned through your fall! The Seed of the woman will one day bruise the head of the great Serpent, and by his suffering he will display the greatness of the glory of the grace of God. You have not undone his plan. Just as Joseph was sold sinfully into slavery, you have sold yourselves for an apple. You have fallen, and now the stage is set for the perfect display of the greatness of the glory of the grace of God.

For not only did sin enter the world, but through sin came suffering and death. Paul tells us that God subjected the world to futility and corruption under his holy curse. He put it like this in Romans 8:20-23:

> The creation was subjected to futility, not willingly, but because of him who subjected it, in hope that the creation itself will be set free from its bondage to decay and obtain the freedom of the glory of the children of God. For we know that the whole creation has been groaning together in the pains of childbirth until now. And not only the creation, but we ourselves, who have the firstfruits of the Spirit, groan inwardly as we wait eagerly for adoption as sons, the redemption of our bodies.

When sin entered the world, horrible, horrible things followed. Diseases, defects, disabilities, natural catastrophes, human atrocities—from the youngest infant to the oldest codger, from the vilest scoundrel to the sweetest saint—suffering is no respecter of persons. That's why Paul said in Romans 8:23, "We ourselves, who have the firstfruits of the Spirit, groan inwardly as we wait eagerly for adoption as sons, the redemption of our bodies."

Ezekiel tells us that God does not delight in this suffering. "As I live, declares the Lord GOD, I have no pleasure in the death of the wicked" (Ezek. 33:11). But the plan remains, and Jeremiah gives us a glimpse into the mysterious complexity of the mind of God in Lamentations 3:32-33, "Though he cause grief, he will have compassion according to the abundance of his steadfast love; for he does not willingly afflict or grieve the children of men." Literally: "He does not *from his heart* [*millibbô*] afflict or grieve the children of men." He ordains that suffering come— "though he cause grief"—but his delight is not in the suffering, but in the great purpose of creation: *the display of the glory of the grace of God in the suffering of Christ for the salvation of sinners.*

The stage has been set. The drama of redemptive history begins to unfold. Sin is now in its full and deadly force. Suffering and death are present and ready to consume the Son of God when he comes. All things are now in place for the greatest possible display of the glory of the grace of God.

Therefore, in the fullness of time God sent his Son into the world to suffer in the place of sinners. Every dimension of his saving work was accomplished by suffering. In the life and death of Jesus Christ, suffering finds its ultimate purpose and ultimate explanation: suffering exists so that Christ might display the greatness of the glory of the grace of God by suffering in himself to overcome our suffering.

Everything—everything—that Christ accomplished for us sinners he accomplished by suffering. Everything that we will ever enjoy will come to us because of suffering.

The Display of the Glory of the Grace of God in the Achievements of Christ by His Suffering

Consider the display of the glory of the grace of God in the achievements of Christ by his suffering.

1. CHRIST ABSORBED THE WRATH OF GOD ON OUR BEHALF— AND HE DID IT BY SUFFERING

Galatians 3:13, "Christ redeemed us from the curse of the law by becoming a curse for us—for it is written, 'Cursed is everyone who is hanged on a tree.'" The wrath of God that should have caused our eternal suffering fell on Christ. This is the glory of grace, and it could only come by suffering.

2. CHRIST BORE OUR SINS AND PURCHASED OUR FORGIVENESS— AND HE DID IT BY SUFFERING

1 Peter 2:24, "He himself bore our sins in his body on the tree." Isaiah 53:5, "He was wounded for our transgressions; he was crushed for our iniquities." The sins that should have crushed us under the weight of guilt were transferred to Christ. This is the glory of grace, and it could only come by suffering.

3. CHRIST PROVIDED A PERFECT RIGHTEOUSNESS FOR US THAT BECOMES OURS IN HIM—AND HE DID IT BY SUFFERING

Philippians 2:7-8, "[He] made himself nothing, taking the form of a servant, being born in the likeness of men. And being found in human form, he humbled himself by becoming obedient to the point of death, even death on a cross." The obedience of Christ by which many are counted righteous (Rom. 5:19) had to be an obedience unto death, even death on a cross. This is the glory of grace, and it would come only by suffering.

4. CHRIST DEFEATED DEATH—AND HE DID IT BY SUFFERING DEATH

Hebrews 2:14-15, "Since therefore the children share in flesh and blood, he himself likewise partook of the same things, that through death he might destroy the one who has the power of death, that is, the devil, and deliver all those who through fear of death were subject to lifelong slavery." "'O death, where is your victory? O death, where is your sting?' The sting of death is sin, and the power of sin is the law. But thanks be to God, who gives us the victory through our Lord Jesus Christ" (1 Cor. 15:55-57). This is the glory of grace, and it would come only by suffering.

5. HE DISARMED SATAN—AND HE DID IT BY SUFFERING

Colossians 2:14-15, "[The record of debts against us] he set aside, nailing it to the cross. He disarmed the rulers and authorities and put them to open shame, by triumphing over them in him." When the record of all our lawbreaking is nailed to the cross and cancelled, the power of Satan to destroy us is broken. Satan has only one weapon that can damn us to hell—unforgiven sin. This weapon Christ stripped from Satan's hand on the cross. This is the glory of grace, and it could only come by suffering.

6. CHRIST PURCHASED PERFECT FINAL HEALING FOR ALL HIS PEOPLE—AND HE DID IT BY SUFFERING

"Upon him was the chastisement that brought us peace, and with his stripes we are healed" (Isa. 53:5). "The Lamb in the midst of the throne will be their shepherd, and he will guide them to springs of living water, and God will wipe away every tear from their eyes" (Rev. 7:17). The Lamb was slaughtered and the Lamb was raised from the dead, and the Lamb together with the Father will wipe every tear from our eyes. This is the glory of grace, and it could only come by suffering.

7. CHRIST WILL BRING US FINALLY TO GOD—AND HE WILL DO IT BY HIS SUFFERING

1 Peter 3:18, "Christ also suffered once for sins, the righteous for the unrighteous, that he might bring us to God." The ultimate achievement of the cross is not freedom from sickness but fellowship with God. This

is what we were made for: seeing and savoring and showing the glory of God. This is the glory of grace, and it could only come by suffering.

The Ultimate Reason Why Suffering Exists

The ultimate purpose of the universe is to display the greatness of the glory of the grace of God. The highest, clearest, surest display of that glory is in the suffering of the best Person in the universe for millions of undeserving sinners. Therefore, the ultimate reason that suffering exists in the universe is so that Christ might display the greatness of the glory of the grace of God by suffering in himself to overcome our suffering and bring about the praise of the glory of the grace of God.

O Christian, remember what Carl Ellis and David Powlison and Mark Talbot and Steve Saint and Joni Eareckson Tada and Dustin Shramek say in this book: they all, in their own way, say that whether we are able or disabled, enduring loss or delighting in friends, suffering pain or savoring pleasure, all of us who believe in Christ are immeasurably rich in him and have so much to live for. Don't waste your life. Savor the riches that you have in Christ and spend yourself no matter the cost to spread your riches to this desperate world.

— Luke 2ff "And They Recognized Him.

Paul: The "backdrops"

Father Damien

Scans of Life
Scans of ministry

CHAPTER 4

Why God Appoints Suffering
for His Servants

JOHN PIPER

W hy did God appoint for Paul to suffer so much as the prototype of
the frontier missionary? He is sovereign. As every child knows he
could toss Satan into the pit today if he wanted to and all his terroriz-
ing of the church would be over. But God wills that the mission of the
church advance through storm and suffering. What are the reasons? I
will mention six.

1. Suffering Deepens Faith and Holiness

Hebrews 12 tells us that God disciplines his children through suffering.
His aim is deeper faith and deeper holiness. "He disciplines us for our
good, that we may share his holiness" (Heb. 12:10). Jesus experienced
the same thing. "Although he was a son, he learned obedience through
what he suffered" (Heb. 5:8). This does not mean that Jesus grew from
disobedience to obedience; the same writer says he never sinned (Heb.
4:15). It means that the process through which he demonstrated deeper
and deeper obedience was the process of suffering. For us there is not
only the need to have our obedience tested and proven deep, but also
purified of all remnants of self-reliance and entanglement with the
world.

This chapter, in slightly different form, originally appeared in John Piper, *Let the Nations Be Glad:
The Supremacy of God in Missions*, 2nd ed. (Grand Rapids, Mich.: Baker, 2003), 86-102. Used with
permission.

Paul described this experience in his own life like this:

> For we do not want you to be ignorant, brothers, of the affliction we experienced in Asia. For we were so utterly burdened beyond our strength that we despaired of life itself. Indeed, we felt that we had received the sentence of death. But *that was to make us rely not on ourselves but on God who raises the dead.* (2 Cor. 1:8-9)

Paul does not concede his suffering to the hand of Satan but says that God ordained it for the increase of his faith. God knocked the props of life out from under Paul's heart so that he would have no choice but to fall on God and get his hope from the promise of the resurrection. This is the first purpose of missionary suffering: to wean us from the world and set our hope fully in God alone (cf. Rom 5:3-4). Since the freedom to love flows from this kind of radical hope (Col. 1:4-5), suffering is a primary means of building compassion into the lives of God's servants.

Thousands of missionaries through the centuries have found that the sufferings of life have been the school of Christ where lessons of faith were taught that could not be learned anywhere else. For example, John G. Paton, who was born in 1824 in Scotland, was a missionary to the New Hebrides (today's Vanuatu) in the South Seas from 1858 almost until his death in 1907. He lost his wife four months after he landed on the island of Tanna at the age of thirty-four. Two weeks later his newborn son died. He buried them alone with his own hands. "But for Jesus, and the fellowship he vouchsafed to me there, I must have gone mad and died beside the lonely grave!"[1] He stayed on the island for a harrowing four years of dangers. Finally there was an uprising mounted against him, and he believed it was right to try to escape. He sought help from the one person he could trust on the island, his friend Nowar. His escape was an unforgettable discovery of grace that left a lifelong spiritual mark. To escape, Nowar told Paton he could not stay in the village; instead, he should hide in a tree, which his son would show him, and there stay till the moon rises.

---

[1] James Paton, ed., *John G. Paton: Missionary to the New Hebrides, an Autobiography* (Edinburgh: Banner of Truth, 1965 [original publication, 1889, 1898]), 80.

Being entirely at the mercy of such doubtful and vacillating friends, I, though perplexed, felt it best to obey. I climbed into the tree and was left there alone in the bush. The hours I spent there live all before me as if it were but of yesterday. I heard the frequent discharging of muskets, and the yells of the Savages. Yet I sat there among the branches, as safe in the arms of Jesus. Never, in all my sorrows, did my Lord draw nearer to me, and speak more soothingly in my soul, than when the moonlight flickered among these chestnut leaves, and the night air played on my throbbing brow, as I told all my heart to Jesus. Alone, yet not alone! If it be to glorify my God, I will not grudge to spend many nights alone in such a tree, to feel again my Savior's spiritual presence, to enjoy His consoling fellowship. If thus thrown back upon your own soul, alone, all alone, in the midnight, in the bush, in the very embrace of death itself, have you a Friend that will not fail you then?[2]

2. Suffering Makes Your Cup Increase

By enduring suffering with patience, the reward of our experience of God's glory in heaven increases. This is part of Paul's meaning in 2 Corinthians 4:17-18.

For this slight momentary affliction is preparing for us an eternal weight of glory beyond all comparison, as we look not to the things that are seen but to the things that are unseen. For the things that are seen are transient, but the things that are unseen are eternal.

Paul's affliction is "preparing" or "effecting" or "bringing about" a weight of glory beyond all comparison. We must take seriously Paul's words here. He is not merely saying that he has a great hope in heaven that enables him to endure suffering. That is true. But here he says that the suffering has an effect on the weight of glory. There seems to be a connection between the suffering endured and the degree of glory enjoyed. Of course the glory outstrips the suffering infinitely, as Paul says in Romans 8:18, "I consider that the sufferings of this present time are not worth comparing with the glory that is to be revealed to us." Nevertheless the weight of that glory, or the experience of that glory,

---

[2] Ibid., p. 200. For a brief overview of Paton's life and ministry, see John Piper, "'You Will Be Eaten By Cannibals!' Courage in the Cause of World Missions: Lessons from the Life of John G. Paton" at www.desiringGod.org.

seems to be more or less, depending in part on the affliction we have endured with patient faith.

Jesus pointed in the same direction when he said, "Blessed are you when others revile you and persecute you and utter all kinds of evil against you falsely on my account. Rejoice and be glad, for *your reward is great in heaven*" (Matt. 5:11-12). This would carry the greatest encouragement to rejoice if Jesus meant that the more we endure suffering in faith, the greater will be our reward. If a Christian who suffers much for Jesus and one who does not suffer much experience God's final glory in exactly the same way and degree, it would seem strange to tell the suffering Christian to rejoice and be glad (in that very day, cf. Luke 6:23) because of the reward he would receive even if he did not suffer. The reward promised seems to be in response to the suffering and a specific recompense for it. If this is not explicit and certain here, it does seem to be implied in other passages of the New Testament. I will let Jonathan Edwards bring them out as we listen to one of the most profound reflections on this problem I have ever read. Here Edwards deals, in a breathtaking way, with the issue of how there can be degrees of happiness in a world of perfect joy.

> There are different degrees of happiness and glory in heaven. . . . The glory of the saints above will be in some proportion to their eminency in holiness and good works here [and patience through suffering is one of the foremost good works, cf. Rom. 2:7]. Christ will reward all according to their works. He that gained ten pounds was made ruler over ten cities, and he that gained five pounds over five cities (Luke 19:17-19). "He that soweth sparingly, shall reap sparingly; and he that soweth bountifully shall reap also bountifully" (2 Corinthians 9:6). And the apostle Paul tells us that, as one star differs from another star in glory, so also it shall be in the resurrection of the dead (1 Corinthians 15:41). Christ tells us that he who gives a cup of cold water unto a disciple in the name of a disciple, shall in no wise lose his reward. But this could not be true, if a person should have no greater reward for doing many good works than if he did but few.
>
> It will be no damp to the happiness of those who have lower degrees of happiness and glory, that there are others advanced in glory above them: for all shall be perfectly happy, every one shall be perfectly satisfied. Every vessel that is cast into this ocean of happiness is full, though there are some vessels far larger than others; and there shall be

no such thing as envy in heaven, but perfect love shall reign through the whole society. Those who are not so high in glory as others, will not envy those that are higher, but they will have so great, and strong, and pure love to them, that they will rejoice in their superior happiness; their love to them will be such that they will rejoice that they are happier than themselves; so that instead of having a damp to their own happiness, it will add to it. . . .

And so, on the other hand, those that are highest in glory, as they will be the most lovely, so they will proportionally excel in divine benevolence and love to others, and will have more love to God and to the saints than those that are lower in holiness and happiness. And besides, those that will excel in glory will also excel in humility. Here in this world, those that are above others are the objects of envy, because . . . others conceive of them as being lifted up with it; but in heaven it will not be so, but those saints in heaven who excel in happiness will also [excel] in holiness, and consequently in humility. . . . The exaltation of some in heaven above the rest will be so far from diminishing the perfect happiness and joy of the rest who are inferior, that they will be the happier for it; such will be the union in their society that they will be partakers of each other's happiness. Then will be fulfilled in its perfections that which is declared in 1 Corinthians 12:22, "If one of the members be honored all the members rejoice with it."[3]

Thus one of the aims of God in the suffering of the saints is to enlarge their capacity to enjoy his glory both here and in the age to come. When their cup is picked up as it were from the "scum of the world" (1 Cor. 4:13), and tossed into the ocean of heaven's happiness, it will hold more happiness for having been long weaned off the world and made to live on God alone.

---

[3] Jonathan Edwards, *The Works of Jonathan Edwards*, 2 vols. (Edinburgh: Banner of Truth, 1974), 2:902. The parable of the workers in the vineyard who all made the same wage (Matt. 20:1-16) need not be in conflict with what Edwards (and the texts he cites!) teaches here. What that text may imply is that all of us are thrown into the same ocean of happiness. Another point of that parable is that God is free to give anyone any degree of blessing more than he deserves, and if there is anyone who is self-pitying in or proud about his endurance, God is indeed free to exalt a person even above him so as to humble him and make him realize all of heaven is all of grace. I think Jonathan Edwards effectively answers Craig Blomberg's question: "Is it not fundamentally self-contradictory to speak of degrees of perfection?" "Degrees of Reward in the Kingdom of Heaven," in *Journal of the Evangelical Theological Society* 35 (June 1992): 162-63. I do, however, want to side with Blomberg over against those who speak of "earning" rewards and who distort the conditional promises of heaven into promises of levels of reward in heaven.

3. Suffering Is the Price of Making Others Bold

God uses the suffering of his missionaries to awaken others out of their slumbers of indifference and make them bold. When Paul was imprisoned in Rome he wrote of this to the church at Philippi. "Most of the brothers, having become confident in the Lord by my imprisonment, are much more bold to speak the word without fear" (Phil. 1:14). If he must, God will use the suffering of his devoted emissaries to make a sleeping church wake up and take risks for God.

The sufferings and dedication of young David Brainerd has had this effect on thousands. Henry Martyn recorded Brainerd's impact on his life again and again in his *Journal*.

> September 11, 1805: What a quickening example has he often been to me, especially on this account, that he was of a weak and sickly constitution!

> May 8, 1806: Blessed be the memory of that holy man! I feel happy that I shall have his book with me in India, and thus enjoy, in a manner, the benefit of his company and example.

> May 12, 1806: My soul was revived today through God's never-ceasing compassion, so that I found the refreshing presence of God in secret duties; especially was I most abundantly encouraged by reading D. Brainerd's account of the difficulties attending a mission to the heathen. Oh, blessed be the memory of that beloved saint! No uninspired writer ever did me so much good. I felt most sweetly joyful to labor amongst the poor natives here; and my willingness was, I think, more divested of those romantic notions, which have sometimes inflated me with false spirits.[4]

Five Inspiring Wives

In our own time it is hard to overstate the impact that the martyrdom of Jim Elliot, Nate Saint, Ed McCully, Pete Fleming, and Roger Youderian has had on generations of students.[5] The word that appeared

---

[4] *Journal and Letters of Henry Martyn*, 240, 326-28.
[5] For their remarkable story, see the following resources: Elisabeth Elliot, *Through Gates of Splendor*, 40th Anniversary Edition (Wheaton, Ill.: Tyndale House, 1986); Elisabeth Elliot, *Shadow of the Almighty: The Life and Testament of Jim Elliot* (San Francisco, Calif.: Harper San Francisco, 1989); Elisabeth Elliot, *The Savage My Kinsmen*, 40th Anniversary Edition (Ann Arbor, Mich.: Servant Publications, 1996); Steve Saint, "Did They Have to Die?" *Christianity Today* 40, no. 10 (September 16, 1996): 20-27; Russell T. Hitt, *Jungle Pilot: The Gripping Story of the Life and Witness of Nate Saint, Martyred Missionary to Ecuador* (Grand Rapids, Mich: Discovery House, 1997).

again and again in the testimonies of those who heard the Huaorani[6] story was "dedication." But more than is often realized it was the strength of the wives of these men that made many of us feel a surge of desire to be dedicated.

Barbara Youderian, the wife of Roger, wrote in her diary that night in January 1956:

> Tonight the Captain told us of his finding four bodies in the river. One had tee-shirt and blue-jeans. Roj was the only one who wore them. . . . God gave me this verse two days ago, Psalm 48:14, "For this God is our God for ever and ever; He will be our Guide even unto death." As I came face to face with the news of Roj's death, my heart was filled with praise. He was worthy of his homegoing. Help me, Lord, to be both mummy and daddy.[7]

It is not hard to feel the biblical point Paul was making. The suffering of the servants of God, borne with faith and even praise, is a shattering experience to apathetic saints whose lives are empty in the midst of countless comforts.

Applications Doubled at His Death

The execution of Wycliffe missionary Chet Bitterman by the Colombian guerrilla group M-19 on March 6, 1981, unleashed an amazing zeal for the cause of Christ. Chet had been in captivity for seven weeks while his wife, Brenda, and little daughters Anna and Esther waited in Bogotá. The demand of M-19 was that Wycliffe get out of Colombia.

> They shot him just before dawn—a single bullet to the chest. Police found his body in the bus where he died, in a parking lot in the south of town. He was clean and shaven, his face relaxed. A guerrilla banner wrapped his remains. There were no signs of torture.

In the year following Chet's death "applications for overseas service with Wycliffe Bible Translators doubled. This trend was continued."[8] It is not the kind of missionary mobilization that any of us would choose. But it

---

[6] This is the name of the tribe formerly called Auca, which means "savage."
[7] Quoted in Elisabeth Elliot, *Through Gates of Splendor* (New York: Harper & Row, 1957), 235-36.
[8] Steve Estes, *Called to Die* (Grand Rapids, Mich.: Zondervan, 1986), 252.

is God's way. "Unless a grain of wheat falls into the earth and dies, it remains alone; but if it dies, it bears much fruit" (John 12:24).

4. Suffering Fills Up What Is Lacking in Christ's Afflictions

The suffering of Christ's messengers ministers to those they are trying to reach and may open them to the gospel. This was one of the ways Paul brought the gospel to bear on the people in Thessalonica. "You know what kind of men we proved to be among you *for your sake.* And *you became imitators of us* and of the Lord, for *you received the word in much affliction*, with the joy of the Holy Spirit" (1 Thess. 1:5-6). They had imitated Paul by enduring much affliction with joy, the sort of endurance that Paul had evidenced among them. So it was his suffering that moved them and drew them to his authentic love and truth.

This is the kind of ministry Paul had in mind when he said, "As we share abundantly in Christ's sufferings, so through Christ we share abundantly in comfort too. If we are afflicted, it is for your comfort and salvation" (2 Cor. 1:5-6). His sufferings were the means God used to bring salvation to the Corinthian church. The Corinthians could see the suffering love of Christ in Paul. He was actually sharing in Christ's sufferings and making them real for the church.

This is part of what Paul meant in that amazing statement in Colossians 1:24, "I rejoice in my sufferings for your sake, and in my flesh I am *filling up what is lacking in Christ's afflictions for the sake of his body*, that is, the church." Christ's afflictions are not lacking in their atoning sufficiency. They are lacking in that they are not known and felt by people who were not at the cross. Paul dedicated himself not only to carry the message of those sufferings to the nations, but also to suffer with Christ and for Christ in such a way that what the people saw were "Christ's sufferings." In this way he followed the pattern of Christ by laying down his life for the life of the church. "I endure everything for the sake of the elect, that they also may obtain the salvation that is in Christ Jesus with eternal glory" (2 Tim. 2:10).

"When We Saw Your Blistered Feet"

While I was working on the first edition of *Let the Nations Be Glad!* in 1992, I had an opportunity to hear J. Oswald Sanders speak. His message touched deeply on suffering. He was eighty-nine years old at the time and still traveled and spoke around the world. He had written a book a year since he turned seventy! I mention that only to exult in the utter dedication of a life poured out for the gospel without thought of coasting in self-indulgence from age sixty-five to the grave.[9]

He told the story of an indigenous missionary who walked barefoot from village to village preaching the gospel in India. After a long day of many miles and much discouragement he came to a certain village and tried to speak the gospel but was spurned. So he went to the edge of the village dejected and lay down under a tree and slept from exhaustion.

When he awoke the whole town was gathered to hear him. The head man of the village explained that they came to look him over while he was sleeping. When they saw his blistered feet they concluded that he must be a holy man, and that they had been evil to reject him. They were sorry and wanted to hear the message that he was willing to suffer so much to bring them.

At the Third Beating the Women Wept

One of the unlikeliest men to attend the Itinerant Evangelists' Conference in Amsterdam sponsored by the Billy Graham Association was a Masai Warrior named Joseph. But his story won him a hearing with Dr. Graham himself. The story is told by Michael Card.

> One day Joseph, who was walking along one of these hot, dirty African roads, met someone who shared the gospel of Jesus Christ with him. Then and there he accepted Jesus as his Lord and Savior. The power of the Spirit began transforming his life; he was filled with such excitement and joy that the first thing he wanted to do was return to his own village and share that same Good News with the members of his local tribe.
>
> Joseph began going from door-to-door, telling everyone he met about the Cross of Jesus and the salvation it offered, expecting to see their faces light up the way his had. To his amazement the villagers not only didn't care, they became violent. The men of the village seized him and held him to the ground while the women beat him with strands of

---

[9] For an organization devoted to helping people nearing retirement give their energy and skill and heart to the cause of Christ, see the Finishers Project (http://www.finishers.org/). Part of their vision statement says, "We can either give them to Jesus to lay up as treasure in Heaven or lose them."

barbed wire. He was dragged from the village and left to die alone in the bush.

Joseph somehow managed to crawl to a waterhole, and there, after days of passing in and out of consciousness, found the strength to get up. He wondered about the hostile reception he had received from people he had known all his life. He decided he must have left something out or told the story of Jesus incorrectly. After rehearsing the message he had first heard, he decided to go back and share his faith once more.

Joseph limped into the circle of huts and began to proclaim Jesus. "He died for you, so that you might find forgiveness and come to know the living God," he pleaded. Again he was grabbed by the men of the village and held while the women beat him reopening wounds that had just begun to heal. Once more they dragged him unconscious from the village and left him to die.

To have survived the first beating was truly remarkable. To live through the second was a miracle. Again, days later, Joseph awoke in the wilderness, bruised, scarred—and determined to go back.

He returned to the small village and this time, they attacked him before he had a chance to open his mouth. As they flogged him for the third and probably the last time, he again spoke to them of Jesus Christ, the Lord. Before he passed out, the last thing he saw was that the women who were beating him began to weep.

This time he awoke in his own bed. The ones who had so severely beaten him were now trying to save his life and nurse him back to health. The entire village had come to Christ.[10]

Surely this is something of what Paul meant when he said, "I fill up what is lacking in Christ's afflictions, for the sake of his body" (Col. 1:24).

5. Suffering Enforces the Missionary Command to Go

The suffering of the church is used by God to reposition the missionary troops in places they might not have otherwise gone. This is clearly the effect that Luke wants us to see in the story of the martyrdom of Stephen and the persecution that came after it. God spurs the church into missionary service by the suffering she endures. Therefore we must not judge too quickly the apparent setbacks and tactical defeats of the church. If you see things with the eyes of God, the Master

---

[10] Michael Card, "Wounded in the House of Friends," *Virtue* (March/April 1991): 28-29, 69.

Strategist, what you see in every setback is the positioning of troops for a greater advance and a greater display of his wisdom and power and love.

Acts 8:1 charts the divine strategy for the persecution: "There arose on that day [the day of Stephen's murder] a great persecution against the church in Jerusalem, and they were all scattered throughout the regions of *Judea and Samaria,* except the apostles." Up until now no one had moved out to Judea and Samaria in spite of what Jesus had said in Acts 1:8: "You will receive power when the Holy Spirit has come upon you, and you will be my witnesses in Jerusalem and in all Judea and Samaria. . . ." It is no accident that these are the very two regions to which the persecution sends the church. What obedience will not achieve, persecution will.

To confirm this divine missionary purpose of the persecution, Luke refers to it in Acts 11:19: "Now those who were scattered because of the persecution that arose over Stephen traveled as far as Phoenicia and Cyprus and Antioch, speaking the word to no one except Jews." But in Antioch some spoke to Greeks also. In other words, the persecution not only sent the church to Judea and Samaria (Acts 8:1) but also beyond to the nations (Acts 11:19).

The Inertia of Ease, the Apathy of Abundance

The lesson here is not just that God is sovereign and turns setbacks into triumphs. The lesson is that comfort and ease and affluence and prosperity and safety and freedom often cause a tremendous inertia in the church. The very things that we think would produce personnel and energy and creative investment of time and money for the missionary cause instead produce the exact opposite: weakness, apathy, lethargy, self-centeredness, and preoccupation with security.

Studies have shown that the richer we are, the smaller the percentage of our income we give to the church and its mission. The poorest fifth of the church give 3.4 percent of their income to the church and the richest fifth give 1.6 percent—half as much as the poorer church members.[11] It is a strange principle, one that probably goes right to the heart

---

[11] The *Minneapolis Star Tribune* carried an article on Friday, May 3, 1991, from which these data are taken.

of our sinfulness and Christ's sufficiency, that hard times, like persecution, often produce more personnel, more prayer, more power, more open purses than easy times.

It is hard for a rich man to enter the kingdom of heaven, Jesus said (Matt. 19:23). It is also hard for rich people to help others enter. Jesus said as much in the parable of the soils. "The cares of the world, and *the delight in riches*, and *the desire for other things* enter in and choke the word and it proves unfruitful" (Mark 4:19, AT)—unfruitful for missions and most every other good work.

Persecution can have harmful effects on the church, but prosperity seems even more devastating to the mission God calls us to. My point here is not that we should seek persecution. That would be presumption—like jumping off the temple. The point is that we should be very wary of prosperity and excessive ease and comfort and affluence. And we should not be disheartened but filled with hope if we are persecuted for righteousness' sake, because the point of Acts 8:1 is that God makes persecution serve the mission of the church.

We must not be glib about this. The price of missionary advance is immense. Stephen paid for it with his life. And Stephen was one of the brightest stars in the Jerusalem sky. His enemies "could not withstand the wisdom and the Spirit with which he spoke" (Acts 6:10, AT). Surely he was more valuable alive than dead, we would all reason. He was needed! There was no one like Stephen! But God saw it another way.

How Joseph Stalin Served the Cause

The way God brought whole Uzbek villages to Christ in the twentieth century is a great illustration of God's strange use of upheaval and displacement. Bill and Amy Stearns tell the story in their hope-filled book, *Catch the Vision 2000.*[12] The key player was Joseph Stalin.

> Thousands of Koreans fled what is now North Korea in the 1930s as the Japanese invaded. Many of these settled around Vladivostok. When Stalin in the late '30s and early '40s began developing Vladivostok as a weapons manufacturing center, he deemed the Koreans a security risk. So he relocated them in five areas around the

---

[12] Bill and Amy Stearns, *Catch the Vision 2000* (Minneapolis: Bethany, 1991), 12-13.

Soviet Union. One of those areas was Tashkent, hub of the staunchly Muslim people called the Uzbeks. Twenty million strong, the Uzbeks had for hundreds of years violently resisted any Western efforts to introduce Christianity.

As the Koreans settled around Tashkent, the Uzbeks welcomed their industry and kindness. Within a few decades, the Koreans were included in nearly every facet of Uzbek cultural life.

As usual in God's orchestration of global events, he had planted within the relocated Koreans strong pockets of believers. Little did Stalin suspect that these Koreans would not only begin enjoying a wild-fire revival among their own people, they would also begin bringing their Muslim, Uzbek, and Kazak friends to Christ.

The first public sign of the Korean revival and its breakthrough effects on the Uzbeks and Kazaks came on June 2, 1990, when in the first open-air Christian meeting in the history of Soviet Central Asia, a young Korean from America preached to a swelling crowd in the streets of Alma-Ata, capital of Kazakhstan.

The result of these roundabout, decades-long maneuverings by God to position his people in inaccessible places is that Muslims, who would not receive missionaries, are confessing that *Isa* (Jesus) is the way the truth and the life. This was a costly strategy for many believers. To be uprooted from their homeland in Korea, and then again from their new home near Vladivostok, must have been a severe test of the Koreans' faith that God is good and has a loving plan for their lives. The truth was that God did have a loving plan, and not only for their lives but also for many unreached Muslims among the Uzbek and Kazak peoples.

Going Forward by Getting Arrested

God's strange ways of guiding the missionary enterprise are seen similarly in the way Jesus told the disciples to expect arrest and imprisonment as God's deployment tactic to put them with people they would never otherwise reach. "They will lay their hands on you and persecute you, delivering you up to the synagogues and prisons, and you will be brought before kings and governors for my name's sake. *This will be a time for you to bear testimony*" (Luke 21:12-13, AT; cf. Mark 13:9).

The June/July 1989 issue of *Mission Frontiers* carried an article signed with the pseudonym, Frank Marshall. He was a missionary in a politically sensitive Latin American country.[13] He told the story of his recent imprisonment. He and his coworkers had been beaten numerous times and thrown in jail before. This time federal agents accused him of fraud and bribing because they assumed he could not have gotten his official documents without lying. They did not believe that he had been born in the country.

In prison the Lord spared him from sexual assault from a huge man wrapped in a towel with four gold chains around his neck and a ring on every finger. When put in the cell with this man, Frank began sharing the gospel with him and praying in his heart, "Lord, deliver me from this evil." The man changed color, shouted at Frank to shut up, and told him to leave him alone.

Frank began to tell others about Christ when the men had free time in the courtyard. One Muslim named Satawa confessed Christ within the first week and invited Frank to answer questions with a group of fifteen other Muslims. In two weeks Frank finally was able to get a lawyer. He also asked for a box of Bibles. The next Sunday forty-five men gathered in the courtyard to hear Frank preach. He spoke about how hard it was for him to be away from his family, and spoke of how much God loved his Son and yet gave him up for sinners so that we could believe and live. Thirty of these men stayed afterwards to pray and ask the Lord to lead them and forgive them. Frank was soon released and deported to the United States. But he now knows firsthand the meaning of Jesus' words, "This will be a time for testimony."

Miracles in Mozambique

During the 1960s the Lord raised up an indigenous leader in the church in Mozambique named Martinho Campos. The story of his ministry, *Life Out of Death in Mozambique*, is a remarkable testimony to God's strange ways of missionary blessing.

Martinho was leading a series of meetings in the administrative area of Gurue sixty miles from his own area of Nauela. The police arrested him and put him in jail without a trial. The police chief, a European, assumed that the gatherings were related to the emerging guerrilla

---

[13] Frank Marshall, "Fear No Evil," *Missions Frontiers*, June 1, 1989.

group Frelimo. But even when the Catholic priest told him that these men were just "a gathering of heretics," he took no concern for justice, though he wondered why the common people brought so much food to the prisoner, as though he were someone important.

One night he was driving his truck with half a dozen prisoners in it and saw "what appeared to be a man in gleaming white, standing in the road, facing him." He swerved so sharply that the truck rolled over and he was trapped underneath. The prisoners themselves lifted the truck so that the police chief could get out.

After brief treatment in the hospital he returned to talk to Martinho because he knew there was some connection between this vision and the prisoner. He entered Martinho's cell and asked for forgiveness. Martinho told him about his need for God's forgiveness and how to have it. The police chief said humbly, "Please pray for me." Immediately the chief called for hot water so that the prisoner might wash, took him out of solitary confinement, and saw to it that a fair trial was held. Martinho was released.

But the most remarkable thing was what followed: "Not only did the chief of police make plain his respect for what Martinho stood for, but he also granted him official permission to travel throughout the whole area under his jurisdiction in order to preach and hold evangelical services."[14] There would have been no way that such a permission would have been given through the ordinary channels. But God had a way through suffering. The imprisonment was for the advancement of the gospel.

God Was Better Served in Prison

On January 9, 1985, Pastor Hristo Kulichev, a Congregational pastor in Bulgaria, was arrested and put in prison. His crime was that he preached in his church even though the state had appointed another man the pastor, one whom the congregation did not elect. Kulichev's trial was a mockery of justice, and he was sentenced to eight months imprisonment. During his time in prison he made Christ known every way he could.

When he got out, he wrote, "Both prisoners and jailers asked many

---

[14] Phyllis Thompson, *Life Out of Death in Mozambique* (London: Hodder and Stoughton, 1989), 111.

questions, and it turned out that we had a more fruitful ministry there than we could have expected in church. God was better served by our presence in prison than if we had been free."[15] In many places in the world, the words of Jesus are as radically relevant as if they had been spoken yesterday. "They will deliver you to prison. . . . This will be a time for you to bear testimony" (Luke 21:12-13, AT). The pain of our shattered plans is for the purpose of scattered grace.

6. The Supremacy of Christ Is Manifest in Suffering

The suffering of missionaries is meant by God to magnify the power and sufficiency of Christ. Suffering is finally to show the supremacy of God. When God declined to remove the suffering of Paul's "thorn in the flesh," he said to Paul, "My grace is sufficient for you, for *my power is made perfect in weakness.*" To this Paul responded, "I will boast all the more gladly of my weaknesses, so that the power of Christ may rest upon me. For the sake of Christ, then, I am content with weaknesses, insults, hardships, persecutions, and calamities. For when I am weak, then I am strong" (2 Cor. 12:9-10).

Paul was strong in persecutions because "the power of Christ" rested upon him and was made perfect in him. In other words, Christ's power was Paul's only power when his sufferings brought him to the end of his resources and cast him wholly on Jesus. This was God's purpose in Paul's thorn, and it is his purpose in all our suffering. God means for us to rely wholly on him. "That was to make us rely not on ourselves but on God who raises the dead" (2 Cor. 1:9). The reason God wants this is because this kind of trust shows his supreme power and love to sustain us when we can't do anything to sustain ourselves.

We began this chapter with this claim: loss and suffering, joyfully accepted for the kingdom of God, show the supremacy of God's worth more clearly in the world than all worship and prayer. This truth has been implicit in the six reasons we've been looking at as to why God appoints suffering for the messengers of his grace. But now we need to make explicit that the supremacy of God is the reason for suffering running through and above all the other reasons. God ordains suffering

---

[15] Herbert Schlossberg, *Called to Suffer, Called to Triumph* (Portland: Multnomah, 1990), 230.

because through all the other reasons it displays to the world the supremacy of his worth above all treasures.

Jesus makes crystal clear how we can rejoice in persecution. "Blessed are you when others revile you and persecute you and utter all kinds of evil against you falsely on my account. Rejoice and be glad, *for your reward is great in heaven*" (Matt. 5:11-12). The reason we can rejoice in persecution is that the worth of our reward in heaven is so much greater than the worth of all that we lose through suffering on earth. Therefore, suffering with joy proves to the world that our treasure is in heaven and not on the earth, and that this treasure is greater than anything the world has to offer. The supremacy of God's worth shines through the pain that his people will gladly bear for his name.

Gladly Will I Boast of Weakness and Calamity

I use the word "gladly" because that's the way the saints speak of it. For example, we just saw Paul saying, "I will boast all the more gladly of my weaknesses . . . insults, hardships, persecutions, and calamities" (2 Cor. 12:9-10). He says the same thing in Romans: "We rejoice in our sufferings." And the reason he gives is that it produces patience and a tested quality of life and an unfailing hope (Rom. 5:3-4). In other words, his joy flowed from his hope just the way Jesus said it should. And Paul makes clear that the reward is the glory of God. "We rejoice in hope of the glory of God" (Rom. 5:2). And so it is the supremacy of God's worth that shines through in Paul's joy in affliction.

We find the other apostles reacting the same way in Acts 5:41 after being beaten for their preaching: "Then they left the presence of the council, rejoicing that they were counted worthy to suffer dishonor for the name" (Acts 5:41). This fearless joy in spite of real danger and great pain is the display of God's superiority over all that the world has to offer.

You Joyfully Accepted the Plundering of Your Property

Again the early Christians who visited their friends in prison rejoiced even though it cost them their possessions. "For you had compassion on those in prison, and you joyfully accepted the plundering of your property, since you knew that you yourselves had a better possession and an abiding one" (Heb. 10:34). Joy in suffering flows from hope in a great reward. Christians are not called to live morose lives of burdensome persecution. We are called to rejoice. "Rejoice insofar as you share Christ's sufferings" (1 Pet. 4:13). "Count it all joy, my brothers, when you meet various trials" (James 1:2).

The Love of God Is Better Than Life

The basis for this indomitable joy is the supremacy of God's love above life itself. "Your steadfast love is better than life. . . ." (Ps. 63:3). The pleasures in this life are "fleeting" (Heb. 11:25) and the afflictions are "light and momentary" (2 Cor. 4:17, NIV). But the steadfast love of the Lord is forever. All his pleasures are superior and there will be no more pain. "In your presence there is fullness of joy; at your right hand are pleasures forevermore" (Ps. 16:11).

Glad Suffering Shines Brighter Than Gratitude

It is true that we should bear testimony to the supremacy of God's goodness by receiving his good gifts with thanksgiving (1 Tim. 4:3). But for many Christians this has become the only way they see their lifestyles glorifying God. God has been good to give them so much; therefore, the way to witness to the reality of God is to take and be thankful.

But even though it is true that we should thankfully enjoy what we have, there is a relentless call in the Bible not to accumulate more and more things, but to give more and more, and to be deprived of things if love demands it. There are no easy rules to tell us whether the call on our lives is the call of the rich young ruler to give away all that we have, or the call of Zacchaeus to give away half of what we have. What is clear from the New Testament is that suffering with joy, not gratitude in wealth, is the way the worth of Jesus shines most brightly.

Who can doubt that the supremacy of Christ's worth shines brightest in a life like this:

> But whatever gain I had, I counted as loss *for the sake of Christ*. Indeed I count everything as loss because of *the surpassing worth of knowing Christ Jesus my Lord*. For his sake I have suffered the loss of all things and count them as refuse *in order that I may gain Christ*. (Phil. 3:7-8, AT)

You cannot show the preciousness of a person by being happy with his gifts. Ingratitude will certainly prove that the giver is not loved. But gratitude for gifts does not prove that the giver is precious. What proves that the giver is precious is the glad-hearted readiness to leave all his gifts to be with him. This is why suffering is so central in the mission of the church. The goal of our mission is that people from all the nations worship the true God. But worship means cherishing the preciousness of God above all else, including life itself. It will be very hard to bring the nations to love God from a lifestyle that communicates a love of things. Therefore, God ordains in the lives of his messengers that suffering sever our bondage to the world. When joy and love survive this severing, we are fit to say to the nations with authenticity and power: hope in God.

How Is Hope in God Made Visible?

Peter talks about the visibility of this hope: "Hallow the Lord Christ in your hearts, ready always to give a reason to everyone who asks you for a word concerning the hope that is in you" (1 Pet. 3:15, AT). Why would people ask about hope? What kind of life are we to live that would make people wonder about our hope? If our security and happiness in the future were manifestly secured the way the world secures its future, no one would ask us about it. There would be no unusual hope to see. What Peter is saying is that the world should see a different hope in the lives of Christians— not a hope in the security of money or the security of power or the security of houses or lands or portfolios, but the security of "the grace that is coming to you at the revelation of Jesus Christ" (1 Pet. 1:13, AT).

Therefore, God ordains suffering to help us release our hold on worldly hopes and put our "hope in God" (1 Pet. 1:21). The fiery trials are appointed to consume the earthly dependencies and leave only the refined gold of "genuine faith" (1 Pet. 1:7). "Therefore let those who suffer according to God's will entrust their souls to a faithful Creator while doing good" (1 Pet. 4:19). It's the supremacy of God's great faithfulness above all other securities that frees us to "rejoice as [we] share in Christ's sufferings" (1 Pet. 4:13, AT). Therefore, joy in suffering for Christ's sake makes the supremacy of God shine more clearly than all our gratitude for wealth.

CHAPTER 5

Sovereignty, Suffering, and the Work of Missions

STEPHEN F. SAINT

I don't know why I am identified with suffering. I guess it is because suffering, like camping and wealth, is relative. No doubt when people hear my life story, they imagine themselves in my position and think, "Wow, he has really suffered." *They can picture themselves in my suffering much more easily than they can understand the incredible blessings and benefits that those painful chapters in my life have provided me.*

Suffering, like many other events in life, *is* relative. I offered to take a friend down to the Amazon to meet my jungle family. Someone overheard our conversation and confided, "I don't think that would be such a good idea. To Kevin, a night at the Hilton is 'camping out.'"

Wealth is also relative. Years ago when my wife, Ginny, and I lived in Dallas, our neighbors frequently referred to the rich people living inside the beltway. Our friends inside the beltway referred to the wealthy people living in the posh neighborhoods just outside downtown Dallas. I guess people hear or read about the minor tragedies in my life, and in relation to their lives it looks like I have suffered. But I compare my life to the experiences of people I have lived with who are persecuted and threatened, who die from minor illnesses because they have little or no access to medical attention, and I think, "Boy, do I have it good."

A Chinese Christian who heard me speak once asked me if I would write a tract about suffering for his fellow believers in the Orient. I told him I would think about it. But when I did, I realized that in comparison to those Chinese believers I knew very little about the topic.

I do know this: *sufferers want to be ministered to by people who have suffered.* When I was a teenager, I knew a family whose son was terribly burned when he ran into a car and the gas tank on his motorcycle exploded. In the hospital burn unit he begged his mother to just let him die. She responded by inviting friends to cheer him up, but he refused to see anyone. Finally one day there was a knock on his hospital room door. When his mother opened the door there was a stranger with hideous scars all over his face and arms standing there.

The mother slammed the door, hoping her son hadn't seen the man. But he had, and insisted that his mother let the man in. His mother resisted, thinking the sight would further discourage her son. Instead of discouraging the boy, however, that man convinced the boy that there was reason to live.

People who suffer want people who have suffered to tell them there is hope. They are justifiably suspicious of people who appear to have lived lives of ease. There is no doubt in my mind that this is the reason that Jesus suffered in every way that we do, while he was here. First Peter 2:21 says, "This [your] suffering is all part of what God has called you to. Christ, who suffered for you, is your example. Follow in his steps" (NLT).

The Reasons for Suffering

The Bible identifies a number of reasons for suffering:

1. God uses suffering *as punishment.* When David was punished for numbering the Israelites in 1 Chronicles 21:12, God gave him three suffering choices: three years of famine, three months of defeats at the hand of Israel's enemies, or three days of pestilence and death at the hands of God's angel.
2. God also uses suffering *to demonstrate his power.* I was perplexed to realize that the poor blind man who begged outside the temple in John 9 had been blind his whole life just so Jesus could prove God's power. That was a lot of suffering in a society without "Americans with Disabilities Act" laws.

3. Suffering also builds *perseverance and strength of character* as revealed in James 1 and Romans 5. I actually hated the verses in James 1 that say, "Whenever trouble comes your way, let it be an opportunity for joy. For when your faith is tested, your endurance has a chance to grow. So let it grow. . . ." (James 1:2-4, NLT).

4. Paul revealed in 2 Corinthians 12:7 that God would not take away his personal suffering caused by a "thorn in the flesh" because it kept him *humble*.

The Avoidance of Suffering

In the United States and most other highly developed and industrialized nations that have been exporters of Christ's gospel, it is generally accepted that the avoidance of suffering is a respected primary objective in life. But in relation to missionary efforts, our lack of suffering is a great obstacle to our effectiveness in communicating Christ's plan for hurting people in third- and fourth-world countries. Suffering people who think we never suffer are understandably cynical about our ability to understand them and care for their physical, emotional, and spiritual hurts.

To be fair, I have to admit that I think there is a great deal of suffering in the United States. Rich people suffer along with poor people, just differently. During the Great Depression, poor people weren't jumping out of tall buildings; the jumpers were rich people who had just become poor. We are the richest country the world has ever produced— ever. And yet our suicide rate and crime rate are extremely high. Suffering is one of the few aspects of life that everyone gets a shot at. And you don't have to be a rocket scientist to figure out that the worst hurts are the ones *you* feel.

I remember spending a night in the hospital after having my appendix removed. I woke up around two o' clock in the morning when they put another patient in my room. As the night wore on, he kept moaning and waking me up. Finally I asked him what could be so terrible that he couldn't be quiet and let me get some sleep. He answered, "*Mi pierna me duele; Mi pierna me duele.*" I turned on the light to see what about his leg could possibly be hurting so badly. It turned out that he had just been hit by a car, and they had amputated his badly man-gled leg. He didn't even know yet that it was gone.

I felt like a schmuck because my worry over the tiny severed appendage on my intestine made me insensitive to a man who had just had his whole leg amputated. But my remorse was short-lived because, despite the significance of his trauma, my tiny operation was the trauma that impacted me.

Two Painful Chapters

Enough of general statements and the theology of suffering. The best way to illustrate that suffering offers significant benefits and should not be resisted is to share two painful chapters from my life. There have been plenty of others, but these two have been especially significant in giving me a passion for ministry to hurting people in what we generally refer to as *missions*.

When I was five years old my mother called me into her bedroom and told me that my hero, the man whom I wanted to grow up and be just like, the man in whom all my dreams and aspirations were centered, was never coming back to live with us again. It was my dad, and I remember thinking: but he promised me that he would teach me to fly. He promised me that. How could he leave? Then Mom said that he had gone to live with Jesus, and I thought, Oh . . . it was something we all look forward to, but I couldn't understand why he didn't come to take us with him, why he just left us behind.

It was an exciting time around our house that last Christmas my dad was home, and I can remember experiencing a great sense of expecta-tion. Actually, Christmas Day had just passed, the memories of which are most vivid in my mind. Then I thought we were going to have another Christmas celebration because these friends of ours—the Elliots, the McCullys, the Youderians—were coming to our house. I thought: this is really good; let's just keep celebrating. But I didn't understand that the excitement was for a different reason: my dad and his four friends were about to try to reach a violent tribe of people in the jungle before an oil company moved in. The tribe had been trying to defend their ter-ritory by killing the oil company's employees. So the oil company had approached the government, explaining that if the country needed oil, they had better get rid of "this problem."

Revelation 5:9-10 says that at the end of time, members of every tribe and nation and tongue will be in God's presence, and that God is going to make a royal priesthood of them. These had to be believers. My dad and his friends understood that and felt compelled to reach these people before the oil company carried out the solution to their problem. But it wasn't fearful compulsion; it was something they were excited about doing.

My dad and his friends knew that they couldn't just walk into the jungle and meet these people; others had tried to do that and failed, including the oil companies. This tribe killed everyone who had ever ventured into their territory. What my dad and his friends didn't know was that the tribe habitually and rampantly killed its own members. The homicide rate within the tribe was the highest that anthropologists have ever studied. More than sixty percent of all the people in this tribe died as a result of being speared or hacked to pieces with machetes by their own people. I don't know a single person in the tribe, similar to me in age, whose father died of natural causes.

My father and his friends knew that a universal way of showing friendship is exchanging gifts. Even though they didn't know how to *exchange* gifts with the Waodani, they did know how to *give* gifts to let them know that they were wanted. Dad had devised a system of flying in tight circles so that, from the plane, they could suspend a bucket tied to a rope that would hang motionless just above the ground. They used this system to give useful gifts to the tribe. After about the third time, the Waodani not only took the gifts out of the bucket, but they also put gifts for us back in. They exchanged gifts in that way for thirteen weeks.

Then Dad found a little sandbar not too far from the village. They landed there and waited for the people to come—Tuesday, Wednesday, Thursday. Suddenly on Friday, after the days of just waiting with nothing happening—plane idle on the sandbar near a little tree house built to run to if they were attacked—they heard voices from across the river. Two women and a man stepped out of the forest and walked across the shallow little river. They spent the day with my dad and his friends as if it was no big deal. We have a video of that movie film and the still pictures taken that day. We called it Friendly Friday. It was just so promising! Dad called my mom and told her what had happened and the word spread among the five wives. We knew that something exciting was going on.

On Saturday my dad flew over the little village to see why the man and two women hadn't come back, but nobody was in the village. Flying back from the Domointado River, across the Tewaeno River, and then to the Awanguno River where they had been landing the plane, he looked down and saw a whole delegation of naked people on the trail. So he called my mom and told her the exciting news: "Looks like they're going to be here for the early afternoon service." Then he landed and told the others, "Hey, they're on the trail." Since they'd already had friendly face-to-face contact, they were so excited.

Three women stepped out of the jungles on the upper end of the beach. Jim and Pete started walking toward them while Dad and Roger and Ed hung back; they didn't want to scare them. Suddenly, members of the tribe rushed out of the jungles—Gikita with Mincaye, Kimo and Dyuwi right behind, and Nimongo and Nampa up ahead just a bit—and they positioned themselves to separate my dad and his friends. Then Gikita struck out after my father, saying, "I'm going to spear the oldest one first." (My dad was the one they recognized from the plane.) One by one they speared my father and his friends and hacked at them, and then they did something even worse by their cultural standards—they took what was left of the bodies and derisively threw them into the river to be eaten by the fish and turtles.

I didn't know the details when I was a little boy, but I can tell you, their deaths still crushed my heart. The incident reshaped my beliefs in a way that I didn't anticipate. Before this, I believed what a lot of you probably believe: when bad things happen, God merely allows them. I found out the details of my father's death after my Aunt Rachel died. During all the years she had lived with the tribe, the death of her brother and the others was never discussed; she didn't want them to think she would seek to avenge those deaths. When Aunt Rachel died, I represented the family at her burial, and that's when a lot of answers came forth. Now that Aunt Rachel was gone, the tribe felt free to talk about the events leading up to the killings and the "family" conflict that precipitated the attack.

The death of the five martyred missionaries, and the amazing change in the Waodani that came about after Aunt Rachel and Elisabeth Elliott were invited into the tribe to teach them God's "carvings," is now a well-known story. Countless lives have been impacted by it; thousands of missionaries name it as the reason their hearts were moved to respond to God's call. Our family has been blessed by the love and friendship—kinship—of the Waodani people.

Someone came up to me at a place where I was speaking and said, "You know, if your father and his four friends had done it differently, they wouldn't have had to die." At first I was repulsed by that suggestion, but then I realized he was right. They didn't even have to go to the jungle. But then, I thought, if I had it to change, I wouldn't change a thing. I simply look at the man standing beside me, one of my dearest friends in the whole world, and I realize that he wouldn't be here now if my dad and Roger and Pete and Ed and Jim hadn't died. We call him Grandfather Mincaye because he has become a dear member of our family.

God Planned My Dad's Death

You know what my conclusion is? I don't think God merely tolerated my dad's death. I don't think he turned away when it was happening. I think he planned it. Otherwise I don't think it would have happened. This was a hard realization for me to come to. I once said that while speaking at a church, and a man came up afterwards and said, "Don't you ever say that again about my God." Afterward I found these verses in Acts 2:

> "Men of Israel, listen to these words. Jesus the Nazarene, a man attested to you by God with miracles and wonders and signs which God performed through him in your midst, just as you yourselves know, you know he was God. You nailed him to a cross, you godless people. But he was delivered up to you by the predetermined plan of God." (vv. 22-23, AT)

Then I thought: Don't anybody tell me that this can't be. If God could plan the death of his own righteous Son, why couldn't he plan the death of my dad?

God Planned My Daughter's Death

I *believe* God planned my daughter's death. In the years prior to her death, people started asking me to go around and speak, and I realized that there was a deficiency in my heart and life: I could not see the world the way God does. *Oh, be careful what you pray for.* I prayed and begged God and told Ginny, "I can't keep doing this. I go out and I'm speaking from my head to people and it doesn't work. I can't keep going. I can't speak unless I feel the passion of this." And so I started praying, "God, please, please let me have your heart for the hurting world out there. I see it, and I empathize a little bit but I don't have a passion for it." Now, don't overrate this. Perhaps a lot of you struggle with the same thing. I just couldn't keep going and talking about what I had seen God do without a passion to share it. And I had no idea if God would give me such a passion or how he would do it. I'm more mechanical; that's what I do well. I fly; it just comes, it's in the genes, I don't have to figure it out—it's just there. But passion is another story, so I begged God to let me see his heart.

We have an idea that if we do what God wants us to do, then he owes us to take the suffering away. I *believed* that; I don't believe that anymore.

Ginny and I had three boys and then we finally had a little girl. I made her promise me that she'd never grow up; she broke her promise and went away to college. And then a time of suffering came because Youth for Christ asked Stephenie, who could play the piano beautifully as well as the bass guitar, to travel around the world for a year with one of their groups sharing the gospel. And you know what? It wasn't worth it to me; I wanted my daughter home. I knew that some day she would probably meet a boy and go off. She was tall and slim, and in my eyes, beautiful. She was Ginny's bosom friend. She was our baby. She started traveling around the world, and it was a painful year. But finally the year was over and she was coming home. Ginny and I met her at the Orlando airport. Grandfather Mincaye was there too. We had made him a sign to hold up, *Welcome Home, Stephenie,* but he couldn't read so he held it upside down. He was jumping around, big holes in his ears, wearing a feather headdress. He wasn't blending! Stephenie came and saw him and tried to pretend that she didn't see us, but Mincaye went up and grabbed her and started jumping around with her. Then we headed out for a welcome home party—it was a joyous time.

Later, I passed Stephenie in the hall, and she just leaned on me and said, "Pop, I love you." I thought: God, just beam me up right now. Let's go at the peak. Does it get any better than this? All of our children are following you, and Stephenie is home. And Ginny and I—we've had a twenty-seven-year honeymoon. Let's just quit right now.

A while later, Ginny said, "Steve, Stephenie's back in her room. Let's go back and be with her." So we ditched everyone else and went back. Stephenie had a headache and asked me to pray for her. Ginny sat on the bed and held Stephenie, and I put my arms around those two girls whom I loved with all my heart, and I started praying.

While I was praying, Stephenie had a massive cerebral hemorrhage. We rushed to the hospital. I rode in the ambulance while our son Jaime and Ginny and Mincaye followed us in the car. Grandfather Mincaye had never seen this type of vehicle with the flashing lights, didn't understand why strangers had rushed into the house and grabbed Stephenie and hurried off with her. Now he saw her at the hospital, lying on a gurney with a tube down her throat and needles in her arm, and he grabbed me and said, "Who did this to her?" And I saw a look on his face that I'd seen before, and I knew that he'd be willing to kill again to save this granddaughter whom he loved.

I didn't know what to say. "I don't know, Mincaye. Nobody is doing this."

And just like that, this savage from the jungles grabbed me again and said, "Babae, don't you see?"

No, I didn't see. My heart was absolutely tearing apart; I didn't know what was going on.

He said, "Babae, Babae, now I see it well. Don't you see? God himself is doing this."

And I thought, what are you saying?

Mincaye started reaching out to all the people in the emergency room, saying, "People, people, don't you see? God, loving Star, he's taking her to live with him." And he said, "Look at me, I'm an old man; pretty soon I'm going to die too, and I'm going there." Then he said, with a pleading look on his face, "Please, please, won't you follow God's trail, too? Coming to God's place, Star and I will be waiting there to welcome you."

Why is it that we want every chapter to be good when God promises only that in the last chapter he will make all the other chapters make sense, and he doesn't promise we'll see that last chapter here? When Stephenie was dying, the doctor said, "There's no hope for recovery from an injury like this." I realized that this was either the time to lose my faith or an opportunity to show the God who gave his only Son to die for my sin that I love and trust him. And then I watched. I watched my sweet wife accept this as God's will and God's plan. And you know what God has done through this? He changed my heart. He broke it. He shredded it. And in the process he helped me see what he sees. I thought the worst thing that could happen in life was that people would go into a Christ-less eternity. There's something worse than that. It is that our loving heavenly Father, the God and Creator of the universe, is being separated every day from those he desperately loves, and he will never be reunited with them again if what this book says is right.

I don't know what role he has for you, but I know he has a role. His great passion is expressed in his Great Commission, and he has given it to messy, wimpy people like you and me. He has made us his ambassadors of reconciliation.

God's Megaphone to the World

Mincaye and I traveled with Steven Curtis Chapman as part of a concert tour back in 2002. Each night after Steve and his band told the story of how Mincaye and I became family, with video and music, Maemae Mincaye and I would spend a few minutes speaking personally to the audience.

One night Mincaye was very intently trying to communicate with the audience. He very dynamically stated, "Waengongi (Creator God) does not see it well that we should walk his trail."

I hesitated to translate what he had just said. That statement directly contradicted what I believed and knew Mincaye believed. Finally, I went ahead and translated what Grandfather had said. Fortunately, he resolved the conflict with one word. He continued, "Waengongi does not see it well that we should walk his trail *alone*!" He continued, "Don't you think Waengongi loves all of his children?"

If we are going to emulate our Savior, we have to identify with the people to whom we take his good news. I don't advocate that we look for suffering; life brings enough of it on its own. But what I do advocate is that suffering is an important prerequisite to ministering to hurting people. Christ took on our likeness and subjected himself to the suffering that plagues us.

I am convinced that we should not make heroic efforts and expend vast resources like the rest of our society does to avoid suffering. Not only would a willingness to experience hurt give us credibility with suffering people, but it would also give God a special opportunity to prove his sufficiency to meet our needs. As a wise man said, "God whispers to us in our pleasures, speaks in our conscience, but shouts in our pains: it is his megaphone to rouse a deaf world."[1]

The poet Martha Snell Nicholson wrote a short poem that expresses this very eloquently. She wrote:

I stood a mendicant of God before His royal throne
And begged him for one priceless gift, which I could call my own.
I took the gift from out His hand, but as I would depart
I cried, "But Lord this is a thorn and it has pierced my heart.
This is a strange, a hurtful gift, which Thou hast given me."
He said, "My child, I give good gifts and gave My best to thee."
I took it home and though at first the cruel thorn hurt sore,
As long years passed I learned at last to love it more and more.
I learned He never gives a thorn without this added grace,
He takes the thorn to pin aside the veil which hides His face.[2]

---

[1] C. S. Lewis, *The Problem of Pain* (New York: Macmillan, 1962), 93.
[2] Martha Snell Nicholson, "The Thorn."

CHAPTER 6

The Sovereignty of God
and Ethnic-Based Suffering

CARL F. ELLIS, JR.

We serve the sovereign God who will accomplish his will no matter what. We find this truth all the way back to creation. When we were created, we were in covenant relationship with God. This was the covenant of creation (others call it the covenant of works). According to the terms of the covenant, obedience would result in blessing. We would experience pleasure as the sovereign will of God was accomplished through us. However, if we broke the covenant, we would be under its curse, and we would experience pain as the sovereign will of God was accomplished through us.

We know from the biblical text that we broke the covenant. The fall was the result, and the path of pain was the outcome. By eating from the forbidden tree, humans were, in essence, attempting to replace God as ultimate judge of good and evil. God said, "You are free to eat from any tree in the garden; but you must not eat from the tree of the knowledge of good and evil" (Gen. 2:16-17, NIV). It wasn't that they didn't understand the nature of good and evil. The real temptation was: what would be the basis for judging good and evil? Would it be the Word of God or human opinion?

What happens just before we fall to temptation? We decide that the thing we desire is good for us. In essence, we reenact the fall every time we give in to temptation. When Adam and Eve ate the forbidden fruit, they were rejecting the Word of God as the basis of life. This was an example of creature-ism—the creature attempts to judge the Creator by creaturely standards.

Instead of immediately sending us to the lake of fire, God showed us grace. He gave us another covenant, the covenant of salvation (the covenant of grace as some call it). The covenant of salvation was designed to deliver us from the curse of the broken covenant of creation. Until salvation was fully applied we would still experience many of the effects of the fall. Among these effects would be *human power differentials*. These power differentials would lead to human power struggles. This is the basis of the ethnic-based strife and suffering.

Let us make some observations about *power*. The Bible tells us that God is all-powerful, and yet there are no power struggles between the persons of the godhead. Why? Because the Father, the Son, and the Holy Spirit are one. Before the fall Adam and Eve had significant power of dominion, yet there were no power struggles between them. Why? Because they were one. Their oneness was like God's oneness only on a human level. This is a perspective on what it means to be in the image of God. Adam was the head, but he was the first among equals.

After the fall their oneness was broken. This is where we began to have our problems. We began to think individualistically, and this led to self-centeredness. Look at what Adam told God after God confronted him about his sin: "The man said, 'The woman whom you gave to be with me, she gave me fruit of the tree, and I ate'" (Gen. 3:12). The man and the woman began to seek dominion and dominance over each other, and inequality was the result.

Thus, the first manifestation of human power struggles was seen in the marriage relationship. When God spoke to the woman in Genesis 3:16, he said, "Your desire will be for your husband, and he shall rule over you." When God said "Your desire shall be for your husband," he was not speaking of the "come hither" kind of desire. The word *desire* here is the exact same word God used when he confronted Cain about his sin. He said, "Sin . . . *desires* to have you, but you must master it" (Gen. 4:7, NIV).

Because of the loss of oneness, power struggles infected the marriage relationship. Eventually it infected all human relationships. Thus, human inequality became universal, not only between individuals like Cain and Abel but also between people groups. It makes no difference how you define people groups, whether ethnically, culturally, linguistically, or generationally. There will be inequalities among them and power struggles between them.

Another result of the fall was *persecution*. We see this in the struggle between the seed of the woman and the seed of the serpent. God said to the serpent, "I will put enmity between you and the woman, and between your seed and her seed. He will crush your head, and you will strike his heel" (Gen. 3:15, AT). The "seed of the woman" refers to the coming of the Savior, and the "seed of the serpent" refers to Satan himself; however, we often fail to see the collective application of this. From this perspective, "the seed of the woman" refers to God's covenant people, and the "seed of the serpent" refers to the enemies of God. God's enemies would persecute and seek to destroy God's people—their heel will be struck. But, God's people would successfully resist this persecution. The people of God would have a power-struggle disadvantage on a human level, yet by God's grace they would persevere and ultimately prevail over God's enemies. The enemy's head would be crushed. This struggle would be painful. Persecution has become a significant manifestation of human power struggles, and it continues to this day.

The Mystery of Suffering

The book of Job deals with the relationship between human suffering and divine justice. This is what the scholars call *theodicy*. Most of us assume a one-to-one relationship between our suffering and our sin, or between prosperity and obedience. This is what Job's friends were trying to say. They were articulating old evangelical clichés: "There must be some sin in your life, brother." Job repeatedly answered, "What else is new!" The account of Job clearly demonstrates that the bad things that happen to us are not necessarily related to our sin, anymore than the good things that happen to us are related to our righteousness, of which we have none (Isa. 64:6). The account of Job shows us that God will not abandon those who suffer for his sake. Job had a "for-realness" about his pain. Likewise, God wants us to have that same "for-realness."

In many ways suffering is a mystery. I take comfort in what Francis Schaeffer told me many times: "We only see the debit side of the ledger now. We don't see the credit side yet. When we see the whole ledger we will say, 'Oh, why didn't I see it that way before?'" This is why the Bible tells us to see now by faith. Though suffering is a mystery to us, it is not a mystery to God. Mysteries may be painful, but they should not perplex us. To God, there is no mystery. He is satisfied because he sees the whole ledger. We will also be satisfied when we see things from God's perspective. Till then, we must learn to be satisfied with God's satisfaction. If we do, we will have peace.

The Basis of Suffering

The cause of suffering is sin. This much is obvious. Suffering from sin has two general categories. First, there are the apparently random effects of sin—storms, earthquakes, floods, tsunamis, wildfires, etc. Then there are the direct results of sin, which come in two categories—ungodliness and oppression. Ungodliness involves sinning and suffering one's own consequences. (Examples are carelessness, laziness, recklessness, irresponsibility, and things like that.) Oppression involves sinning and forcing others to suffer the consequences, or imposing our sin on others. God says a lot about oppression in Scripture.

Let us make some observations. Oppression is sin plus power. If you've ever been in a dominant position over people, and you sin against them, you have oppressed them. The power to oppress doesn't require a particular skin color, ethnicity, or economic status.

I'll never forget when God opened my eyes to this. God has given me the privilege of raising two children, a boy and a girl. I'm very proud of them. They both love the Lord. When my girl was little, it was my job to braid her hair. I must admit, I became quite skilled at it. As a father, I was in a dominant position over her. One Sunday morning, her hair was looking particularly good. When I was almost finished, she said, "Daddy, the braid is too tight. It hurts!" Of course it was not my intention to inflict pain on her, yet pain was the result.

Because I was in a dominant position over her I just dismissed her pain. "Oh Nikki, it doesn't hurt."

Then she repeated, "Daddy, it hurts!" And then she started to cry. As her tears began to flow, I began to realize what I had done: I oppressed my own daughter when I denied her reality.

I strongly disagree with those who narrowly define oppression only in terms of race. Though racial oppression is real, oppression itself is universal.

Because oppression is sin plus power, it is driven by power struggles. How does oppression affect individual victims? Based on my observations, it increases their proportion of bad choices and decreases their proportion of good choices. For example, let's suppose each of us has ten choices to make in life. If we are not oppressed, we would expect eight of the ten choices to be good ones and two to be bad. However, oppression might cause eight choices to be bad and two to be good. Given the law of averages, how likely is one to make bad choices? It should not surprise us that oppressed people end up in prison in higher proportions.

As we mentioned earlier, one of the foundations of oppression is *creature-ism*, which is judging the Creator by the standard of the creature. Creature-ism has several applications:

- *me-ism*—judging others by the standard of myself
- *cultural imperialism*—judging other cultures by the standard of my culture
- *sexism*—judging the other gender by the standard of my gender
- *racism*—judging the other races by the standard of my race
- *ethno-centrism*—judging other people groups by the standard of my people group

If I am guilty of any of those, I will see others as inferior. Why? Because no one else can be me as well as I can be me; no other culture can be my culture as well as my culture can; no other race can be my race as well as my race can. When we use ourselves as the standard of judgment instead of the Word of God, we begin to think of others as inferior, not worthy of our respect. Power differentials serve to aggravate the situation.

Manifestations

Israel was plagued by ethnocentrism. God repeatedly showed them they were to be Jews because they were chosen. To be a Jew was a response to God's saving grace. But they foolishly assumed that they were chosen because they were Jews. They assumed they would always have the status of dominant culture in the kingdom of God. And they did not tolerate anything that would contradict this notion.

Let us look at Acts 13:14-48 from this perspective. In this passage we see that Paul and his companions went to Pisidian Antioch. On the Sabbath day they entered the synagogue and sat down, and after the reading of some of the Scriptures, the brothers in the synagogue asked if they had a message of encouragement: "Standing up, Paul motioned with his hand and said: 'Men of Israel and you Gentiles who worship God, listen to me!'" (v. 16, NIV).

He began to review Israel's history: from Egypt to the conquest of Canaan (vv. 18-28); from the judges to King David (vv. 20-22); then to the Savior, Jesus Christ, descended from David and greater than all the prophets (vv. 23-25). We would expect resistance to Paul's message, but none materialized. Paul continued: Jerusalem failed to recognize Jesus and condemned him to death. Yet this fulfilled the Scripture and God raised Jesus from the dead (vv. 26-31). Still there was no negative reaction to all this new theology. Paul explained that the resurrection of Jesus Christ was the fulfillment of Scripture and that Jesus is greater than King David (vv. 32-37). Yet they did not react.

Then Paul stated that forgiveness of sin comes through Jesus, and justification cannot come by the works of the law of Moses (vv. 38-39). Even this did not upset them. Paul wrapped up his message: "Take care that what the prophets have said does not happen to you: 'Look, you scoffers, wonder and perish. I am going to do something in your days that you would never believe, even if someone told you'" (vv. 40-41).

Notice the reaction to the message: "As Paul and Barnabas were leaving the synagogue, the people invited them to speak further about these things on the next Sabbath" (v. 42). So far the situation looked promising, but watch what happened next: On the next Sabbath day, almost the whole city gathered to hear the Word of the Lord. When the Jews saw the crowds they were filled with jealousy and began to talk abusively against what Paul was saying (v. 44). The Jews took the response of the whole town as a threat to their position of dominance when it came to the things of God. This was a manifestation of power struggles.

A similar thing happened in Acts 21–22:

- On his visit to the temple in Jerusalem Paul was spotted, seized, and accused of teaching against Israel and the law. Furthermore, he was accused of defiling the temple by bringing Greeks into it. (21:17-29)
- Paul was dragged out of the temple and almost killed by mob violence. The commander of the Roman troops saved Paul by taking him into custody. (21:30-36)
- Paul was able to get permission to address the crowd. (21:37-40)
- Paul introduced himself as a Jew. He showed forth his pedigree: born and raised in Tarsus, taught by Gamaliel, persecuted the church in his zeal for God. (22:1-5)
- Paul explained his encounter with Jesus and his dramatic conversion on the Damascus Road: "Saul! Saul! Why do you persecute me?"

  "Who are you, Lord?" I asked.

  "I am Jesus of Nazareth, whom you are persecuting." (22:6-13)

The crowd did not react. Then Paul replied to the Lord, "These men know that I went from one synagogue to another to imprison and beat those who believe in you. And when the blood of your martyr Stephen was shed I stood there giving my approval and guarding the clothes of those who were killing him" (22:19-20).

There was still no reaction, but watch this: "Then the Lord said to me, 'Go, *I will send you far away to the Gentiles.*' The crowd listened to Paul until he said this. Then they raised their voices and shouted, 'Rid the earth of him! He's not fit to live'" (vv. 21-22).

The Jewish crowd was willing to deal with all that testimony about Jesus. But when testifying to the Gentiles came into play, the dominance of the Jews was threatened. They got upset. The violence of the crowd became so intense that Paul had to be rescued by Roman soldiers (vv. 23-24).

Ethnic-based suffering comes out of these power struggles, out of dominant/sub-dominant dynamics. There is a lot of talk today about reconciliation. But, if we ignore the dominant/sub-dominant dynamics, we will never bridge the gap. We will wonder why racial reconciliation does not seem to work, and people will continue to suffer. These passages in Acts should give us insights as to why.

Dimensions

One of the results of oppression is *marginalization*. Marginalization happens when that which is valid is regarded as invalid merely because it differs from the prevailing standards of creature-ism. Thus, people who fit this description are relegated to a position of insignificance, devalued importance, minor influence, or diminished power. How does marginalization affect human interaction?

Every society has a dominant culture and at least one sub-dominant culture. Each of these has a corresponding cultural agenda and intra-cultural consciousness. Those in the dominant culture tend not to realize they have a culture, and those in the sub-dominant culture know very well that everybody has a culture.

All in the sub-dominant culture are exposed to the dominant cultural agenda. But few in the dominant culture are even aware that there is a sub-dominant cultural agenda. Therefore, to those in the dominant culture, the concerns of the sub-dominant culture tend to be marginalized. We can define these dominant and sub-dominant cultures in terms of race, generation, gender, geography, language, etc.

This begs the question: who is going to show the world how to deal with these kind of power differential dynamics? It must be the body of Christ. There are four dimensions of marginalization: (1) *relational (face-to-face) marginalization*—like what I did with my daughter; (2) *systemic marginalization,* which is marginalization by way of time-honored conventions and protocols; (3) *marginalization by design,* which is intentional marginalization resulting from subjugation; and (4) *marginalization by default,* which is marginalization resulting from a lack of either real or perceived power.

When you pair these four dimensions in all the possible combinations, you come out with the window of marginalization (Figure 1). The top two panes of the window are relational; the bottom two panes, systemic; the left two panes, marginalization by design; the right two, marginalization by default.

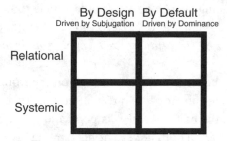

Figure 1: The Window of Marginalization

One thing that exacerbates ethnic-based suffering in the world today is the lack of a full understanding of marginalization. For example, we tend to think of only one manifestation—relational by design—which we find in the upper left-hand quadrant. We don't think much about what's in the other three quadrants. If we in the church are going to have something prophetic to say to the issue of ethnic-based suffering, we must deal with all four panes of the window.

Every subdominant group has a distinct paradigm for marginalization. For example, the African-American experience has largely been a struggle against racism and its effects—an application of creature-ism. Therefore, racism is regarded as *the* paradigm for all marginalization. We may know that marginalization does not ultimately require a racist motive. However, from an African-American perspective, marginalization is assumed to have a racist motive.

Anglo-Americans without this paradigm tend to view African-American protest against marginalization as "playing the race card." African-Americans, on the other hand, may view Anglo-Americans' protest as being in denial. When this happens we will speak past each other, because we do not understand that marginalization is the foundation of ethnic-based suffering. The theology of the Christian community has been weak in that area. If we are going to be a prophetic voice against marginalization, we will need to address it with some serious theology.

Blossoms

A young lady named Camara Phyllis Jones wrote a fascinating article called "Levels of Racism: A Theoretical Framework and a Gardener's

Tale."[1] I am not going to review the whole article, but I will share some of her insightful illustrations. According to Ms. Jones, there are three levels of racism: (1) *institutionalized*, (2) *personally mediated*, and (3) *internalized*.

Jones bought a house in a major city, and on the front porch were two flower boxes. One already had dirt in it, and the other was empty. She did not realize the existing soil was poor and rocky. Because she wanted to plant flowers in both boxes, she filled the empty box with rich potting soil and planted six flower seeds in each box. The growth of the flowers in the boxes showed her how racism develops and functions.

To illustrate her point, Jones supposed the following: (1) the gardener decided to plant flowers yielding red blossoms in one box and flowers yielding pink blossoms in the other; (2) she knows which box has the rich potting soil and which has the poor soil; (3) the gardener prefers red blossoms over pink.

In this case, the gardener would plant seeds for red blossoms in the rich soil and seeds for pink blossoms in the poor soil. All six seeds sprout in the rich soil. The three strongest seeds grew tall. The weaker seeds grew to middling height. In the poor soil, only the strongest seeds grew, but only to middling height (Figure 2).

• Initial historical insult
• Structural barriers
• Inaction in face of need
• Societal norms
• Biological determinism
• Unearned privilege

Figure 2: Institutionalized Racism

This is how she illustrates *institutionalized* racism. It starts with what she calls *an initial historical insult*—the decision was made to plant the red flowers in the better soil. It is carried on by *structural barriers*—the two boxes separate the two soils. It involves inaction in the face of

---

[1] Camara Phyllis Jones, "Levels of Racism: A Theoretical Framework and a Gardener's Tale," *American Journal of Public Health* 90 (August 2000): 1212-15.

need—the poor, rocky soil needs fertilizer, but "it does not matter because they are just pink flowers anyway." It reflects societal norms. Everybody knows that if you have sick plants, you don't waste your time on them. Your best efforts should be directed to the best plants. Institutionalized racism also involves *biological determinism* (the red blossoms are considered superior to the pink blossoms). Finally, it involves *unearned privilege* (the red flower seeds are planted in the good soil, but they did not earn this privilege).

Ms. Jones illustrates *personally mediated* racism in the following way. The weak pink blossoms and the strong red ones are about to produce pollen. However, the gardener does not want good, strong plants to be pollinated by obviously weak, inferior ones. So the gardener will pluck the pink blossoms off before they can pollinate. As a result, the weak plants will wither and die (Figure 3).

- Intentional
- Unintentional
- Acts of Commission
- Acts of Omission
- Maintains structural barriers
- Condoned by social norms

Figure 3: Personally Mediated Racism

This is equivalent to relational marginalization by design. Thus, personally mediated racism is *intentional* and *unintentional*. It involves *acts of commission* and *acts of omission*. It maintains the structural barriers, in this case the two different soils. It is also condoned by societal norms. After all, everybody knows the weak blossoms are plucked off before they can pollinate.

The third level is the most devastating—*internalized racism*. In this case, the "pink blossoms" themselves begin to believe that "red pollen" is superior. When people are marginalized long enough, when people are under the yoke of oppression long enough, they begin to believe in their own inferiority. This is what makes internalized racism so tragic.

Suppose a bee carrying pollen was to land on one of the pink blossoms. What kind of pollen would it prefer: pink or red? It would say, "Stop! I prefer red pollen. I don't want any of that inferior pink pollen!" Why this response? Because it believes in its own inferiority (Figure 4).

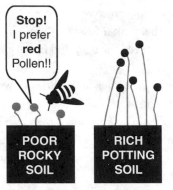

• Reflects systems of privilege
• Reflects social values
• Erodes Individual sense of value
• Undermines collective action

Figure 4: Internalized Racism

The pain of ethnic-based suffering is bad enough. It is devastating when they begin to think of themselves as inferior, not deserving respect.

Thus, internalized racism reflects the system of privileges and societal values. It erodes the individual sense of value and undermines collective action. The pink flowers are so convinced that they are inferior that they begin to despise each other. Pink-on-pink crime becomes a problem.

Let me share with you two biblical examples of internalized oppression. They both happened while the Hebrews were under the yoke of Egyptian slavery.

The First Example of Internalized Oppression

Most of us know the story of how Moses, a Hebrew, grew up in Pharaoh's palace ("the big house"). Contrary to the depiction of Moses in Cecil B. deMille's movie *The Ten Commandments,* the biblical text indicates that Moses' Egyptian mother never hid his true identity from him. The Hebrews in Goshen ("the hood") evidently were aware of who Moses was also.

One day, after he had grown up, Moses decided to go to the "hood" and hang out—to "kick it" with the brothers (Ex. 2:11-14). He saw a fellow Hebrew being brutally beaten by an Egyptian. Moses intervened, and in the struggle he killed the Egyptian.

He returned to the "hood" the next day and saw two Hebrews fighting. He said to the one in the wrong, "Why are you hitting your fellow Hebrew?" This man replied, "Who made you ruler and judge over us? Are you thinking of killing me as you killed the Egyptian?"(Ex. 2:14, NIV).

If we do not understand internalized oppression, we will miss one of the subtle things that God shows us. After four hundred years of slavery and humiliation, the Hebrews had come to believe they were inferior; they had contempt for themselves. Therefore, if Moses had been an Egyptian, the angry Hebrew would have respected him, but the man in the wrong knew Moses was Hebrew, so he totally disrespected him. He asked, "Are you thinking of killing me like you killed *the* Egyptian?" Notice he didn't say, "*your fellow* Egyptian." In other words, the man was saying, "Who do you think you are? You're still a Hebrew." In those days Hebrew was a derogatory term.

The Second Example of Internalized Oppression

When God appeared to Moses on Mount Sinai, God told him to go to the Pharaoh and say, "The LORD, *the God of the Hebrews*, has met with us. Let us take a three-day journey into the desert to offer sacrifices to the LORD our God" (Ex. 3:18, NIV). Perhaps one of the reasons the children of Israel complained and murmured against God was because he identified with them; in their minds, any God who would identify with the Hebrews had to be inferior. Thus, when Moses was overdue returning from the mountaintop, the Hebrews quickly made an idol and wanted to return to Egypt (Ex. 32:1-9).

God's Awareness of Suffering

Isaiah 53:3 (NIV) says the suffering Servant "was despised and rejected by men, a man of sorrows, and familiar with suffering." Mary and Martha were overcome with grief at the death of Lazarus. Jesus knew that he was going to resurrect Lazarus, but he identified with their grief and wept with them (John 11:33). If we follow Jesus, we too should be in touch with the sorrow of those in pain and the suffering of the oppressed.

Listen to what God says to King Jehoiakim in Jeremiah 22:3, 15-16.

> This is what the LORD says, "Do what is just and right. Rescue from
> the hand of his oppressor the one who has been robbed." (v. 3a)

Remember, people were robbed, not only by thugs, but by the corrupt
legal system.

> Do no wrong or violence to the alien, the fatherless or the widow, and
> do not shed innocent blood in this place. (v. 3b)

That has application across the board. And then he says:

> Does it make you a king to have more and more cedar? (v. 15a)

In other words, is "bling-bling" the thing?

> "Did not your father have food and drink? He did what was right and
> just, so all went well with him. *He defended the cause of the poor and*
> *needy, and so all went well. Is that not what it means to know me?"*
> declares the LORD. (vv. 15b-16, NIV)

Daniel understood this perspective when he advised Nebuchadnezzar:

> "Therefore, O king, be pleased to accept my advice: Renounce your
> sins by doing what is right, and your wickedness by being kind to
> the oppressed. It may be that then your prosperity will continue."
> (Dan. 4:27, NIV)

The issue here was not whether or not the king had quiet times or said
grace before he ate.

How Should We Respond to Suffering?

According to Cornelius Van Til, we are called to restrain sin and destroy
the consequences of sin in this world as much as possible:

> It is our duty not only to seek to destroy evil in ourselves and in
> our fellow Christians, but it is our further duty to seek to destroy
> evil in all our fellow men. It may be, humanly speaking, hopeless

in some instances that we should succeed in bringing them to Christ. This does not absolve us, however, from seeking to restrain their sins to some extent for this life. We must be active first of all in the field of special grace, but we also have a task to perform with respect to the destruction of evil in the field of common grace.

Still further we must note that our task with respect to the destruction of evil is not done if we have sought to fight sin itself everywhere we see it. We have the further obligation to destroy the consequences of sin in this world as far as we can. We must do good to all men, especially to those of the household of faith. To help relieve something of the sufferings of the creatures of God is our privilege and our task.[2]

An aspect of restraining evil involves seeking to minimize the dominant/sub-dominant dynamics in human relationships in general and within the body of Christ in particular. We may not be able to do a lot about the consequences of sin in the fallen world, but we can certainly do something about it within the household of faith.

Remember what the apostle James says:

> My brothers, as believers in our glorious Lord Jesus Christ, don't show favoritism. Suppose a man comes into your meeting wearing a gold ring and fine clothes [the bling-bling], and a poor man in shabby clothes also comes in. If you show special attention to the man wearing fine clothes and say, "Here's a good seat for you," but say to the poor man, "You stand there" or "Sit on the floor by my feet," have you not discriminated among yourselves and become judges with evil thoughts?" (James 2:1-4, NIV)

Being sensitive to the cultural, core concerns of sub-dominant people groups is an application of this passage. By core concerns, I mean life-controlling and life-defining concerns. The core concerns of the dominant culture tend to revolve around preservation of the status quo, while the concerns of the sub-dominant culture revolve around changing the status quo.

I used to play King of the Mountain when I was a young boy. I am

---

[2] Cornelius Van Til, *Christian Theistic Ethics*, vol. 3 of *In Defense of the Faith* (Nutley, N.J.: Presbyterian and Reformed, 1977), 87.

sure many of you men used to play this game also. One of us would stand on top of the hill, and the other players would struggle to push him off and replace him. Whoever succeeded would become the new king and the one to knock off the hill. Who would be the most conservative player in the game? Who would most want to preserve the status quo? The king, of course. Why? Because he was in the dominant position. His attitude was, "let there be tranquility," while everybody else clamored for self-empowerment by seeking to be king. When we played this game, we never thought of race or ethnicity, which shows that these dominant/sub-dominant dynamics transcend all people-group categories.

These dynamics speak to the issue of cultural diversity. Diversity is not just a matter of clapping our hands on "one-and-three" or "two-and-four." It also involves whether we look at things from a dominant or sub-dominant perspective. The Bible has much to say about power differentials. If we understand the issue of ethnic-based suffering from the perspective of power differentials, our insights will be light-years ahead of those the world offers.

Perhaps our inability to model solutions to this issue comes from having lost the doxological dimension of spirituality. What should distinguish the body of Christ is gratitude to God for his saving grace. This gratitude should be characterized by two expressions. The first is faith, which is our response of trusting Christ and his saving grace. The second expression is works, the resulting demonstration of our faith and thanksgiving to Christ for his saving grace.

These two expressions of gratitude should be empowered by two motivations. The first is a *salvific* motivation for faith. By "salvific" I mean an ongoing, strong desire to grow in our knowledge and experience of God's salvation. The second motivation is a *doxological* motivation for works. By "doxological" I mean an ongoing strong desire to show the excellence of God's glory.

The relationship between these dimensions can be seen in the "Window of Practical Spirituality" (Figure 5).

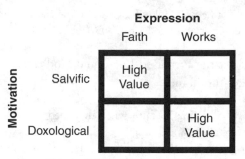

Figure 5: The Window of Practical Spirituality

When our motivation is salvific, faith has high value; when our motivation is doxological, works have high value. This is why Jesus said, "Let your light shine before others, so that they may see your good works and give glory to your Father who is in heaven" (Matt. 5:16). This is a doxological statement.

We do faith fairly well, but we don't do works well at all. Why? Because *we have lost the doxological motivation in spirituality*. Maybe it is time for a new reformation. The first Reformation rediscovered the salvific dimension. The new reformation will rediscover the doxological dimension. Doxology was what distinguished the Reformed movement. But somehow we've lost it. This is why our works have become shabby. This is why we have not had a strong prophetic voice regarding issues like ethnic-based suffering. And the world is poorer for it.

The People of God and Suffering

Since the fall, God has worked through his people as a sub-dominant group. Have you ever thought of yourself this way? As far as the world system is concerned, we in the body of Christ are a sub-dominant people group. Remember, Jesus our leader said, "My kingdom is not of this world system" (John 18:36, AT). God reminds us to consider ourselves strangers and aliens in the context of this world system.

> By faith Abraham obeyed when he was called to go out to a place that he was to receive as an inheritance. And he went out, not knowing where he was going. By faith he went to live in the land of promise, as in a foreign land, living in tents with Isaac and Jacob, heirs with him

of the same promise. For he was looking forward to the city that has
foundations, whose designer and builder is God. (Heb. 11:8-10)

Today, the whole world is the Promised Land, and God calls us to be
strangers and aliens like Abraham:

> All these people were still living by faith when they died. . . . They
> admitted that they were aliens and strangers on earth. . . . They were
> longing for a better country, a heavenly one. Therefore God is not
> ashamed to be called their God, for he has prepared a city for them.
> (Heb. 11:13, 16, NIV)

Peter refers to the elect as strangers in this world: "Since you call on a
Father who judges each man's work impartially, live your lives as
strangers here in reverent fear" (1 Pet. 1:17, NIV). Again Peter says:
"Dear friends, I urge you, as aliens and strangers in the world, to abstain
from sinful desires, which war against your soul" (1 Pet. 2:11, NIV).

As strangers and aliens, we in the body of Christ should have no real
vested interest in the world system as it exists. We should be completely
focused on our sovereign God and his kingdom. We are called to be
change-agents for the kingdom in this world. Thus, to identify with suffering should be as natural as breathing. Ethnic-based suffering should
be a rare occurrence within the body of Christ. Indeed, we have a long
way to go.

We have lost the concept of what it means to be the worldwide
church. Christians do things in this country that directly hurt and harm
our fellow Christians in other parts of the world, especially the Muslim
world. We should be champions of kingdom empowerment and kingdom transformation. Israel, the Old Testament church, was to be a community marked by righteousness, social justice, and compassion for the
oppressed. And these covenant requirements also apply to the church,
the New Testament Israel. When Jesus said, "Let your light shine"
(Matt. 5:16), it was against the backdrop of these same covenant
requirements. Isaiah says:

> Is not this the kind of fasting I have chosen: to loose the chains of injus-
> tice and untie the cords of the yoke, to set the oppressed free and break
> every yoke? Is it not to share your food with the hungry and to pro-

vide the poor wanderer with shelter—when you see the naked, to clothe him, and not to turn away from your own flesh and blood? *Then your light will break forth like the dawn.* . . . (Isa. 58:6-8, NIV)

As the downtrodden looked to Christ in the first century, so should they be able to look to the body of Christ today. But we must let our light shine. God is calling us to model what it means to be a people without ethnic-based suffering.

What is the purpose of ethnicity anyway? We get a glimpse of this in Haggai 2:7 (NIV), "I will shake all nations, and the desired of all nations will come, and I will fill this house with glory," says the LORD Almighty. The "desired of the nations" is the best the nations have to offer. All people groups have a unique contribution to make to the glory of God. We see the fulfillment of this in Revelation 7:9-10:

> After this I looked, and behold, a great multitude that no one could number, from every nation, from all tribes and peoples and languages, standing before the throne and before the Lamb, clothed in white robes, with palm branches in their hands, and crying out with a loud voice, "Salvation belongs to our God who sits on the throne, and to the Lamb!"

May God give us the grace to glorify him by discipling the nations. May God give us the grace to disciple the nations by demonstrating the true meaning of ethnicity rather than imitating the world with ethnic power struggles, marginalization, and oppression. We need to glorify God by being on the vanguard of spiritual unity with ethnic diversity.

Yes, there is ethnic-based suffering. Yes, we can understand it. Yes, by grace we can make a difference to the glory of God.

Part 3:
The Grace of God in Suffering

CHAPTER 7

God's Grace and Your Sufferings

DAVID POWLISON

How does God meet you in trouble, loss, disability, and pain? You probably already know the "right answer." He does not immediately intervene to make everything all better. Yet he continually intervenes, according to gracious purposes, working both in you and in what afflicts you. If you've read Psalms, if you've heard a sermon on the second half of Romans 8, if you've worked through 1 Peter in a Bible study, if you've read the earlier chapters of this book, then you've got the gist already.

How does God's grace engage your sufferings? We may know the right answer. And yet we don't know it. It is a hard answer. But we make it sound like a pat answer. God sets about a long slow answering. But we try to make it a quick fix. His answer insists on being lived out over time and into the particulars. We act as if just saying the right words makes it so. God's answer insists on changing you into a different kind of person. But we act as if some truth, principle, strategy, or perspective might simply be incorporated into who we already are. God personalizes his answer on hearts with an uncanny flexibility. But we turn it into a formula: "If you just believe _____. If you just do _____. If you just remember _____." No important truth ever contains the word "just" in the punch line.

How *does* God's grace meet you in your sufferings? We can make the right answer sound old hat, but I guarantee this: God will surprise you. He will make you stop. You will struggle. He will bring you up short. You will hurt. He will take his time. You will grow in faith and in love. He will deeply delight you. You will find the process harder than you ever imagined—and better. Goodness and mercy will follow you all the days of your life (Ps. 23:6). No matter how many times you've heard it, no matter how long you've known it, no matter how well you can say it, God's answer will come to mean something better than you could ever imagine.

Significant Suffering

Think of this chapter as a workshop. You have to put yourself into it in order to get something out of it. Insert your own story into what is said. Walk it out—on the margins of these pages, when you put the book down, when you pray, when you talk with your best friend tomorrow. The title of the chapter might have tipped you off: I'm not going to discuss the general topic of God and suffering. Instead, we will consider how God's grace enters *your* sufferings.

What is the most significant experience of suffering that you have gone through? That you are now going through?

_____

_____

_____

What has happened? How did it affect you? How did your life change? Don't rush on. Pull out a pen or pencil. Take five or ten minutes. Ponder. Remember. Write. *You* are responsible for half of this chapter! If you do your part well, it will be the better half.

Let me prime the pump a bit more. Perhaps one catastrophic event leapt to mind. But as you thought further, maybe something else pressed forward into consciousness. Perhaps the searing moment was not as significant as a difficult and disappointing relationship that lasted a long, long time. There are many kinds of significant suffering. It's no accident that James mentions "various trials" (1:2) within which God works. He invites you to consider the variety of life-altering afflictions, and then to make it personal. Nobody suffers in general. Each person suffers in some particular way. Put your particulars on the table.

What marked you? What most changed you? More specifically, what marked you for good? Profound good in our lives often emerges in a crucible of significant suffering. Jesus himself "learned obedience through what he suffered" (Heb. 5:8). Often faith and love shine most clearly, simply, and courageously in a dark place. And what marked you for bad? Often our typical sins emerge in reaction to betrayal, loss, or pain. Hammered by some evil, we discover the evils in our own hearts (Rom. 12:17). And perhaps most often, in the hands of our kind and purposeful Father, the bad and the good both come out. A trial brings out what is most wrong in you, and God brings about what is most right as he meets you and works with you (Ps. 119:67). The endurance of faith is one of the Spirit's finest fruits—and you only learn to endure when you must live through something hard.

"How Firm a Foundation . . ."

Hold that significant suffering in one hand. In the other hand, hold a wise old hymn. Listen to God's grace speaking in the words of "How Firm a Foundation":

> How firm a foundation, you saints of the Lord,
> is laid for your faith in his excellent Word!
> What more can he say than to you he has said,
> to you who for refuge to Jesus have fled?
>
> "Fear not, I am with you, O be not dismayed;
> for I am your God, and will still give you aid;
> I'll strengthen you, help you, and cause you to stand,
> upheld by my righteous, omnipotent hand.
>
> "When through the deep waters I call you to go,
> the rivers of sorrow shall not overflow;
> for I will be with you, your troubles to bless,
> and sanctify to you your deepest distress.
>
> "When through fiery trials your pathway shall lie,
> my grace, all-sufficient, shall be your supply;

the flame shall not hurt you; I only design
your dross to consume and your gold to refine.

"E'en down to old age all my people shall prove
my sovereign, eternal, unchangeable love;
and when hoary hairs shall their temples adorn,
like lambs they shall still in my bosom be borne.

"The soul that on Jesus has leaned for repose,
I will not, I will not desert to his foes;
that soul, though all hell should endeavor to shake,
I'll never, no never, no never forsake."[1]

I'll make several introductory comments before we explore each stanza. First, one of the subtle charms of this hymn is that it is anonymous. Only God and the author know who wrote it. In a world obsessed with taking credit and receiving payment for achievements, this hymn is only an unknown person's honest offering to God. What significant sufferings had that person faced? We don't know. But every stanza breathes firsthand experience with God's hand in life's hardships. Was the author male or female? Young or old? Married or single? Black, brown, or white? Rich, poor, or middling? Baptist, Presbyterian, or Anglican? We have no idea. Whoever the person, whatever the affliction, we hear timely words from the God of intervening grace. What is written will speak into *your* significant suffering. The anonymity adds appropriateness to the invitation to make this hymn your very own as a means of grace.

Second, though we might not notice this, every hymn adopts a point of view, a "voice" identifying a listener and a speaker. Most often we sing *to God*, making requests or expressing praise: "Be Thou my vision, O Lord of my heart." Often we sing *about God* and what he has done, bearing witness to others and reminding ourselves: "Amazing grace, how sweet the sound, that saved a wretch like me." Sometimes we sing *to each other*, exhorting and encouraging: "O come, all ye faithful." Occasionally, just like Psalm 103, we sing *to ourselves*: "Be still, my soul,

---

[1] This version of the lyrics is updated to more modern language, from *Trinity Hymnal* (Suwanee, Ga.: Great Commission Publications, 1990), #94. It can be sung to several well-known tunes. My favorite is *Adeste Fideles* (also the tune of "O Come, All Ye Faithful"), which doubles the last line in each stanza.

the Lord is on thy side." Each of these voices expresses our faith in a different way.

Most of "How Firm a Foundation" operates in an unusual voice. Only in the first stanza do we express our faith by exhorting each other to listen to what God has said. Notice what's different about the last five stanzas. Each begins with a quotation mark. Why is this? *God* is doing the talking. Though we sing the words, we are placed in the role of listeners. God is talking *to you*. You sing this hymn by listening. What does he talk about? Interestingly, he speaks directly into significant suffering. He tells you who he is and what he is like—pointedly with respect to what *you* are going through. He tells *you* his purposes. He promises the very things *you* most need. Most hymns express our faith to God, to each other, and to ourselves. This hymn is more elemental. God's voice invites faith. He's calling to you.

This is particularly appropriate when it comes to suffering. The hymn writer demonstrates a profound feel for the struggles and needs of sufferers. A sufferer's primal need is to hear God talking and to experience him purposefully at work. That changes everything. Left to ourselves, we blindly react. Our troubles obsess us and distract us. We grasp at straws. God seems invisible, silent, far away. Pain and loss cry out loud and long. Faith seems inarticulate. Sorrow and confusion broadcast on all the channels. It's hard to remember anything else, hard to put into words what is actually happening, hard to feel any force from who Jesus Christ is. You might mumble right answers to yourself, but it's like reading the phone book. You pray, but your words sound rote, vaguely unreal, like pious generalities. You'd never talk to a real person that way. Meanwhile, the struggle churning within you is anything but rote and unreal. Pain and threat are completely engrossing. You're caught in a swirl of apprehension, anguish, regret, confusion, bitterness, emptiness, uncertainty.

This struggle is not surprising. Exodus 6:9, for example, describes how "despondency and cruel bondage" (NASB) deafened the people. Moses' words made no impression because they were so crushed and disheartened. But God worked patiently. He continued to say what he does and to do what he says. The people's sufferings, deafness, and blindness did not vanish in the twinkling of an eye. But by Exodus 15:1-18, the people were seeing and hearing, and they sang with hearty, well-founded joy. How much more in our times. The Holy Spirit works powerfully and intimately in this age of new creation to write God's words on our hearts. Sufferers awaken to hear their Father's voice and to see their Savior's hand in the midst of significant suffering.

You need to hear what God says, and to experience that he does what he says. You need to feel the weight and significance of what he is about. He never lies. He never disappoints (though he wisely sets about to disappoint our false hopes). Though you walk through the valley of the shadow of death, you need fear no evil, for he is with you. Goodness and mercy will follow you. This *is* what he is doing. God's voice speaks deeper than what hurts, brighter than what is dark, more enduring than what is lost, truer than what happened.

You awaken. You take it to heart, and you take heart. You experience that this is so. The world changes. You change. His voice changes the meaning of every hardship. What he does—has done, is doing, will do—alters the impact and outcome of everything happening to you. Your faith grows up into honest, intelligent humanness, no longer murky and inarticulate. You grow more like Jesus: the man of sorrows acquainted with grief, the man after God's own heart, who having loved his own loved them to the end.

1. Listen

> How firm a foundation, you saints of the Lord,
> is laid for your faith in his excellent Word!
> What more can he say than to you he has said,
> to you who for refuge to Jesus have fled?

In 2 Timothy 2:19 (NASB), Paul wrote: "The firm foundation of God stands, having this seal, 'The Lord knows those who are His.'" This excellent Word never changes. This hymn is going to speak standing on that firm foundation. Consider three things about the exhortation of this opening stanza.

First, "What more can he say than to you he has said?" Let that rattle around a minute. I don't know how you read Scripture. But there is a way to read Scripture that leaves you wishing God had said a whole lot more. How did Satan become evil? Why does Chronicles add zeros to the numbers in Samuel and Kings? How did Jonah avoid asphyxiation? Who wrote the book of Hebrews? And those aren't even the questions that most often divide and perplex the church. Wouldn't it have been great if the Lord had slipped in one killer verse that pinned down the eschatological timetable; that resolved once and for all every question about baptism; that specifically told us how to organize church leadership and government; that told us exactly what sort of music to use in worship; that explained how God's absolute sovereignty neatly dovetails with full human responsibility? Only one more verse! And think what he could have told us with an extra paragraph or chapter! If only the Lord had shortened the genealogies, omitted mention of a few villages in the land distribution, and condensed the spec sheet for the temple's dimensions, dishware, décor, and duties. Our Bible would be exactly the same length—even shorter—but a hundred of our questions could have been anticipated and definitively answered. Somehow, God in his providence didn't choose to do that.

It comes down to what you are looking for as you read and listen. When you get to what most matters, to life-and-death issues, *what more can he say than to you he has said?* Betrayal by someone you trusted? Aggressive, incurable cancer? Your most persistent sin? A disfiguring disability? The meaning and purpose of your life? Good and evil? Love and hate? Truth and lie? Hope in the face of death? Mercy in the face of sin? Justice in the face of unfairness? The character of God? The dynamics of the human heart? What more can he say than to you he has said? Listen well. There is nothing more that he needed to say.

Second, this opening stanza describes you, the listener, in profound ways. You are among the "saints" of the Lord. In a nutshell, it means, "God says, 'You are mine. You belong to me.'" In popular usage, the word "saint" has been debased to describe extraordinary, individual spiritual achievements. But in the Bible—the way God views sainthood—the word describes ordinary people who belong to a most extraordinary Savior and Lord. Our Redeemer achieves all the extraordinary things. At our best (and too often we are at our worst, or bumping along in the middle!), "we have done only that which we ought to have done" (Luke 17:10, NASB). God calls you "saint" to point out who owns you, not to honor you for going above and beyond the call of duty. It's not the Medal of Honor; it's your enlistment papers and dog tag. When God has written his name on you, suffering qualitatively changes.

Pain, loss, and weakness are no longer the end of the world and the death of your hopes. If you are not a saint, then sufferings are omens of the end of your world. All that you live for will die when you die (Prov. 10:28). But when you are in Christ, sufferings become the context to awaken your truest hopes and bring them to fulfillment.

There's more. You have taken refuge in the Lord. You are a "refugee." You fled for your life and found every sort of aid and protection in Jesus. In September 2005, hundreds of thousands of people were displaced by Hurricane Katrina. Many escaped with nothing and lost everything. They were vulnerable. They needed food, housing, medical care, clothes, money, police protection, a new start. But a public official caused an uproar when he referred to the evacuees as "refugees." The term was seen as demeaning. It called to mind the degraded conditions in refugee camps for those fleeing genocide in Sudan or Rwanda.

Refugee might connote degradation; but in Christ it becomes an affirmation of glory and hope. We *are* refugees. The Bible turns many typical associations upside down. Words for degradation and powerlessness—"slave, crucifixion, child, weakness"—invert into symbols of joy. A refugee absolutely depends on outside mercies. And you have found all you need and more than you could ever imagine in the Lord, the only true refuge. The opposite of a refugee? It is the current cultural ideal: self-confidence, self-sufficiency, independence, right of ownership, freedom to boldly assert your opinions, freedom to do what you want as long as it doesn't hurt someone else.

To be "dependent" on God often implies something warm and comfortable. That is a partial truth. A child on his mother's lap simply rests in trust (Psalm 131). But often dependency doesn't feel very good. You *need* help. You're helpless in yourself. When the psalmist cries to God, "Help. If you won't listen to me, I will die" (Ps. 28:1, AT), that's not a comfortable feeling. You feel threatened, battered, vulnerable. You are powerless, with nowhere else to turn. Jesus' first beatitude says that the "poor in spirit" are the blessed. He turns another bad word upside down. "Poor" means poverty-stricken, destitute, people with nothing, street people. "Poor in spirit" means conscious awareness of dire and pressing need for help that God most freely and generously gives. Insoluble suffering (like insoluble sin) brings you to this foundation of all blessing. God does not turn away from the afflictions of the afflicted. Do not be afraid, little flock, he is giving you the kingdom (Luke 12:32).

Our discipleship materials often don't teach us much about this. We learn how to have a quiet time. We discover our spiritual gifts. We study good doctrine. We learn how to study the Bible and memorize Scripture. We don't necessarily learn how to need help. "How Firm a Foundation" teaches you to need help. God uses significant suffering to teach us to need him.

2. I Am with You

"Fear not, I am with you, O be not dismayed;
for I am your God, and will still give you aid;
I'll strengthen you, help you, and cause you to stand,
upheld by my righteous, omnipotent hand."

How do you react to serious suffering? "Fear and dismay" cover the ground pretty well! If you are honest, you feel rocked, overwhelmed, preoccupied, confused, upset, endangered. You "struggle"—always. If you do not feel the weight or knife-edge of what is happening, you are a stone, not a human being. Image-bearers of God are not impervious. But here's the problem: distress and apprehension often become God-less. The anguish of faith vanishes into godless dismay. As troubles settle in, they claim your thought life, conversations, emotions, future, faith. They occupy wakeful hours at night. If you fall asleep, they wake up with you first thing in the morning. "Dismay" well covers a whole range of temptations: from troubled to unglued, from disappointed to hopeless, from worried to panicky, from frustrated to enraged.

There are also many dishonest reactions that aim to avoid experiencing dismay in the face of life's troubles. You meet many people who have become cynical, hard-boiled, brutal, invulnerable. (Most are not readers of books with "suffering" in the title!) They callous themselves against any fresh experience of suffering (thereby also hardening themselves from compassion on the sufferings of others). They fear and loathe any "weakness" in themselves or others. In the pages of Scripture, perhaps Pilate expresses this worldly-wise, cynical self-interest. Hard people justify themselves as "realists." In fact, they are dehumanized. Jesus is far more realistic, and he chose to enter into weakness and affliction in order to love needy people. You also meet people who recoil from life (perhaps this is your tendency?). It's the opposite of cynical, but it is also dishonest. They become so blinded by pain, so fearful of further rejection and loss, so vulnerable, that they withdraw into a shell of excruciating self-protection. And still others (your tendency perhaps?) escape into the "feel-goods," the false refuges that numb or stimulate or distract. Entertainment, recreation, and addiction seem like good hiding places.

Honesty is able to feel the weight of things that arouse fear and dismay. The problem is not that we feel troubled by trouble and pained by pain. Something hurtful should hurt. The problem is that God slides away into irrelevance when we obsess over suffering or compulsively avoid it. God inhabits a vague afterthought—weightless and distant in comparison to something immediately pressing. Or, if God-words fill our minds and pour forth from our lips, it's easy to make the "god" we cry out to someone who will magically make everything better if we can only catch his ear.

The real God is up to better things. He says and does weighty and immediate things that engage what you are facing. He pursues purposes that are better than you imagine. He refuses to become your lucky charm who makes all the bad things disappear from your world.

Suffering tends to trigger a cascade of bad reactions. God gives a cascade of better reasons that invite the finest responses of which a human being is capable. These very reasons patterned Jesus' consciousness, motives, emotions, words, and actions as he faced his own significant suffering. In this second stanza, God makes seven promises. Our hymn writer didn't just make it up. The stanza closely paraphrases Isaiah 41:10. God said exactly these words, and our hymn accurately quotes the source:

> I am with you.
> I am your God.
> I will still give you aid.
> I will strengthen you.
> I will help you.
> I will cause you to stand.
> I will uphold you by my all-good, all-powerful hand.

Jesus, the pioneer and perfecter of faith, heard this voice, and took it to heart. He now says these same things to you.

What makes it hard for us to hear? There are times we have a hard time slowing down to listen. There are times we simply don't want to listen. There are times we are busy listening to ten thousand other voices, including our own. There are times we feel so weary and disheartened that we don't feel up for listening. But whatever the particulars, our essential problem is deafness to God's voice. We become absorbed in the world of our own experiences, thoughts, feelings, and opinions. The early church used a wonderful phrase to capture the essential inward-turning nature of sinfulness: *curvitas in se*. We curve in on ourselves. Sin's *curvitas in se* pointedly turns away from God. When you or others suffer, you experience or witness the strength of this incurving tendency. It's hard not to be self-preoccupied.

God willingly keeps talking. Listen to how near he sounds in this hymn. The Lifegiver willingly gives ears to hear. The incurving can be reversed. Psalms cry out rather than turning in. Jesus is a most excellent teacher. In the extremity of his agony, there was no *curvitas in se*. He heard God's voice and remembered. He turned towards God in neediness, generosity, and trust: "My God, my God, why have you forsaken me? Forgive them, for they don't know what they are doing. Father, into your hands I commit my spirit." He turned towards people in practical love: "Today you will be with me in paradise. Behold your son. Behold your mother." He gave voice to honest experience of his ordeal: "I am thirsty. It is finished."[2] This is the Jesus to whom we have fled for refuge. This most careful and thoughtful of listeners walked ahead of us. He deals gently with our ignorance and waywardness. He now willingly walks with us, fully aware of our temptations to be forgetful, distracted, and inattentive. He addresses the biggest problem first. That's why this hymn speaks in the first person. The words of new life first create ears that listen.

God is talking. His sheep hear his voice, even in the valley of the shadow of death. Are you listening?

The starting point of this stanza is well chosen. "I am with you" is a central promise when speaking pastorally with sufferers. It's no acci-

---

[2] Matthew 27:46; Luke 23:34, 43, 46; John 19:26-28, 30.

dent that Psalm 23 says, "I fear no evil, for you are with me" (v. 4 NASB). It's no accident that this is the central promise of the entire Bible, the one hope of sinners and sufferers. It is the only thing Moses really wanted—without it the so-called Promised Land was only mediocre real estate. It is the essential reason that David's life flourished. It came to a point in Emmanuel, in whom all God's promises become Yes and Amen (2 Cor. 1:20).

I will unpack one pastoral implication of this omni-relevant promise: suffering often brings a doubled pain. In the first place there is "the problem" itself—sickness, poverty, betrayal, bereavement. That is hard enough (and this promise speaks comfort). But it is often compounded by a second problem. Other people, even well-meaning, often don't respond very well to sufferers. Sufferers are often misunderstood, or meddled with, or ignored. These reactions add relational and psychological isolation to "the problem." For example, Job suffered the deaths of his children, financial disaster, and unrelenting physical pain. But then he had to deal with the attitudes of his wife and friends. They exacerbated his suffering. He became utterly isolated because they misunderstood and mistreated him. When Job's life was hardest, he was also most alone. Similarly, Jesus faced betrayal, mockery, and torture at the hands of his enemies. But his truest friends? First they argued about who was most important. Then they lapsed into sleepy incomprehension. Then they disintegrated into confusion, panic, flight, and denial. When Jesus' life was most painful, he also had to go it alone. God speaks into this: "I am with you."

This doubled hardship is a common experience. A young woman is bereaved of her father whom she dearly loves. Her friends are initially very supportive. But they get tired of her grief long before her grief is over. They give up on her as a friend. Or, parents of a severely disabled child face lifelong hardships of many sorts. They also face how they are treated by others. Friends and family distance themselves, or feel awkward and don't know what to say, or offer laughably (weepably?) inappropriate help, or don't want to be bothered, or offer a thousand suggestions and fixes that reveal utter incomprehension of the realities. Disability is compounded by isolation. But "I am with you."

Here's another way this happens. People who love you often focus exclusively on "the problem." They ask about "the problem." They pray that God would solve "the problem." They offer advice for solving "the problem." They care for you! These are well-meaning attempts to be helpful. But the effect can become unkind. For example, many significant sufferings have no remedy until the day when all tears are wiped away. Your disease or disability is incurable. The injustice will not be remedied in your lifetime. Your loved one is dead. The marriage is over. The money is gone. There may be partial helps along the way. There may be partial redemptions. There will be no fix. Often the biggest problem for any sufferer is not "the problem." It is the spiritual challenge the problem presents: "How are *you* doing in the midst of what you are going through? What are you learning? Where are you failing? Where do you need encouragement? Will you learn to live well and wisely within pain, limitation, weakness, and loss? Will suffering define you? Will faith and love grow, or will you shrivel up?" These are life-and-death issues—more important than "the problem" in the final analysis. They take asking, thinking, listening, responding. They take time. Other people are often clumsy and uncomprehending about the most important things, while pouring energy and love into solving what is often insoluble. "I am with you."

This double suffering commonly occurs when a health problem eludes diagnosis and cure. Jesus met a woman who "had a hemorrhage for twelve years, and had endured much at the hands of many physicians, and had spent all that she had, and was not helped at all, but rather had grown worse" (Mark 5:25-26, NASB). Her story has a decidedly contemporary ring! Bleeding was a real medical problem. But attempts to help multiplied her misery. The subsequent two thousand years have not eliminated the phenomenon: faulty diagnoses, misguided treatments, negative side effects, contradictory advice, huge waste of time and money, false hopes repeatedly dashed, false fears pointlessly rehearsed, no plausible explanation forthcoming, blaming the victim, and declining sympathy as compassion fatigue sets in for would-be helpers! The woman was sick; other people made it worse. "I am with you."

J. I. Packer once noted that "a half-truth masquerading as the whole truth becomes a complete untruth."[3] We can extend his logic. A half-

---

[3] J. I. Packer, *A Quest for Godliness: The Puritan Vision of the Christian Life* (Wheaton, Ill.: Crossway Books, 1994), 126.

kindness masquerading as the whole of kindness becomes a complete unkindness. The desire to explain and solve "the problem" is surely a kindness. But it can miss the person who must in any case come to grips with what is happening. The first line of this stanza displays a remarkable pastoral intuition. God speaks first to the fear, dismay, and isolation that attend hardships.

This is a workshop chapter. Take your most significant of sufferings. Try out these sentences. I am not afraid of _____. I am not dismayed by _____. Can you say this and mean it? What gets in the way? What gives you reasons to say it, mean it, and live it out all your days?

3. *"I'm with You for a Purpose"*

"When through the deep waters I call you to go,
the rivers of sorrow shall not overflow;
for I will be with you, your troubles to bless,
and sanctify to you your deepest distress."

Words from Isaiah 43:2 weave through this stanza. Your troubles are envisioned as "deep waters" and "rivers." Isaiah alludes to when God's people faced the Red Sea with enemies at their back, and to when they faced the Jordan River at flood stage. No human being could carve a path through such difficulties. God restates his core promise with an eye to the future: "I will be with you." That itself is significant, because the effects of most significant sufferings extend into an indeterminate future. We need much more than help in the present moment. What exactly does it mean that God will be "with" you amid destructive forces?

In promising this, God explicitly does *not* mean that he will give you mere comfort, warm feelings because a friend is standing at your side through tough times. God plays a much more active and powerful role. This stanza fills in the meaning with four vast truths:

- God himself calls you into the deep waters in your life.
- God sets a limit on the sorrows.
- God is with you actively bringing good from your troubles.
- In the context of distressing events, God changes you to become like him.

This is heady stuff. High and purposeful sovereignty. A big God—who comes close to speak tenderly, work personally, make you different, finish what he begins.

In other words, your significant sufferings don't happen by accident. No random chance. No purposeless misery. No bad luck. Not even (and understand this the right way) a tragedy. Tragedy means ruin, destruction, downfall, an unhappy ending with no redemption. Your life story may contain a great deal of misery and heartache along the way. But in the end, in Christ, your life story will prove to be a "comedy" in the good old sense of the word, a story with a happy ending. You play a part in the *Divine Comedy*, as Dante called it, with the happiest ending of any story ever written. Death, mourning, tears, and pain will be no more (Rev. 21:4). Life, joy, and love get last say. High sovereignty is going somewhere. People miss that when they make "the sovereignty of God" sound as if it implied fatalism, like Islamic *kismet*, like *que sera sera*, like being realistic and resigned to life's hardships. God's sovereign purposes don't include the goal of getting you to just accept your troubles. He's not interested in offering you some perspective to just help get you through a rough patch.

This stanza expresses the kind purposes of the most high God. But it does not make light of your hardships. There is no chilly objectivity in God's words. He carefully refers to the pain of deep sufferings in every line. He speaks poignantly, not matter-of-factly: "deep waters, rivers of sorrow, troubles, deepest distress." In fact, the original hymn (with "thee and thou") put the second line even more graphically: "The rivers of woe shall not thee overflow." Woe is the keenest edge of anguish, the extremity of distress, sorrow raised to the highest degree of pain.

Those rivers of woe sweep many good things away. Your deepest distress is deeply distressing. But the God who loves you is master of your significant sorrow. He calls you to go through even this hard thing. Though it feels impossible and devastates earthly hopes, he sets a boundary (not where we would set it). He convinces you that this hard thing will come out good beyond all you can ask, imagine, see, hear, or conceive in your heart (Eph. 3:20; 1 Cor. 2:9). You will pass through the valley of the shadow of death filled with evils, but you will say that goodness and mercy followed you all the days of your life.

Again, take in hand the significant suffering that contributes to your half of this chapter. Insert it into this stanza. "When I call you to go through _____, you will not drown in the rivers of woe. I will be with you to bring blessing out of _____. I will take _____, and sanctify it to you. I will transform _____ into the crucible in which you become like Jesus, whose self-giving love enters the real troubles of the human condition."

God is God. He exerts a high and purposeful sovereignty. But we often misapply God's sovereignty when it comes to actually helping sufferers—both ourselves and others. Here is a common misapplication: "God is in control, therefore what's happening is his will. You need to just trust the Lord and accept it. Ignore your feelings. Remember the truth, gird your loins, and get with the program." Somehow stoic conclusions are fashioned from a most unstoic truth about a most unstoic God!

Here's the classic text whose pastoral application too often misfires in this way: "Let those who suffer according to God's will entrust their souls to a faithful Creator while doing good" (1 Pet. 4:19). Even as you read those words, does it sound like the Bible puts the damper on heartache? Does God teach a sanctified version of calm detachment and dutiful self-discipline? Is Peter saying, "It doesn't matter that you're suffering. God's in control, so just keep up your quiet time and fulfill your responsibilities"? Does God make the deep waters only waist deep? Does he canalize the rivers of woe, so they flow gently between banks of riprap? Does he sanctify distress by making it unstressful? Does he call you to ignore what's going on around you in order to get on with being a Christian? Look carefully at *how* to entrust your soul to a faithful Creator. You'll never read 1 Peter 4:19 in the same way.

Consider David's Psalm 28. "To you, LORD, I call. My Rock, do not be deaf to me. If you don't answer me, I will die. Hear the voice of my supplications, my cry for help to you" (vv. 1-2, AT). This is an example of what it means to "entrust your soul" to the sovereign God. It's not sedate. David does not mentally rehearse the fact that God is in control in order to quietly press on with unflinching composure. Instead, trust pleads candidly and believingly with God: "This is big trouble. You must help me. I need you. You are my only hope." Prayer means "ask for something you need and want." Supplication means "*really* ask." Frank supplication is the furthest thing from keeping everything in perspective so you can move on with life as normal. The sovereign God does not intend that you maintain the status quo while suffering. Pain disrupts normal. It's supposed to disrupt normal. It's supposed to make you feel a need for help. Psalm 28 is not an orderly "quiet time." It's noisy and needy. When you let life's troubles get to you, it gets you to the only one who can help. As Psalm 28 unfolds, David specifically names the trouble he's in, what he's afraid of, what he wants (vv. 3-5). His trust in God's sovereignty moves to glad confidence (vv. 6-7). Finally, his faith works out into love as he starts interceding on behalf of others (vv. 8-9).

Consider how Psalm 10 trusts a faithful God. Your life is being threatened by predatory people who give you good reason for apprehension. You begin to entrust your soul by crying out, "Why do you stand far away from me, O Lord? Where are you? Why do you hide yourself in times of trouble?"(v. 1, AT).[4] Faith in God's sovereign rule, promises, and purposes talks out the implications. Instead of ignoring the situation and the feelings of threat, instead of finding a quiet (but unreal) solace, instead of getting on with business as usual, the psalmist even takes time to think carefully about the thought processes of wicked men (vv. 2-11, 13). His scope of concern reaches beyond his own plight: the afflicted, the unfortunate, the innocent, the orphan, the oppressed. He thinks through how God's hand rests differently on evildoers and on sufferers (vv. 12, 14-18). We might say that the things of earth definitely do *not* grow strangely dim. Instead, they grow much clearer in the light of his glory and grace! This psalm comes out in a place of resolution and confidence. But trust never anesthetizes the threat. So entrusting to a faithful Creator ends with a plea: "Do justice for the fatherless and the oppressed, so that man who is of the earth will no longer cause terror" (v. 18, AT). That's not calm, cool, and collected. It's faith working through love.

Finally, Psalms 22:1 and 31:5 were out loud on Jesus' lips, because these psalms were in his heart as he entrusted his soul to God. Hebrews 5:7 (NASB) refers to this time as characterized by "loud crying and tears to the One able to save him from death." Jesus hardly ignored his feel-

---

[4] That's not a bitter rant: "Where was God when I needed him? It's God's fault that I'm suffering, because he could have stopped it." Both stoics and ranters take a mechanical view of God's sovereign control, detaching it from his living purposes. For stoics, God's control over suffering rationalizes cool detachment. For ranters, it becomes reason for hot accusation.

ings or viewed them as the inconvenient by-product of cognitive processes! These are psalms of intense affliction. You see what was on Jesus'
mind when he poured out his heart. He cried, "My God, my God, why
have you forsaken me?" because he believed that the sovereign God does
not treat lightly "the affliction of the afflicted"; God won't shrink back
in dismay from our troubles; God doesn't turn away and ignore naked
need (Ps. 22:24). He does not forsake us. He hears and acts. Other people often do distance themselves from suffering. They minimize it, recoil
in distaste, look the other way, or blame the victim. But this God will
hear our cry.

In Jesus' final act of trust he expressed himself in words from Psalm
31:5: "Into your hands I commit my spirit." Taken out of context, these
words might sound calm, cool, and collected. But taken in context, it is
anything but calm. This is a plea of need from a man fully engaged with
both his troubles and his God. The emotions of Psalm 31 expressing
faith in the act of trust run the gamut from fear to courage, from sorrow to joy, from hate to love, from neediness to gratitude. "Commit"
(Luke 23:46) and "entrust" (1 Pet. 4:19) are the same Greek word. Peter
intentionally calls forth our experience into the pattern of Jesus' experience on the cross.

God's high sovereignty? Of course, it takes all the panic out of life.
Any reason for despair washes away. But, grasp it rightly, and you'll never
be matter-of-fact and coolly detached. God's purposes are to "sanctify"
you. And his kind of sanctification aims for vibrant engagement with the
real and immediate conditions of life, both the good and the bad. "All
that is within me, joyously bless his name" and "Hear my anguished cry
for help" are both what sanctification produces. Christ fiercely opposes
matter-of-fact detachment. It is the opposite of what he is like. God will
teach you to experience life the way the psalms express it.

4. "My Loving Purpose Is Your Transformation"

"When through fiery trials your pathway shall lie,
my grace, all-sufficient, shall be your supply;
the flame shall not hurt you; I only design
your dross to consume and your gold to refine."

This stanza makes God's purpose even more explicit. He designs your significant suffering for three reasons: to reveal his abiding generosity, to remove all that is ungenerous in you, to make you abidingly generous. He is "with us" to work out this purpose. The metaphor of "fiery trials" that cannot finally harm you comes from Isaiah 43:2. But this stanza's core promise arises from 1 Peter 1:6-9. Peter uses the metaphor of a smelting furnace. You are a mixed—mixed-up!—creature, and experiences of suffering purify you. His love works to take away all that is wrong ("dross"). The outcome is a torrent of love and joy towards God in Christ, and a sincere, fervent love for others ("gold"). Peter says that this is the fruit of faith, because you have never actually seen Jesus. But he becomes more and more real in the context of fiery trials. We will look first at the dross, and then at the gold.

Most of the time we are right to separate sufferings from sins. What you do is different from what happens to you. Your sins are bad things about you as a moral agent. Your sufferings are bad things that happen to you. Agent and victim are opposite in principle. So far so good. Most of this book (like this chapter) has rightly focused on the things that happen *to* us. Christians, as new creation in Christ, live in an essentially different relationship to their sufferings.

But it is worth noting that Christians, as new creations in Christ, also live in an essentially different relationship to their own sinfulness. Your sin now afflicts you. The "dross" no longer defines or delights you. Indwelling sin becomes a form of significant suffering. What you once instinctively loved now torments you. The essential change in your relationship with God radically changes your relationship to remaining sinfulness. In Christ, in order to sin, you must lapse into temporary insanity, into forgetfulness. It is your worst cancer, your most crippling disability, your most treacherous enemy, your deepest distress. It is the single most destructive force impacting your life. Like nothing else in all creation, this threatens your life and well-being.

This is not to justify or excuse our sins. Your sin is your sin. When you get your back up in an argument, when you vegetate in front of the TV, when you spin a fantasy world of romance or eroticism, when you grumble about the weather, when you obsess about your performance in the eyes of significant others, when you worry, nag, or gossip, *you* do these things. No evil twin, no hormone, no satanic agency, and no aspect of your upbringing can take credit or blame for the works of your flesh.

You do it. You wanted to do it . . . but you don't *really* want to, when you come to your senses. And you do come to your senses. The conflicted dual consciousness of the Christian always lands on its feet. You commit sin, but you are more committed to the Lord, because he is absolutely committed to you. Many psalms capture this tension that always resolves the right way. They confess the dark vitality of indwelling sin while confessing love for the triumphant mercies and goodness of the Lord.[5]

In moments of sane self-knowledge, you view your dark tendencies as an affliction: "I am what I do not want to be. I do what I do not what to do. I think what I do not want to think. I want what I do not want to want." You feel the inner contradiction: "I want to love God joyously, but meander in self-preoccupation. I want to love others freely, but lapse into lovelessness. I want to forgive, but brood in bitterness. I want to give to others, but find that I take from them or ignore them. I want to listen and learn, but find I am opinionated and narrow-minded. My biggest problem looks at me from the mirror." But indwelling sin does not define you. It opposes you. It is an aberration, not an identity. Self-will is a living contradiction within you. So you look far beyond the mirror: "The love of Christ for me will get last say. He is merciful to me for *his* name's sake, for the sake of *his* own goodness, for the sake of *his* steadfast love and compassion (Psalm 25). When he thinks about me, he remembers what *he* is like, and that is my exceeding joy. My indestructible hope is that he has turned his face towards me, and he will never turn away."

All the promises of our hymn apply to the significant suffering of indwelling evil, as well as to the evils that come at you from outside. You probably did not initially identify a pattern of indwelling sin as your most significant suffering. But put the two together. How does God use the very trouble you identified as a context that reveals what he is working on? How do you know that he will deliver you from the sins that afflict you?

Second, what does the "gold" look like? Earlier we portrayed how

---

[5] Most people associate psalms of confession (e.g., 32, 38, 51) with this theme. But Psalm 119 most vividly captures the dual consciousness that lands on its feet. See "Suffering and Psalm 119" in David Powlison, *Speaking Truth in Love* (Winston-Salem, N.C.: Punch Press, 2005), 11-31. Psalm 25 and Romans 6–8 are also filled with this holy ambivalence that lands on God's side of the struggle.

faith thinks and speaks according to the intelligent passion of the psalms. And that faith leads somewhere very, very good. We will examine two key aspects of the love that faith produces. The most remarkable good things that the planet has ever seen or will ever see can only come out in the context of suffering. We will look first at fearless endurance and then at wise love.

Grace means courage. When God says, "Fear not," his aim is not that you would just calm down and experience a relative absence of fear. He does not say, "Don't be afraid. Everything will turn out okay. So you can relax." Instead he says, "Don't be afraid. I am with you. So be strong and courageous." Do you hear the difference? The deep waters have not gone away. The opposite of fear is fearlessness. Fearlessness is active and enduring. It carries on constructively in the midst of stressful things that don't feel good at all. Courage means more than freedom from anxious feelings. Endurance is a purposeful "abiding under" what is hard and painful, considering others even when you don't feel good.

There are countless ways to simply lessen anxiety feelings: vigorous exercise, getting all the facts, Prozac, cognitive behavioral therapy, finding the best possible doctor, yoga, a vacation in Bermuda, a glass of wine, getting some distance from the problem, finding support from fellow sufferers, throwing yourself into work. Some of these are fine in their place. But none of them will make you fearless in the face of trouble. None of them creates that fruit of the Spirit called "endurance," which is mentioned repeatedly when the New Testament talks about God's purposes in suffering. None of the strategies for personal peace gives you the disposition and power to love another person considerately in the small choices of daily life. None of them gives you high joy in knowing that your entire life is a holy experiment as God's hands shape you into the image of his Son. None of them changes the way you suffer by embedding it in deeper meaning. None gives you a reason to persevere in fruitfulness through all your days, even if the scope of your obedience is constricted to your interactions with nurses at your bedside.

Grace also teaches wise love. In fact, fearless endurance is for the purpose of wise love. God is making you like Jesus in the hardships of real life. Jesus combines two qualities that rarely go together: true compassion and life-rearranging counsel. He intends to combine them in you. Some helpers care intensely, but don't know what to say. They feel helpless compassion. They offer platitudes. They reinforce the self-pity and entitlement of the victimized. Other helpers have advice to offer, but don't enter the plight of sufferers. They offer cold counsel. They become impatient when a sufferer is slow to change. They dismiss the significance of the affliction of the afflicted. Neither is able to really comfort; neither is able to really guide.

But when you've passed through your own fiery trials, and found God to be true to what he says, you have real help to offer. You have firsthand experience of both his sustaining grace and his purposeful design. He has kept you through pain; he reshaped you more into his image. You've found that what this entire hymn says is *true*. What you are experiencing from God, you can give away in increasing measure to others. You are learning both the tenderness and the clarity necessary to help sanctify another person's deepest distress.

Second Corinthians 1:4 says it best: "[God] comforts us in all our affliction so that we will be able to comfort those who are in any affliction with the comfort with which we ourselves are comforted by God." That word "comfort" (or "encourage" in other translations) does not simply mean solace or inspiration. It means God's transformative compassion, the perfect union of kindness and candor. He speaks the truth in love so that we grow up to do the same. Notice how wise love is a "generalizable skill." What you learn from God in your *particular* affliction becomes helpful to others in *any* affliction. This is why a hymn written 250 years ago can help us in any affliction, though we don't know exactly what particulars the author experienced.

God's personal tenderness, unchangeable truth, and high purposes are united so that he simultaneously accomplishes seemingly contradictory things. He profoundly comforts us as sufferers, strengthening us for endurance. He mercifully challenges us as sinners, humbling us with our ongoing need for the blood of the Lamb. He powerfully changes us as his sons and daughters, making us fearless, making us wise to help other sufferers, other sinners, other sons and daughters. There is inevitably an aloneness in suffering because no one can fully enter another's experience. Each person "knows the affliction of his own heart" (1 Kings 8:38; cf. Prov. 14:10). God ensures that human aid will never substitute for the Lord who alone comes fully near. But we can bear each other's burdens with love, and we can counsel each other with truth. The give and take of wise love is one of life's most significant joys.

5. *"I Will Prove My Love to the End of Your Life"*
    "E'en down to old age all my people shall prove
    my sovereign, eternal, unchangeable love;
    and when hoary hairs shall their temples adorn,
    like lambs they shall still in my bosom be borne."

All that we've looked at continues even down to old age. This is remarkable. It shows great sensitivity to the human condition to write a hymn about growing old. Readers already "adorned" with gray or white hair—big fans of Psalm 71!—will immediately appreciate why a hymn for sufferers must tackle aging. A friend of mine in his seventies puts it this way: "Growing old is not for the fainthearted." Every single reader, should you live so long, will experience a landslide of losses and disabilities. Live long enough, and you may outlive everyone you love: parents, friends, spouse, even children, perhaps grandchildren. You may outlive your money. You outlive your usefulness in the workplace and other productive arenas. You outlive your relevance. You are no longer part of what's happening. You outlive your health as every bodily system breaks down. You might outlive your ability to walk, your toilet training, your ability to feed yourself. You may outlive your memory, and, in the extreme, might lose your ability to put thoughts together, to relate to others the way you wish you could, and even to remember who you are. Should you live long enough, you will lose every earthly good. And then you will certainly lose your life. The last enemy still kills. Our hymn only mentions the outward indicators: the years, the white hairs. But those allusions tip you off to a story of weakness, hardship, and finally the loss of life itself. It is in this context that God gently and persistently promises to prove his "sovereign, eternal, unchangeable love . . . like lambs they shall still in my bosom be borne." He tenderly carries the helpless.

A dear friend had experienced many losses in her life. She recently faced one more: a disfiguring cancer surgery. She put her grief plaintively, "I didn't expect the scarring after the bandages came off. It's upsetting to look in the mirror. It's one more loss. And I feel so much uncertainty about whether the cancer will return. Then there's the loss of people, the isolation, the loss of human society, the parts of life in which I can no longer participate." She is a woman of articulate faith. She is honest about the pain of loss. But her God speaks the final, decisive word about her: "I will carry you and never let you go." That is perhaps the deepest comfort communicated by this hymn's way of communicating God's voice. He gets first say, and he gets last say. So everything in the middle—about which he expects us to have lots to say!—is anchored in sovereign, eternal, unchangeable love.

How does faith learn what to trust? God teaches faith the words to trust and what to say. Think back to the very first promise in the second stanza, "Fear not, I am with you." This fifth stanza (like the fourth, like the third, and like the sixth to come!) says essentially the same thing. Each gives us different details, unpacks further implications, uses metaphors that evoke a different nuance of God's inexhaustible riches of wisdom. Psalm 23:4 has probably provided more comfort to more suffering and dying people than any other passage of Scripture: "Though I walk through the valley of the shadow of death, I will fear no evil, for you are with me." Notice that through this entire hymn, God has been telling that same truth from the opposite direction. "Fear not, I am with you" allows Psalm 23 to say, "I fear not, for you are with me." Faith listens well, and lives it back to God.

I bring this up here because of the other details in Psalm 23:4—"shadow of death" and "no evil" (i.e., any one of the many evils). Most likely, the particular "shadow" of oncoming death that threatened David was an enemy (most likely Saul) who was out to kill him. Like a sheep stalked by wolves, David lives, but under a "shadow" of looming death. David generalizes this experience to "any evil" that we might fear. The metaphor powerfully applies to hardships of aging. Death is coming nearer. Aging casts numerous specific shadows of approaching death: sickness, losses, weakness, helplessness, futility. In fact, if you think about it, whether you are young or old, *every* form of significant suffering, *every* evil, leaves something of the bitter taste of death in your mouth. So "shadow of death" is not simply an evocative metaphor, and "no evil" does not intend a generality. Those shadows and evils are person-specific: your significant sufferings. You don't theoretically need God's grace to reach into your sufferings. In suffering, you immediately feel your need. A shadow reaches towards you. It covers you. Its inner logic whispers or shouts of death.

Can you say, "I fear no evil"? Can you honestly say, "I do not fear _____"? It all depends on actually hearing the God who says the same truth from the opposite direction, so that you become able to say it back. If the God of life is in fact *with* you, carrying you as a newborn lamb, you will become fearless in any suffering. (I'm not mentioning the ups and downs, the painful struggle of a lifetime to come towards such a place. I'm describing the destination toward which to struggle.) If God pledges his absolute fidelity to you, if indestructible love will see you through to a good end, then you are able to walk a very hard road. You will have to walk a very hard road. Death sends out many messengers, even to the very young. If you listen, you will become fearless. If you listen, you will endure. If you listen, you will fight the good fight in the most terrible of wars. If you listen, you will know that you need to be rescued. You will know that you need to be carried into the battle, and carried through the battle, and finally carried from the battlefield. If you listen, you will live.

6. *"I Will Never Fail You"*
"The soul that on Jesus has leaned for repose,
I will not, I will not desert to his foes;
that soul, though all hell should endeavor to shake,
I'll never, no never, no never forsake."

A predator is after you. The velociraptors are out. The roaring lion prowls. Psalm 10, as we saw earlier, directly faced exactly this form of significant suffering. Ultimately, you face the same. At the beginning of this chapter, you selected some significant suffering in your life. We have held that in view as we worked through this hymn stanza by stanza. Perhaps you noticed that the fourth stanza pushed the envelope in a surprising direction: by grace, your sinfulness has also become a significant suffering. The gracious Lord actually uses the outward sufferings as a catalyst to free you from the enemy within. The fifth stanza further pushed the envelope: aging will bring you into the shadow of death, and finally you will be swallowed into the darkness of the last enemy. The sixth stanza pushes one more time: you have foes from hell. The fact that you will die is not an impersonal fact. It registers the personal animosity of a killer. There is a lord of darkness, who is father to both sin and death. He personifies every aspect of the evils that come upon us and the evils that arise from within us.

When you think about hellish foes coming after you, our hymn writer (like the Bible) is talking about reality—not the "horror" genre in videos and books. He means ordinary, everyday life lived under the shadow of death. White hairs and birthday candles testify that a predator is coming soon. The Evil One is both the accuser and murderer of sinners. He holds the power of death (Heb. 2:14). He willingly conceals his workaday identity behind veneers of horror and superstition. It makes people unsuspecting. They don't notice that he's in the mortality business however it happens.

When you think about the power of moral evil, our hymn writer (again like the Bible) is talking about all-pervasive reality—not lurid stories of Satan worship. He means garden-variety sin, unbelief, and self-will, spun out into ten thousand forms. The fair and honest wage paid for ordinary sin is death (Rom. 6:23). The Evil One is both the liar and tempter who works skillfully in and with the facts of life. It matters little to him whether or not people even believe he exists. He willingly conceals his real malignancy behind wild tales. It makes people unsuspecting. They don't notice that he's in the unbelief business whatever form it takes.

You suffer in a world in which immediate sufferings point to deeper, darker, deadlier things: the enemy within, the final enemy, and The Enemy. These significantly afflict every one of us. They characterize the human condition. "The whole world lies *in* the evil one" (1 John 5:19, literal translation). It is a slave world. A dark world. A death world.

But you suffer in a world in which all dark, deadly things exist within an even deeper design and calling. The drama of evil occasions the revelation of good: the holy justice and the sacrificial love of God. He will bring all enemies to final justice. And he has shown wholly unmerited mercy. When we were helpless, when we were ungodly, when we were sinners, when we were enemies, Christ died for us. You are now free. You are light in the Lord. You live. "We are *of* God. . . . We are *in* him who is true, *in* his Son, Jesus Christ. This is the true God and eternal life" (1 John 5:19f).

If you "lean for repose" on Jesus, you will live. "Repose" here does not mean a restful state of peace and tranquility. It means actively placing the weight of your life on Jesus. Put your entire faith, confidence, and trust in him. Our Savior Christ Jesus abolished death, and brought life and immortality to light. . . . I know whom I have believed, and I am convinced that he is able to guard what I have entrusted to him until that day (2 Tim. 1:10, 12). That is the language of repose.

This final stanza aims to make you free and fearless, no matter what you now face or will face. *I will never forsake you.* God is willing to say it until you get it! The final line of the hymn sends us out with another of the Bible's core promises. In fact, it completes a quartet, two promises and two commands that God frequently links: "I am with you. Don't be afraid. Be strong and courageous. I will never forsake you."[6] We've discussed the other promise and the two commands in previous sections.

Here one final promise gets last say. There is a particular appropriateness to closing with *I will never forsake you.* Sufferers feel apprehension about the future, for good reason. Some evils won't go away. Shadows multiply and darken. The night is coming. This word of comfort looks to the future. It speaks right into our temptation to fear and dismay.

Notice how God's words press into you. The hymn has unfolded in a double crescendo. Our awareness of suffering, pain, weakness, and danger has steadily intensified. Our awareness of God's powerful love at work has steadily intensified. Sin, misery, and death abound. Grace, joy, and life abound all the more. Mercy will have final say. But we easily quail. We *feel* the force of things that undo us and would unglue us. They shake us up. They immediately hurt. Is God's saving voice only words? Is it really so? The hymn writer knows our vulnerability to dismay. "I'll never, no never, no never forsake. I'll never, no never, no never forsake."[7] If you have ever sung this hymn with your brothers and sisters, these last lines come out fiercely triumphant.

In the pages of the Bible, God explicitly promises, "I will not forsake you" (e.g., Josh. 1:5). Once you know to look for it, you see that he says the same truth in a hundred other ways, too. "God is faithful" and "His

---

[6] See Deuteronomy 31:6, 8; Joshua 1:5; 1 Chronicles 28:20.
[7] This powerful last line doubles when sung to *Adeste Fideles*.

steadfast love endures forever" and "The Lord is my refuge" are varia-
tions on a theme. What God says for himself, his spokesmen often proclaim about him, "He will not forsake you" (e.g., Deut. 31:6, 8). So with
good reason his children cry out to him in their troubles and distresses,
Don't forsake me! Again, hearing, we believe and speak. Scripture gives
many particular examples of this dynamic. Are you elderly, suffering
the weakness, pain, disability, and losses of aging? *Don't abandon me!*
(Ps. 71:9, 18). Do you feel lonely and vulnerable as you face powerful
interpersonal hostility, bereft of anyone who can protect you? *Don't
desert me!* (Ps. 27:9-10). Do you feel dismayed because of your sins,
that God has every reason to give up on you? *Don't give up on me!*
(Ps. 119:8). Are you doubly dismayed, both because of your sins and
because of the hostilities of others? *Don't let me go!* (Ps. 38:17-21).

Our hymn takes God's simple "I will not" and says it ten times in a
row: "I will never, no, never, no, never, never, no, never, no, never forsake you." Not a mere doubling, but a promise to the power of ten. This
is pastoral wisdom, helping us to hear the fierceness and triumph of
God's lovingkindness. You will never be abandoned. You will never be
alone. He will never give up on you.

Never forget this. Never forget. Never, never, never forget that he
will not forsake you.

Coda

So often the initial reaction to painful suffering is *Why me? Why this?
Why now? Why?* You've now heard God speaking with you. The real
God says all these wonderful things, and does everything he says. He
comes for you, in the flesh, in Christ, into suffering, on your behalf. He
does not offer advice and perspective from afar; he steps into your significant suffering. He will see you through, and work with you the whole
way. He will carry you even *in extremis.* This reality changes the questions that rise up from your heart. That inward-turning "why me?" qui-
ets down, lifts its eyes, and begins to look around.

You turn outward and new, wonderful questions form. Why you?
Why you? Why would you enter this world of evils? Why would you go
through loss, weakness, hardship, sorrow, and death? Why would you
do this for me, of all people? But you did. You did this for the joy set

before you. You did this for love. You did this showing the glory of God in the face of Christ. As that deeper question sinks home, you become joyously sane. The universe is no longer supremely about you. Yet you are not irrelevant. God's story makes you just the right size. Everything counts, but the scale changes to something that makes much more sense. You face hard things. But you have already received something better which can never be taken away. And that better something will continue to work out the whole journey long.

The question generates a heartfelt response: Bless the Lord, O my soul, and do not forget any of his benefits, who pardons all your iniquities and heals all your diseases, who redeems your life from the pit, who crowns you with lovingkindness and compassion, who satisfies your years with good things so that your youth is renewed like the eagle. Thank you, my Father. You are able to give true voice to a *thank you* amid all that is truly wrong, both the sins and the sufferings that now have come under lovingkindness.

Finally, you are prepared to pose—and to mean—almost unimaginable questions: Why not me? Why not this? Why not now? If in some way, my faith might serve as a three-watt night-light in a very dark world, why not me? If my suffering shows forth the Savior of the world, why not me? If I have the privilege of filling up the sufferings of Christ? If he sanctifies to me my deepest distress? If I fear no evil? If he bears me in his arms? If my weakness demonstrates the power of God to save us from all that is wrong? If my honest struggle shows other strugglers how to land on their feet? If my life becomes a source of hope for others? Why not me?

Of course, you don't want to suffer, but you've become willing: "If it is possible, let this cup pass from me; yet not as I will, but as you will." Like him, your loud cries and tears will in fact be heard by the one who saves from death. Like him, you will learn obedience through what you suffer. Like him, you will sympathize with the weaknesses of others. Like him, you will deal gently with the ignorant and wayward. Like him, you will display faith to a faithless world, hope to a hopeless world, love to a loveless world, life to a dying world. If all that God promises only comes true, then why not me?

CHAPTER 8

Waiting for the Morning during the Long Night of Weeping

DUSTIN SHRAMEK

G ood theology is essential if we are going to suffer well. It will help us persevere during our trials, and it will give us hope. We believe that "Weeping may tarry for the night, but joy comes with the morning" (Ps. 30:5). It is faith in our good and sovereign God that enables us to wait until the morning. But we must never forget that often the night is long and the weeping uncontrollable.

No amount of good theology is able to take the pain out of suffering. Too often we allow ourselves to believe that a robust view of God's sovereignty in all things means that when suffering comes it won't hurt. God's sovereignty doesn't take away the pain and evil that confront us in our lives; it works them for our good.

The pain of suffering is both dark and deep. This is crucial to see, for when we minimize the pain we fail to love others and we fail to honor God. When we minimize the pain of suffering we can no longer understand the apostle Paul, who said, "For this slight momentary affliction is preparing for us an eternal weight of glory beyond all comparison" (2 Cor. 4:17). There is nothing astounding about such a statement if Paul is speaking about hangnails, stubbed toes, and his favorite shirt getting stained.

But we know better. Paul's statement is so amazing because he *did* suffer, far more than most of us ever will. He was imprisoned multiple times, suffered "countless beatings, and [was] often near death" (2 Cor. 11:23).

Five times I received at the hands of the Jews the forty lashes less one. Three times I was beaten with rods. Once I was stoned. Three times I was shipwrecked; a night and a day I was adrift at sea; on frequent journeys, in danger from rivers, danger from robbers, danger from my own people, danger from Gentiles, danger in the city, danger in the wilderness, danger at sea, danger from false brothers; in toil and hardship, through many a sleepless night, in hunger and thirst, often without food, in cold and exposure. And, apart from other things, there is the daily pressure on me of my anxiety for all the churches. (2 Cor. 11:24-28)

He endured awful physical pain through beatings, lashings, and a stoning. He went hungry and at times did not have adequate shelter against the cold. He experienced the grief of seeing his friends near death (Phil. 2:27-30). He was even betrayed by friends (2 Tim. 4:10, 16). Then there was the "daily pressure" for the churches. It is only when we understand the depth of Paul's suffering and the pain he endured, both physical and emotional, that we will stand amazed that he could call such things slight and momentary. By embracing the depth of his pain we are enabled to marvel at the eternal weight of glory. What glory it must be if pain this deep and protracted is slight and momentary!

So it is good for us to delve into the depths of our pain in suffering, for in so doing we will be teaching ourselves the far greater value of the eternal weight of glory.

The Reality of Pain

We also need to delve into the depths of our pain in suffering so that we can be honest. There are times in our lives that we can barely make it out of bed in the morning and we have no energy to do anything. Our pain and grief is so great that we are unable to concentrate. We have no energy for prayer, let alone Bible reading. God feels distant and unloving. Questions about his goodness and purposes run through our minds without stopping.

This was certainly what my wife and I experienced after our son Owen died in 2003. We were living in the Middle East, and as Kellie went into labor we were medically evacuated to Istanbul, Turkey, where premature babies have a better chance of survival. He was born October 3, but he only lived for twenty minutes. I saw him kicking and moving and heard him give one little cry, but that was it. Our firstborn was dead.

The pain was unlike anything we had ever experienced. We felt alone. A few nights after Owen died, my wife stayed up for hours scouring the Scriptures for hope and comfort. She finally fell asleep more discouraged than ever because she found none. Of course it was there, but when we are in the depths of pain we often can't see it, let alone *feel* it.

We struggled with anger toward God, wondering why he didn't comfort us. We had prayed; indeed, people literally all over the world had prayed for the life of our son, but God chose a different path for us. So why wouldn't he comfort us on this path?

Many people said things to us like, "Look to Jesus! Trust in his promises. He does care for you. You need to get in the Word and pray and fight for your joy. You need to talk with others about this and have them pray for you." We knew that this is true and right; yet, when we were overwhelmed with grief, it felt hollow and unhelpful. We needed to know that they too had been changed by our pain; that, in some sense, it was also their pain.

We don't love others in the midst of this kind of pain by pretending that it isn't all that bad or by trying to quickly fix it with some pat theological answers. We love them by first weeping with them. It is when we enter into their pain and are ourselves changed by it that we can speak the truth in love. When their pain becomes our pain (as Paul said, "If one member suffers, all suffer together" [1 Cor. 12:26]), we are able to give the encouragement of the Scriptures.

My hope for this chapter is twofold. First, for those who are not in the midst of suffering, I hope to help you see the depth of the pain of those who are suffering. By entering into their pain you will be more equipped to weep with those who weep. For those who are in the midst of terrible suffering, I hope you will see that God has not abandoned you in the pit. He knows it is dark and seemingly bottomless, but he has left you a lifeline—himself. My prayer is that by looking at the depth of pain in Scripture, God might give you even a tiny sliver of hope.

The Problem with Pain

The problem that we deal with here in the West is that we don't like to confront grief or suffering. Through medicine and wealth we have avoided a lot of the suffering that the rest of the world still experiences (though our façade of invincibility was at least temporarily washed away with 9/11 and Hurricane Katrina). Suffering is a universal experience so we can't avoid it forever. However, when it does come, we fast-paced Westerners like to "deal with it" as quickly as possible.

In some cultures, after the death of a loved one there are many days of mourning, and this mourning includes loud wailing and lamentations. In fact, after Jacob died in the land of Egypt we are told that the "*Egyptians* wept for him *seventy* days" (Gen. 50:3. I emphasize "Egyptians" because Jacob and his family were shepherds, and we are told in Genesis 46:34 that shepherds are an abomination to the Egyptians). When his family came to his burial place "they lamented there with a *very great* and *grievous* lamentation" (Gen. 50:10). We, on the other hand, have about a week before we are expected to return to work and put up the front that we are okay. Even worse, in America most of us work hard at holding back the loud cries during funerals. Indeed, we even try to hold back the tears.

When my mother died of cancer, I was sixteen years old. I had been a believer for two years and everyone was telling me how strong I was and how well I was handling her death. No one saw me cry, and their comments made me feel as though I *shouldn't* cry. I had to be the strong one for my family, and strong people don't grieve (at least that is what they unintentionally [?] led me to believe). It wasn't until three months after my mother's death that I cried for the first time. The dam broke and I sobbed like a baby. God used those tears to help begin my healing as I was finally able to release some of the pain that had been building up inside of me.

The problem, though, was that this experience made me a grief-avoider. There are many of us in the world (especially among men). I learned to do whatever was necessary to avoid dealing with the grief in my heart so that I could remain strong and not cry.

I believe this avoidance of grief in our culture results from not knowing how to deal with pain. We get uncomfortable when we hear people question God. We like to give easy answers to try to minimize the pain. When someone says that they feel God has forsaken them, we think we must quickly preach the truth that he will never leave us nor forsake us (Heb. 13:5), or they will fall away and lose their faith.

Part of the problem is that we do not see such pain and deep grief as normative in the Christian life. Yes, we all know that suffering is normative, but we don't take the time to really talk about the pain involved in suffering. After all, it isn't suffering if it doesn't hurt.

When we read about great saints of the past, we hear about their suffering, which is immediately followed by their triumph through Christ. Rarely do we truly enter with them into their dark night of the soul, when all around them nothing makes sense.

Consider the nineteenth-century theologian, Robert Dabney. In a matter of about a month he lost two of his sons, Jimmy and Bobby. This is what he says: "When my Jimmy died, the grief was painfully sharp, but the actings of faith, the embracing of consolation, and all the cheering truths which ministered comfort to me were just as vivid." This is what we like to hear. We like to hear that the truths of the gospel encouraged him and that his faith was strong.

But he goes on in the same letter, "But when the stroke was repeated, and thereby doubled, I seem to be paralyzed and stunned. I know that my loss is doubled, and I know also that the same cheering truths apply to the second as to the first, but I remain numb, downcast, almost without hope and interest."[1] When we hear this we get uncomfortable. The great truths of the gospel fell flat after his second son died and he remained "numb, downcast, almost without hope and interest." It is true that God carried him through and that Dabney proved to be faithful. He did triumph. He experienced the truth of Psalm 34:19, "Many are the afflictions of the righteous, but the LORD delivers him out of them all." But let us not so quickly go from the affliction to the deliverance and thus minimize the pain in between. God's promise of deliverance does not mean that he will *immediately* deliver us. For many, deliverance only comes with death.

---

[1] Thomas Cary Johnson, *The Life and Letters of Robert Lewis Dabney* (Edinburgh: Banner of Truth, 1977), 172.

The Depth of Pain

What we need is to validate and give voice to the depth of pain. I don't want to merely sound the triumphant horn of the gospel (though I do want to do that); I also want us to recognize that there is a reason it is called suffering, affliction, and tribulation. We may be shocked when suffering people speak openly of their pain, and concerned when it sounds like they are questioning God's goodness, wisdom, or power. But if that makes us uncomfortable, then the Bible will make us uncomfortable. As we will see, the pain of some of the psalmists was raw and at times quite disturbing.

There are many psalms where we read about pain, but the most remarkable one is Psalm 88, which some could argue is the most discouraging chapter in the Bible:

> O Lord, God of my salvation;
>   I cry out day and night before you.
> Let my prayer come before you;
>   incline your ear to my cry!
>
> For my soul is full of troubles,
>   and my life draws near to Sheol.
> I am counted among those who go down to the pit;
>   I am a man who has no strength,
> like one set loose among the dead,
>   like the slain that lie in the grave,
> like those whom you remember no more,
>   for they are cut off from your hand.
> You have put me in the depths of the pit,
>   in the regions dark and deep.
> Your wrath lies heavy upon me,
>   and you overwhelm me with all your waves.
>   *Selah*
>
> You have caused my companions to shun me;
>   you have made me a horror to them.
> I am shut in so that I cannot escape;
>   my eye grows dim through sorrow.
> Every day I call upon you, O Lord;
>   I spread out my hands to you.

Do you work wonders for the dead?
  Do the departed rise up to praise you?
    Selah

Is your steadfast love declared in the grave,
  or your faithfulness in Abaddon?
Are your wonders known in the darkness,
  or your righteousness in the land of forgetfulness?

But I, O LORD, cry to you;
  in the morning my prayer comes before you.
O LORD, why do you cast my soul away?
  Why do you hide your face from me?
Afflicted and close to death from my youth up,
  I suffer your terrors; I am helpless.
Your wrath has swept over me;
  your dreadful assaults destroy me.
They surround me like a flood all day long;
  they close in on me together.
You have caused my beloved and my friend to shun me;
  my companions have become darkness.

The first verse is the only verse in the entire psalm that has any sense of hope. He begins, "O LORD, God of my salvation." He had not rejected God, and he still knew (at least intellectually) that God is the God of his salvation. Yet as we read further it sounds as though this profession of faith felt empty for him.

"I cry out day and night before you. Let my prayer come before you; incline your ear to my cry! For my soul is full of troubles and my life draws near to Sheol" (vv. 1-3). His pain was so great that he cried out day and night, begging God to incline his ear and hear. He desperately wanted for God to hear his cry and act on his behalf. But he didn't feel heard. He didn't feel like anyone was listening. His soul was filled with troubles and trials; he was near death, either literally or because of the pain he was enduring. It is no small thing to be near death and feel that the God you have served has put his hands over his ears so that he does not hear.

In verse four he admits that he is a "man who has no strength." Grief and pain do this to us. They suck away our energy and leave us as though dead, unable to even get dressed in the morning. In the deepest and darkest moments of our suffering we are people without strength. He takes it a step further and says that he is like a dead man, "like those whom you remember no more, for they are cut off from your hand" (v. 5). The pain is so great and overwhelming it caused him to believe God had already forgotten him and counted him as dead. Even worse than not being remembered was the reason he felt he was no longer remembered. He believed he had been cut off from God's hand, that is, that he had been cut off from the covenant blessings of God. So it isn't just that God didn't hear—God was treating him like he was a dead *Gentile*, cut off from the covenant people of God.

"You have put me in the depths of the pit, in the regions dark and deep" (v. 6). There are times when we feel so alone and cut off from everyone, even God, that we seem to be in the depths of the pit. No one else can possibly understand our pain, and there is no glimmer of hope. We can't see even a shred of light—surely the pit must be hundreds of miles deep. The darkness is so deep it feels heavy all around as though the darkness itself could be measured by a scale.

But the problem wasn't just that he felt alone and lost in the pit. It was worse than that. He felt that God's *wrath* was heavy upon him. "Your wrath lies heavy upon me, and you overwhelm me with all your waves" (v. 7). He was overwhelmed, for the waves were crashing over him and he knew that any moment he could go under them for the last time.

Part of the reason he felt so alone was because his companions had shunned him—he was a horror to them (v. 8). Whatever the cause of his pain, it also made his friends leave him. Perhaps this was because they were horrified at what they saw when they looked at him, or perhaps it was simply because they didn't know what to say. The reason they shunned him is irrelevant because for him the result was the same—he was alone.

Yet even in the midst of such great pain, he was not negligent in prayer. "Every day I call upon you, O LORD; I spread out my hands to you" (v. 9). Every day he spread out his hands and called upon God because he expected God to answer. But he didn't receive an answer. His hands remained empty day after day. This was when the pain was at its deepest. Many of us can endure the worst kinds of suffering if God himself is filling our hands (and hearts) with comfort. But when we cry out for comfort and receive nothing, we are undone. Surely the Sovereign One who has ultimately brought about this suffering could at least comfort me in the midst of it, couldn't he? When this doesn't happen the suffering is magnified beyond our imaginings.

The psalmist goes on to describe his despair and rejection in verses 13-16: "But I, O LORD, cry to you; in the morning my prayer comes before you. O Lord, why do you cast my soul away? Why do you hide your face from me? Afflicted and close to death from my youth up, I suffer your terrors; I am helpless. Your wrath has swept over me; your dreadful assaults destroy me."

O God, I cry out to you, why don't you answer? Why have you rejected me and cast me away from you? I seek you, and yet you hide your face from me. Why O Lord? Why? Don't you see my affliction? I cry out for mercy from you, but instead of mercy I suffer your terrors and am helpless. Your wrath sweeps over me and you are assaulting me, destroying me. Where are you? Who are you?

He then ends the psalm with this statement: "You have caused my beloved and my friend to shun me; my companions have become darkness" (v. 18). Even the one closest to him had turned away and now there was nothing but darkness.

That's it. There is nothing more, the psalm has ended. He did not move from pain and grief to joyful triumph. He had not experienced the deliverance he cried out for. He was still just as discouraged then as he was when he began writing.

This is raw and disturbing. But if we let ourselves enter into his pain (as well as our own) we will see that his experience isn't so unique. So what encouragement is there in a text like this? Why would this be included in the Bible? There is no triumph here. Only pain, despair, and fear.

We also read in Psalm 77:7-9, "Will the Lord spurn forever, and never again be favorable? Has his steadfast love forever ceased? Are his promises at an end for all time? Has God forgotten to be gracious? Has he in anger shut up his compassion?"

Have you felt the Lord turn his back on you so that you questioned whether he would ever look your way again? Have you felt that his love for you has ended and that his promises were null and void? In the midst of your pain have you cried out, "God where is your grace? Why will you not comfort me?"

Of course we know intellectually that God does not forget to be gracious and that he will indeed be compassionate. We know that he hasn't rejected us and that his steadfast love is forever. But there are times when our pain is so deep that truths in our mind just can't seem to penetrate the darkness that surrounds our hearts.

Why Such Pain Is in the Bible

Where is the hope in Psalm 88? Didn't Paul say in Romans 15:4, "For whatever was written in former days was written for our instruction, that through endurance and through the encouragement of the Scriptures we might have hope"? Why, then, is such a hopeless psalm like Psalm 88 in the Bible?

It is in the Bible for the time when your son has just died after living for only twenty minutes and all that runs through your mind are questions such as: "God, what were you thinking?" "Why didn't you help me?" "Why didn't you save him?" "Why would you punish us for moving halfway around the world in obedience to you to a place where premature babies have no chance of survival?"—plus a million other thoughts that you would never want another person to know, because you are supposed to be a Christian who exults in the sovereignty of God.

This text is in the Bible so that when suffering and pain come and we are between the affliction and the triumph in the midst of the questions, pain, and clouds of doubt, we may see that what we are feeling is normal. It has all been felt before, and all the questions have been asked before. We are not the first. We are not alone. And we are not in danger of losing our faith (at least not yet).

God is a big God who can handle our questions, our anger, and our pain. This is clear from the fact that God has many psalms and verses in his Word in which godly people are struggling with doubts about his goodness and care for them. It is especially clear from Psalm 88, which doesn't even end with a message of hope.

God cares about us in the midst of the pain. His goal isn't just to get us out of the pain to the joy; he also wants us to see that he is for us and with us *in* the pain. It is true that weeping may tarry for the night, but joy comes in the morning (Ps. 30:5). The morning will dawn and God will remove every tear (Rev. 21:4), but God is not just concerned about the morning, the new day when you can shout for joy. He is with us even in the night when there is nothing but weeping, when the tears are so thick that we can't see. When we are in the deepest pit and darkness weighs on our souls and God feels so absent that we wonder if he is even real, this psalm reminds us that he is with us even then.

The Pain of Jesus

Even more remarkable than the experience of the psalmist in Psalm 88 is the experience of the Son of God on Calvary. The night he was betrayed he went to Gethsemane in order to pray. He brought Peter, James, and John with him that they might pray for him and comfort him, for he told them, "My soul is very sorrowful, even to death; remain here, and watch with me" (Matt. 26:38).

Jesus, the Divine Son, was full of sorrow, and his sorrow was so deep that it was like death. Isaiah said he was "a man of sorrows, and acquainted with grief; and as one from whom men hide their faces" (Isa. 53:3). He sought comfort from his friends, and yet they failed him by falling asleep in his time of need and then abandoning him when he was arrested. He was left alone to face the pain and suffering. Does this not sound like the experience of the psalmist?

His agony was so intense and severe that his "sweat became like great drops of blood falling down to the ground" (Luke 22:44). The author of Hebrews tells us, "In the days of his flesh, Jesus offered up prayers and supplications, with *loud cries and tears,* to him who was able to save him from death, and he was heard because of his reverence" (5:7). Jesus offered up "loud cries and tears," which are not incompatible with faith in God. In his cries and tears, Jesus was heard by the one able to save him from death, yet he still died. He asked for the cup to pass, but was resigned to do his Father's will, even though it would cost him his life. God heard his prayers, but rather than save him from pain and death, he chose for Jesus to walk on the road of suffering so that he might receive the greater joy of resurrection.

And let us not forget that his death was no ordinary death. First of all, it was death on a cross, one of the most excruciating forms of execution ever devised. But even more, it was a death in which he bore the wrath of God for all the people of God. The intensity of this wrath is remarkable, for it would take us all of eternity to pay the penalty for our sins and God's wrath would never be quenched, yet Christ bore God's complete wrath for billions and he did it in a matter of hours. No wonder he cried out, "My God, my God, why have you forsaken me?" (Matt. 27:46).

When we read the story of Christ's passion, we often gloss over this astounding statement. The Son of God who is the Father's beloved and delight was forsaken. He was abandoned and left all alone. Being forsaken by his friends was one thing, but being forsaken by his Father was quite another. The depth of this pain is greater than we can know. There has been no greater pain in all of history.

Why is the depth of Christ's pain significant for us? Because "we do not have a high priest who is unable to sympathize with our weaknesses, but one who in every respect has been tempted as we are, yet without sin" (Heb 4:15). In the midst of our pain we may feel alone and believe that no one has hurt as badly as we hurt. But it isn't true. Jesus Christ has felt such pain; indeed, he has felt pain that would have destroyed us. He is able to sympathize. "Let us then with confidence draw near to the throne of grace, that we may receive mercy and find grace to help in time of need" (Heb. 4:16).

Hope for the Pain

I hope you see that this depth of pain is normal. I want us to see that Jesus knows how badly it hurts. We don't need to feel shame because there is pain in our suffering. As I said before, if there was no pain, it wouldn't be called suffering.

Jesus' cry, "My God, my God, why have you forsaken me?" was not only a spontaneous outburst of emotion, it was also a quote from Psalm 22, which has much to say about Christ and his suffering as well as his hope.

David wrote Psalm 22 about himself and as a messianic prophecy. "My God, my God, why have you forsaken me? Why are you so far from saving me, from the words of my groaning? O my God, I cry by day, but you do not answer, and by night, but I find no rest" (vv. 1-2). His experience was very similar to what we saw in Psalm 88, but he goes a step further. He feels forsaken, has not received an answer, and finds no rest, but then he says, "*Yet* you are *holy*, enthroned on the praises of Israel" (v. 3).

He was abandoned, but he did not forget one very important thing—the fact that God is holy. How does regarding God as holy help us in the midst of our suffering? What help is this when we are trapped in the pit and the darkness threatens to suffocate us?

It helps us in two ways. First, in the midst of our pain, God's holiness is a life preserver that we can cling to in order to keep us from falling into the abyss. Second, it is because God is holy that he *himself* will keep us from falling into the abyss.

Isaiah had a remarkable glimpse of God's holiness when he heard the seraphim calling out to one another, "Holy, holy, holy is the LORD of hosts; the whole earth is full of his glory!" (Isa. 6:3). What did they see about God that led them to make such a declaration?

The seraphim were compelled to make the declaration of God's holiness on the basis of his entire character and all of his attributes. It is his divine perfection that causes them to humble themselves by covering their eyes and feet. They see God's utter uniqueness, that he is totally unlike any other thing, but even more they see that he is glorious in his uniqueness. As Moses declared in Exodus 15:11, "Who is like you, O LORD, among the gods? Who is like you, majestic in holiness, awesome in glorious deeds, doing wonders?" John Piper expresses this well:

> God is holy in His absolute uniqueness. Everything else belongs to a class. We are human; Rover is a dog; the oak is a tree; Earth is a planet; the Milky Way is one of a billion galaxies; Gabriel is an angel; Satan is a demon. But only God is God. And therefore He is holy, utterly different, distinct, unique. All else is creation. He alone creates. All else begins. He alone always was. All else depends. He alone is self-sufficient. And therefore the holiness of God is synonymous with His infinite value. His glory is the shining forth of His holiness. His holiness is His intrinsic worth—an utterly unique excellence.[2]

So it isn't just that God is absolutely unique, but his absolute uniqueness makes him supremely valuable. And all of this is meant to be conveyed in the word "holy." God's holiness is not simply one of

---

[2] John Piper, *Brothers, We Are Not Professionals* (Nashville: Broadman & Holman, 2002), 12-13.

many attributes; it is the beauty of all he is. So when we say God is holy, what we mean is that God is God, the only God.

This is our hope in the midst of suffering. There is no one more powerful. There is no one more loving. There is no one more merciful. There is no one more compassionate. There is no other God but God. He alone is Savior, and he alone is Lord. It is because God is holy that we can have confidence that he will fulfill his promises to us, that his power will be used to help us, that his mercy will be poured out on us, and that his wisdom will design our suffering and everything else in our lives to work together for our good.

After the death of our son Owen, my wife and I often had deep, haunting questions about God and his purposes. But any time we were tempted to turn away from him, we were always confronted with the question, "If not God, then who? If not God, then what?"

Could we abandon the truth and turn to some other religion? There is no hope for us there, for then we would have to save ourselves. Could we become atheists? There is no hope for us there, for then life would be futile. Could we turn to materialism? There is no hope for us there, for material things can't bring back our son, nor can they keep us from suffering in the future. There is no hope anywhere else because God alone is God and he alone is holy.

So in our suffering we cling to God in his holiness. And quite honestly, there are times when we cling to him simply because we see that there isn't anything else to hold on to. But I think this is okay. God *wants* us to see that there isn't anything else to cling to.

Where Is God in Our Pain?

But there is more hope for us, for it is because God is holy that he holds onto us. Isaiah writes:

> Fear not, for I have redeemed you; I have called you by name, you are mine. When you pass through the waters, I will be with you; and through the rivers, they shall not overwhelm you; when you walk through fire you shall not be burned, and the flame shall not consume you. For I am the LORD your God, the *Holy One* of Israel, your Savior." (Isa. 43:1-3)

God tells us that we need not fear. Why? Because he himself is the one who helps us. He is the one who holds our right hand and doesn't let go. Our Redeemer isn't just anyone. Our Redeemer is the Holy One of Israel. It is because God is holy that we can have confidence that he will fulfill his promises to us. If he isn't holy, he can make all the promises in the world and yet not have any intention or even ability to fulfill them. But he is holy, and therefore his promises are sure. When he says that he will never leave us nor forsake us, he means it. When he says that he works all things together for the good of those who love him, he does it.

Clinging to God in the Midst of Pain

Experiencing grief and pain is like falling off a cliff. Everything has been turned upside down, and we are no longer in control. As we fall, we see one *and only one* tree that is growing out from the rock face. So we grab hold of it and cling to it with all our might. This tree is our holy God. He alone can keep us from falling headfirst to our doom. There simply aren't any other trees to grab. So we cling to this tree (the holy God) with all our might.

But what we didn't realize is that when we fell and grabbed the tree our arm actually became entangled in the branches, so that in reality, the tree is holding us. We hold on to keep from falling, but what we don't realize is that we can't fall because the tree has us. We are safe. God, in his holiness, is keeping us and showing mercy to us. We may not be aware of it, but it is true. He is with us even in the deepest and darkest pit.

Conclusion

Indescribable pain and grief is normal, even for Christians; indeed, Peter tells us, "Beloved, do not be surprised at the fiery trial when it comes upon you to test you, as though something strange were happening to you" (1 Pet. 4:12). Our fears, anger, doubts, and everything else we feel in our pain don't make God nervous or uncomfortable with us. God still loves us, and he is still for us.

When we are in the pit of despair we must look around and see that only God can bring us out. There is no other hope. And what's more is that God himself is committed to bringing us out. He alone is holy and therefore he alone can help us. Yes, the night is long and the weeping intense, but the morning is coming. And as we wait for the coming dawn, the return of the Son of God, we can know that we are not alone. Jesus himself endured the long night of weeping, and God promises to carry us even when we don't feel his arms around us.

While we are on earth, there often will be deliverance from many of our sufferings—there will be many mornings that will dawn and bring with them joy. But the ultimate morning comes when Jesus returns. That is when the true shout for joy will come and when all tears will be wiped away (Rev. 21:4). "And the city [will have] no need of sun or moon to shine on it, for the glory of God [will give] it light, and its lamp [will be] the Lamb. . . . And night will be no more" (Rev. 21:23; 22:5).

CHAPTER 9

Hope . . . the Best of Things

JONI EARECKSON TADA

Sometimes hope is hard to come by. Like the other week when I visited my friend Gracie Sutherlin in the hospital. Gracie has been volunteering at our Joni and Friends Family Retreats for many years, and despite her age of sixty-one, she's always been energetic and active with the disabled children at our camps. All that changed a month ago when she broke her neck in a tragic accident. Gracie has always been happy and buoyant, but when I wheeled into the intensive care unit to visit her, I did not even recognize the woman lying in the hospital bed. With tubes running in and out of her, a ventilator shoved down her throat, and Crutchfield tongs screwed into her skull, Gracie looked completely helpless. She couldn't even breathe on her own. All she could do was open and close her eyes.

I sat there by Gracie's hospital bed. I read Scriptures to her. I sang to her: "Be still my soul, the Lord is on thy side." I leaned as far forward as I could and whispered, "Oh, Gracie, Gracie, remember. Hope is a good thing, maybe the best of things. And no good thing ever dies." She blinked at that point, and I knew she recognized the phrase. It's a line from the movie *The Shawshank Redemption*.

The Shawshank Redemption is a story about two men—Andy Dufresne, who is unjustly convicted and sentenced to life imprisonment, and his friend Red. After many hard years in prison, Andy opens up a path of promise for himself and for Red. One day in the prison yard, he instructs Red that if he is ever freed from Shawshank, he should go to a certain town and find a certain tree in a certain cornfield, to push aside the rocks to uncover a little tin can, and to use the money in the can to make it across the border to a little Mexican fishing village. Not long after this conversation, Andy escapes from prison and Red is paroled. Red, dutiful friend that he is, finds the cornfield, the tree, the rocks, the tin can, the money—and a letter, in which Andy has written, "Red, never forget. Hope is a good thing, maybe the best of things. And no good thing ever dies." At that moment, Red realizes he has two choices: "Get busy livin' or get busy dyin'."

Sadly, right now, it appears as though my friend Gracie is busy dying. She is stuck at UCLA waiting for surgery on her neck, and an infection in her body is running rampant. The doctors are trying to get her white blood cell count down, but it doesn't look promising. Now when visitors come in to see her, she shuts her eyes against them. *Oh, Gracie, hold onto hope. It's a good thing, maybe the best of things.*

Hope Is Hard to Come By

But hope is hard to come by. I should know. I remember the time when I was once busy dying. It wasn't long after I had broken my neck in a diving accident that I spent one particularly hopeless week in the hospital. I had endured long surgeries to shave down the bony prominences on my back, and it was a long recovery. I had lost a great deal of weight. And for almost three weeks I was forced to lie facedown on what's called a Stryker frame—a long, flat canvas sandwich where they put you faceup for three hours and then strap another piece of canvas on you and flip you facedown to lie there for another three hours.

Trapped facedown, staring at the floor hour after hour, my thoughts grew dark and hopeless. All I could think was, "Great, God. Way to go. I'm a brand-new Christian. This is the way you treat your new Christians? I'm young in the faith. I prayed for a closer walk with you. If this is your idea of an answer to prayer, I am never going to trust you with another prayer again. I can't believe that I have to lie facedown and do nothing but count the tiles on the floor on this stupid torture rack. I hate my existence." I asked the hospital staff to turn out the lights, close the blinds, close the door, and if anybody came in—visitor, parent, nurse—I just grunted. I justified it all. I rationalized that God shouldn't mind that I would be bitter—after all, I was paralyzed. And I didn't care how much joy was set before me. This was one cross I was not going to bear without a battle.

My thoughts got darker because no longer was my bitterness a tiny trickle. It had become a raging torrent, and in the middle of the night I would imagine God holding my sin up before my face and saying lovingly but firmly, "Joni, what are you going to do about this? What are you going to do about this attitude? It is wrong. This sin is wrong. Get rid of it." But I, hurting and stubborn, preferred my sins. I preferred my peevish, snide, small-minded, mean-spirited comments, grunting at people when they walked in or out, and letting food drool out of my mouth. Those were sins that I had made my own.

You know what it's like when you make sin your own. You housebreak it. You domesticate it. You shield it from the Spirit's scrutiny. I did not want to let go of the sick, strange comfort of my own misery.

So God gave me some help. About one week into that three-week stint of lying facedown, staring at the floor, waiting for my back to heal, I got hit with a bad case of the flu. And suddenly, not being able to move was peanuts compared to not being able to breathe. I was claustrophobic. I was suffering. I was gasping for breath. I could not move. All was hopeless. All was gone. I was falling backward, head over heels, down for the count, decimated.

And I broke. I thought, "I can't do this. I can't live this way. I would rather die than face this." Little did I realize that I was echoing the sentiments of the apostle Paul, who in 2 Corinthians 1:8 talks of being "so utterly burdened beyond [his] strength that [he] despaired of life itself." Indeed, he even had in his heart the sentence of death. "O God, I don't have the strength to face this. I would rather die. Help me." That was my prayer. That was my anguish.

God Can Raise Us Out of Hopelessness

That week a friend came to see me in the hospital while I was still facedown counting the tiles. She put a Bible on a little stool in front of me, and stuck my mouth stick in my mouth so that I could flip its pages, and my friend told me to turn to Psalm 18. There I read: "In my distress I called upon the LORD; to my God I cried for help. From his temple he heard my voice, and my cry to him reached his ears. Then the earth reeled and rocked. . . . Smoke went up from his nostrils. . . . He bowed the heavens and came down. . . . He sent from on high, he took me. . . . He rescued me"—and here's the best part—"because he delighted in me" (vv. 6-19).

I had prayed for God to help me. Little did I realize that God was parting heaven and earth, striking bolts of lightning, and thundering the foundations of the planet to reach down and rescue me because he delighted in me. He showed me in 2 Corinthians 1:9 that all this had happened so that I would "rely not on [myself] but on God who raises the dead." And that's all God was looking for. He wanted me to reckon myself dead—dead to sin—because if God can raise the dead, you'd better believe he could raise me out of my hopelessness. He would take it from there. And he has been doing the same for nearly four decades.

Meeting Suffering on God's Terms

Now don't be fooled—that was no isolated incident. I didn't just leave my desperation back there in the hospital. No, desperation is part of a quadriplegic's life each and every day. For me, suffering is still that jackhammer breaking apart my rocks of resistance every day. It's still the chisel that God is using to chip away at my self-sufficiency and my self-motivation and my self-consumption. Suffering is still that sheepdog snapping and barking at my heels, driving me down the road to Calvary where otherwise I do not want to go. My human nature, my flesh, does not want to endure hardship like a good soldier (2 Tim. 2:3) or follow Christ's example (1 Pet. 2:21) or welcome a trial as friend. No, my flesh does not want to rejoice in suffering (Rom. 5:3) or be holy as he is holy (1 Pet. 1:15). But it is at Calvary, at the cross, where I meet suffering on God's terms.

And it happens almost every morning. Please know that I am no expert at this wheelchair thing. I'm no professional at being a quadriplegic. There are so many mornings when I wake up and I can hear my girlfriend come to the front door to help me get out of bed and get ready for the day. She goes to the kitchen, turns on the water, and starts brewing coffee. I know that in a few moments she's going to come gliding into the bedroom, where she'll greet me with a happy, "Good morning!" And I am lying there with my eyes closed, thinking, "O God, I can't do this. I am so tired. I don't know how I'm going to make it to lunchtime. O God, I'm already thinking about how good it's going to feel when I get back to bed tonight and put my head on this pillow."

I'm sure you have felt that way at some point. Maybe you feel that way every morning. But Psalm 10:17 says, "O LORD, you hear the desire of the afflicted; you will strengthen their heart; you will incline your ear." "O God," I often pray in the morning, "God, I cannot do this. I cannot do this thing called quadriplegia. I have no resources for this. I have no strength for this—but you do. You've got resources. You've got strength. I can't do quadriplegia, but I can do all things through you as you strengthen me [Phil. 4:13]. I have no smile for this woman who's going to walk into my bedroom in a moment. She could be having coffee with another friend, but she's chosen to come here to help me get up. O God, please may I borrow your smile?"

And just as he promises, he hears the cry of the afflicted, and before even 7:30 in the morning he has sent joy straight from heaven. Then, when my girlfriend comes through the door with that steaming cup of coffee, I can greet her with a happy "Hello!" borrowed from God.

To this you, too, were called. To this *you* were called because Christ suffered for you, leaving *you* this kind of example that you should follow. He endured the cross for the joy that was set before him (Heb. 12:2). Should we expect to do less? So then, join me; boast in your afflictions. Delight in your infirmities. Glory in your weaknesses, for then you know that Christ's power rests in you (2 Cor. 12:9). You might be handicapped on all sides, but you're not crushed. You might be perplexed, but you're not in despair. You might be knocked down, but you're not knocked out. Because it says in 2 Corinthians 4:7-12 that every day we experience something of the death of the Lord Jesus Christ, so that in turn we might experience the power of the life of Jesus in these bodies of ours.

Do you know who the truly handicapped people are? They are the ones—and many of them are Christians—who hear the alarm clock go off at 7:30 in the morning, throw back the covers, jump out of bed, take a quick shower, choke down breakfast, and zoom out the front door. They do all this on automatic pilot without stopping once to acknowledge their Creator, their great God who gives them life and strength each day. Christian, if you live that way, do you know that James 4:6 says God opposes you? "God opposes the proud, but gives grace to the humble."

And who are the humble? They are people who are humiliated by their weaknesses. Catheterized people whose leg bags spring leaks on somebody else's brand-new carpet. Immobilized people who must be fed, cleansed, dressed, and taken care of like infants. Once-active people crippled by chronic aches and pains. God opposes the proud but gives grace to the humble, so then submit yourselves to God. Resist the devil, who loves nothing more than to discourage you and corrode your joy. Resist him and he will flee you. Draw near to God in your affliction, and he will draw near to you (James 4:6-8). Take up your cross daily and follow the Lord Jesus (Luke 9:23).

I must qualify that last statement. Please know that when I take up my cross every day I am not talking about my wheelchair. My wheelchair is not my cross to bear. Neither is your cane or walker your cross. Neither is your dead-end job or your irksome in-laws. Your cross to bear is not your migraine headaches, not your sinus infection, not your stiff joints. That is not your cross to bear. My cross is not my wheelchair; it is my attitude. Your cross is your attitude about your dead-end job and your in-laws. It is your attitude about your aches and pains. Any complaints, any grumblings, any disputings or murmurings, any anxieties, any worries, any resentments or anything that hints of a raging torrent of bitterness—these are the things God calls me to die to daily. For when I do, I not only become like him in his death (that is, taking up my cross and dying *to* the sin that he died *for* on his cross), but the power of the resurrection puts to death any doubts, fears, grumblings, and disputings. And I get to become like him in his life. I get to experience the intimate fellowship of sharing in his sufferings, the sweetness and the preciousness of the Savior. I become holy as he is holy. O God, "you will make me full of gladness with your presence" (Acts 2:28).

And to be in God's presence is to be holy. Not to be sinless, but to *sin less*. To let suffering sandblast you to the core, revealing the stuff of which you are made. And it's never pretty—the sin we housebreak and domesticate and try to make our own—is it? No. Suffering sandblasts that stuff, leaving us bare and falling head over heels, down for the count and decimated.

Meeting Joy on God's Terms

It is when your soul has been blasted bare, when you feel raw and undone, that you can be better bonded to the Savior. And then you not only meet suffering on God's terms, but you meet joy on God's terms. And then God—as he does every morning at 7:30 when I cry to him out of my affliction—happily shares his gladness, his joy flooding over heaven's walls filling my heart in a waterfall of delight, which then in turn always streams out to others in a flood of encouragement, and then erupts back to God in an ecstatic fountain of praise. He gets your heart pumping for heaven. He injects his peace, power, and perspective into your spiritual being. He imparts a new way of looking at your hardships. He puts a song in your heart.

I experienced this kind of elation last year when I was in Thailand. I am the senior disability representative with the Lausanne Committee for World Evangelization, and last year thirty-six disability ministry workers from around the world, most of them disabled themselves, gathered at the Lausanne conference in Thailand. There was a tall, beautiful African from Cameroon named Nungu Magdalene Manyi, a polio survivor who has made it her life's ambition to rescue other disabled infants who are left on riverbanks to starve to death because a disability is viewed as a curse or a bad omen by local witch doctors. Pastor Noel Fernández, blind, using his white cane, came all the way from Cuba. Therese Swinters, another polio survivor in a wheelchair, joined us from Belgium. There was Carminha Speirs from Portugal, walking with her crutches. There we came from around the world—thirty-six of us. And we were celebrating the kinds of things I've been talking about in this chapter—how when we boast in our affliction and glory in our weaknesses, God's power is poured out upon us.

By the end of the week, we happy people, our ragtag group of disabled individuals, looked around at this conference and saw that nobody else seemed to be having fun. The conference was a bit stuffy, as conferences can be when we rehearse theology *at* one another rather than live it *with* one another. Well, our group of thirty-six was having so much fun praising the Lord, our joy just spilled out of our workshop room. It flooded down the hallway. It spilled over the hotel mezzanine level. And before we knew it, there we were in this fancy resort hotel lobby, and we were a procession of praise, singing, "We are marching in the light of God, we are marching in the light of God." I wish you could have heard me singing and seen me dancing. Our procession of praise was an audiovisual display of 2 Corinthians 2:14-15: "Thanks be to God, who in Christ always leads us in triumphal procession, and through us spreads the fragrance of the knowledge of him everywhere."

You see, we are to God the fragrance of Christ. The world can't see Jesus endure suffering with grace because he's not here on earth, but you and I are. And we can fill up in our flesh what is lacking in his afflictions (Col. 1:24), and in so doing become that sweet fragrance, that perfume, that aroma of Christ to God. What a blessing, a privilege, an honor! What elation! And if I am to remind the Father of his precious Son who suffered, the apple of his eye turning brown with the rot of my sin; if I am to follow in his steps, then it is a gift to suffer alongside him, to take up my cross daily and follow him.

"Since therefore Christ suffered in the flesh, arm yourselves with the same way of thinking, for whoever has suffered in the flesh has ceased from sin" (1 Pet. 4:1). I'm so glad the apostle Peter included that, because without it we would look at suffering and think that it gives us cause for bitterness, worry, self-indulgence, or some other sin, because we have "earned it." But do not use your affliction as an excuse to sin. Rather, "whoever has suffered in the flesh has ceased from sin." So we can endure hardship like a good soldier (2 Tim. 2:3). We can welcome a trial as a friend. We can face the fiery ordeal that is about to set us ablaze (1 Pet. 4:12). We can rejoice in the hope of the glory of God (Rom. 5:2). Not only so, but we can rejoice in our sufferings because we know that suffering produces perseverance (Rom. 5:3).

Hope Never Disappoints

Tomorrow morning I will wake up, and I guarantee you I'm going to be tired, my neck is going to hurt, my back is going to ache, and I'm going to say, "O Lord God, I just cannot fly all the way across the ocean. O Lord, sixteen hours on a plane. I cannot do that. Jesus, I can't do that." But I will do it because suffering produces endurance, and endurance produces character, and character produces hope, and hope never, ever, ever disappoints us (Rom. 5:3-4). Nothing can disappoint us. Nothing can rob his joy in us, and nothing can rob our joy in him, neither height nor depth nor things to come nor things past nor muscular dystrophy nor osteogenesis imperfecta, not spinal cord injury, or multiple sclerosis (Rom. 8:39), for all things are yours (1 Cor. 3:21). For you are of Christ, and Christ is of God (1 Cor. 3:23). Therefore, you can be sorrowful yet always rejoicing; you can have nothing and yet possess everything (2 Cor. 6:10).

Passing on the Hope to Others

We are so rich. We've been given so much insight, so much knowledge. And to whom much is given, much shall be required; to whom much is entrusted, much shall be demanded (Luke 12:48). I may have a wheelchair, but there is a need for eighteen million wheelchairs around the world. So I cannot sit here in America on my backside and be content. No. Ken and I will head to Africa with our Wheels for the World team to deliver not only terrain-appropriate wheelchairs, but also Bibles, and to give the good news and to teach disability ministry training in churches and to let people there know that cerebral palsy is not a curse from a local witch doctor. We will shed the light of Jesus who always tells the truth—not only about redemption but about rickets, not only about the atonement but about autism. We will shine his light. The way I see it, I've been given so much, I must pass on the blessing. We simply must, must pass on the hope to others.

We must pass on the hope to people like Gracie, with her eyes shut in UCLA, at this point perhaps hoping that God will take her home before that operation. To people like her and to people like Beverly and Ron. Beverly is a woman who wrote me the following e-mail a while back:

> Dear Joni,
>   I'm out of hope. [But I am wondering if] you might be able to help my husband, Ron, who was in an accident last year.
>   My husband is a pastor. The accident left him a quadriplegic. When he came home from the hospital he continued to pastor from his wheelchair, but then two months later he was back in the hospital with an infection. And there have been many infections since then and many visits to the hospital. My husband, Ron, began to become depressed. He has now resigned from his church, and he does not get out of bed.

He does not talk. And if he answers a question, he only says, "I don't know."

I am at a loss. He does not want the lights on in his room and no TV. He does not want to live, and he does not care about our family. We have no medical insurance. We all seem to be falling through the cracks. My husband feels useless and hopeless. We need help.

How do you respond to something like that? Well, I responded by dialing 411 and tracking down Ron and Beverly's phone number. I gave them a call, Beverly answered, and I shared with her that I had received her e-mail. I talked and prayed with her over the phone. Finally I asked, "Any chance your husband, Ron, might want to talk to a fellow quadriplegic?" She was delighted that I was even interested. She knocked on his door, and he allowed her to tuck the phone receiver under his ear. And although he would not respond, I talked a little bit of shop about quadriplegia. I talked about urinary infections and bowel programs and difficulties breathing, and I thought I detected a grunt on the other end.

I wanted to move beyond those topics, however, and bridge the conversation to spiritual things. I thought, "This man's a pastor. Surely he knows the Word of God." So I started to share with him several favorite Scriptures that have sustained me through the toughest of times, for example, James 1:2-4 ("Count it all joy, my brothers, when you meet trials of various kinds, for you know that the testing of your faith produces steadfastness. And let steadfastness have its full effect, that you may be perfect and complete, lacking in nothing") and Romans 8:18 ("For I consider that the sufferings of this present time are not worth comparing with the glory that is to be revealed to us"). Still silence on the other end. I even sang to him. Nothing.

Finally I did the only thing I could think of that I hadn't already tried. I asked Ron if he had ever seen a movie called *The Shawshank Redemption*.

"Why, yes, I have," he said. I couldn't believe it. He had responded. So I went on, "Well, Ron, do you remember when Red found Andy Dufresne's letter? Do you remember what it said?"

"I . . . I think so. 'Hope is a good thing, maybe the best of things. And no good thing ever dies.'"

"Ron, there are ten thousand other quadriplegics like you and me across America, not to mention who knows how many beyond the borders of this country. And all of them were lying in bed this morning wondering whether or not they should get busy living or get busy dying. Ron, I'm going to make a choice to get busy living. Do you want to join me today?"

"Yes, ma'am. Yes, I do."

"Good for you, Ron, because now you're in the fellowship of sharing not only my suffering but Christ's sufferings. And he'll give you the grace one day at a time, one day at a time. Sufficient unto this day are the evil and the trials and the troubles that you're going to face."

He put his wife back on the phone, and I proceeded to tell her about our family retreats. I asked, "Beverly, do you think you could get your husband, Ron, to one of our family retreats?" I promised her that our office would provide scholarship money, which we always do to families who are struggling with medical expenses. And sure enough, that summer Ron and Beverly went to a Joni and Friends family retreat in Texas. Shortly after they returned home, I received another e-mail from Beverly:

> Dear Joni,
>   Ron asked me to be sure and write you because this past month has been wonderful. Camp was a huge blessing, and I don't think we realized how much of a blessing it was until we got home. We have made new friends for a lifetime. Ron wants to find things that he can do which will get him out of the house more. I told him that whenever he's ready we can hook up our camper to our truck and go minister so he can share his testimony all over the United States. For the first time in a year he did not say no. He grinned. Thank you. We have hope.

"Hope is a good thing, maybe the best of things. And no good thing ever dies." But we live in a dark, diseased world under the curse of sin. Hell is real. And God owes this utterly rebellious planet absolutely nothing. But aren't you glad that he is a God of love, not wanting anyone to perish? And he is out to convince this unbelieving, sarcastic, skeptical world of his power to save, his abilities to sustain, and his desire to share his hope.

Misery May Love Company but Joy Craves a Crowd

We have been given so much. Jesus said, "To you it has been given to know the secrets of the kingdom of heaven" (Matt. 13:11). And "everyone to whom much was given, of him much will be required, and from him to whom they entrusted much, they will demand the more" (Luke 12:48). God mandates that we go out into the streets and the alleys and the highways and the byways. He mandates that we find the poor, the blind, the disabled, and the lame, and help them get busy living, because misery might love company, but joy craves a crowd. And the Father and the Son and the Holy Spirit crave a crowd of joy, joy spilling over and splashing and filling the hearts of thirsty people in this world who are absolutely dehydrated from a lack of hope. They need help from God on high. The Father and the Son and the Holy Spirit's plan is to rescue humans. The Father is gathering a crowd, an inheritance that is pure and perfect and blameless, to join him in the river of joy and the whirlwind of pleasure. And he is heaven-bent on gathering glad and happy souls who will make it their eternal ambition to worship his Son in the joy of the Holy Spirit. God is love. And the wish of love is to drench with delight those who have stepped into the fellowship of sharing in his Son's suffering.

And soon, perhaps sooner than we think, the Father, the Son, and the Holy Spirit are going to get their wish. Perhaps sooner than we think, God will close the curtain on sin and suffering and disease and death, and we are going to step into the Niagara Falls that will be.

And one day I'm going to leave this wheelchair behind. I cannot wait. I may have suffered with Christ on earth, but one day in heaven I'm going to reign with him. I may have tasted the pains of living on this planet, but one day I'm going to eat from the tree of life in the pleasure of heaven, and it's all going to happen in the twinkling of an eye. The Lord's overcoming of this world will be the lifting of the curtain on our five senses, and we shall see him and we shall be like him, and we shall see the whole universe in plain sight.

I think at first the shock of the joy that will come from reveling in the waterfall of love and pleasure that is the Trinity may burn with a brilliant newness of being glorified, but in the next instant we will be at peace. We will be drenched with delight. We will feel at home as though it were always this way, as though we were born for such a place—because we were!

I will look up. And walking toward me will be my husband, Ken. I know he loves me on earth, but I am just a hint, an omen, a foreshadowing of the Joni that I'll be in heaven. And when he sees me he'll say, "So this is what I loved about you all those years on earth." And I will see Ron and Beverly striding toward me, their souls' capacities stretched because of suffering, stretched for joy and pleasure and worship and service in heaven. Their souls will be large and spacious because they chose to boast in their affliction rather than wallow in sadness and self-pity.

It is my prayer that Jesus will look at Gracie and he will say to her, "I know you. You came to me hemorrhaging human strength, and I felt power go out of me, and I touched you and gave you grace upon grace upon grace."

Romans 8:18 says that we can consider our present sufferings not worth comparing with the glory that will be revealed in us. I have shared this before, but I must say it again. For I sure hope I can bring this wheelchair to heaven. Now, I know that's not theologically correct. But I hope to bring it and put it in a little corner of heaven, and then in my new, perfect, glorified body, standing on grateful glorified legs, I'll stand next to my Savior, holding his nail-pierced hands. I'll say, "Thank you, Jesus," and he will know that I mean it, because he knows me. He'll recognize me from the fellowship we're now sharing in his sufferings. And I will say, "Jesus, do you see that wheelchair? You were right when you said that in this world we would have trouble, because that thing was a *lot* of trouble. But the weaker I was in that thing, the harder I leaned on you. And the harder I leaned on you, the stronger I discovered you to be. It never would have happened had you not given me the bruising of the blessing of that wheelchair."

Then the real ticker-tape parade of praise will begin. And all of earth will join in the party.

And at that point Christ will open up our eyes to the great fountain of joy in his heart for us beyond all that we ever experienced on earth. And when we're able to stop laughing and crying, the Lord Jesus really will wipe away our tears. I find it so poignant that finally at the point when I do have the use of my arms to wipe away my own tears, I won't have to, because God will.

Hope may well be the greatest of things, because Romans 5:2 says, "We rejoice in hope of the glory of God." I get so excited thinking about how Jesus and the Father and the Holy Spirit are anticipating on tiptoe that wonderful day when we, the bride of Christ, spotless and pure and blameless, will join them and swim with them in their river of pleasure. I rejoice in that hope—the hope of God's being glorified in himself and our getting a chance to join him. The hope we wait for is our only hope, the blessed hope, the glorious appearing of our great God and Savior, Jesus Christ (Titus 2:13). It is Jesus for whom we have prevailed through all of this suffering, and, oh, for the sweetness of melding one heart into his in that intimacy that is so precious.

Is hope *really* all that hard to come by? I don't think so. Our hope is for the Desire of the nations. Our hope is the Healer of broken hearts, the Friend of sinners, the God of all encouragement, the Father of all comfort, the Lord of all hope. And it is my prayer that the eyes of your heart might be enlightened so that you might know this hope to which he has called you.

Appendices

Don't Waste Your Cancer

John Piper and David Powlison

Five months after the Suffering and the Sovereignty of God conference, two of the speakers—John Piper and David Powlison—were diagnosed with prostate cancer. On the eve of his prostate surgery (February 13, 2006) John Piper wrote the following article to reflect on his situation and in order to minister grace and truth to others. (It should be noted that these reflections constitute one way to minister pastorally to those in need, but it's not the only way to do so, and it is not the only thing that needs to be said.) Shortly thereafter, David Powlison was diagnosed with prostate cancer (March 3, 2006), and he provided additional insights for this article.

John Piper:

> I believe in God's power to heal—by miracle and by medicine. I believe it is right and good to pray for both kinds of healing. Cancer is not wasted when it is healed by God. He gets the glory and that is why cancer exists. So not to pray for healing may waste your cancer. But healing is not God's plan for everyone. And there are many other ways to waste your cancer. I am praying for myself and for you that we will not waste this pain.

1. You will waste your cancer if you do not believe it is designed for you by God.

John Piper:

> It will not do to say that God only *uses* our cancer but does not design it. Not that his first design for creation was a Garden of Eden with cancer. But the fall did not take God off guard. He

was planning redemption before creation (2 Tim. 1:9). He saw it coming and permitted it. What God permits, he permits for a reason. And that reason is his design. If God foresees molecular developments becoming cancer, he can stop it or not. If he does not, he has a purpose. Since he is infinitely wise, it is right to call this purpose a design. Satan is real and causes many pleasures and pains. But he is not ultimate. So when he strikes Job with boils (Job 2:7), Job attributes it ultimately to God (2:10) and the inspired writer agrees: "They . . . comforted him for all the evil that the LORD had brought upon him" (42:11). If you don't believe your cancer is designed for you by God, you will waste it.

David Powlison:

Recognizing God's designing hand does not make you stoic or dishonest or artificially buoyant. Instead, the reality of his design elicits and channels your honest outcry to your one true Savior. God's design invites honest speech, rather than silencing us into resignation. Consider the honesty of the Psalms, of King Hezekiah (Isaiah 38), of Habakkuk 3. These people are bluntly, believingly honest because they know that God is God and set their hopes in him. Psalm 28 teaches you passionate, direct prayer to God. He must hear you. He will hear you. He will continue to work in you and your situation. This outcry comes from your sense of need for help (28:1-2). Then name your particular troubles to God (28:3-5). You are free to personalize with your own particulars. Often in life's "various trials" (James 1:2), what you face does not exactly map onto the particulars that David or Jesus faced, but the dynamic of faith is the same. Having cast your cares on him who cares for you, then voice your joy (Ps. 28:6-7): the God-given peace that is beyond understanding. Finally, because faith always works out into love, your personal need and joy will branch out into loving concern for others (28:8-9). Illness can sharpen your awareness of how thoroughly God has already and always been at work in every detail of your life.

*2. You will waste your cancer if you believe it is a curse
and not a gift.*

John Piper:

"There is therefore now no condemnation for those who are in
Christ Jesus" (Rom. 8:1). "Christ redeemed us from the curse
of the law by becoming a curse for us" (Gal. 3:13). "There is
no enchantment against Jacob, no divination against Israel"
(Num. 23:23). "The LORD God is a sun and shield; the LORD
bestows favor and honor. No good thing does he withhold from
those who walk uprightly" (Ps. 84:11).

David Powlison:

The blessing comes in what God does for us, with us, through us.
He brings his great and merciful redemption onto the stage of the
curse. Your cancer, in itself, is one of those ten thousand "shadows of death" (Ps. 23:4) that come upon each of us: all the
threats, losses, pains, incompletion, disappointment, evils. But in
his beloved children, our Father works a most kind good through
our most grievous losses: sometimes healing and restoring the
body (temporarily, until the resurrection of the dead to eternal
life), always sustaining and teaching us that we might know and
love him more simply. In the testing ground of evils, your faith
becomes deep and real, and your love becomes purposeful and
wise (James 1:2-5; 1 Pet. 1:3-9; Rom. 5:1-5; 8:18-39).

*3. You will waste your cancer if you seek comfort from your odds
rather than from God.*

John Piper:

The design of God in your cancer is not to train you in the ratio-
nalistic, human calculation of odds. The world gets comfort
from their odds. Not Christians. Some count their chariots (percentages of survival), and some count their horses (side effects
of treatment), but we trust in the name of the Lord our God (Ps.
20:7). God's design is clear from 2 Corinthians 1:9: "We felt

that we had received the sentence of death. But that was to make us rely not on ourselves but on God who raises the dead." The aim of God in our cancer (among a thousand other good things) is to knock props out from under our hearts so that we rely utterly on him.

David Powlison:

God himself is your comfort. He gives himself. The hymn "Be Still My Soul" (by Katerina von Schlegel) reckons the odds the right way: we are 100 percent certain to suffer, and Christ is 100 percent certain to meet us, to come for us, comfort us, and restore love's purest joys. The hymn "How Firm a Foundation" reckons the odds the same way: you are 100 percent certain to pass through grave distresses, and your Savior is 100 percent certain to "be with you, your troubles to bless, and sanctify to you your deepest distress." With God, you aren't playing percentages, but living within certainties.

4. You will waste your cancer if you refuse to think about death.

John Piper:

We will all die, if Jesus postpones his return. Not to think about what it will be like to leave this life and meet God is folly. Ecclesiastes 7:2 says, "It is better to go to the house of mourning [a funeral] than to go to the house of feasting, for this is the end of all mankind, and the living will lay it to heart." How can you lay it to heart if you won't think about it? Psalm 90:12 says, "Teach us to number our days that we may get a heart of wisdom." Numbering your days means thinking about how few there are and that they will end. How will you get a heart of wisdom if you refuse to think about this? What a waste, if we do not think about death.

David Powlison:

Paul describes the Holy Spirit as the unseen, inner "down payment" on the certainty of *life*. By faith, the Lord gives a sweet taste of the face-to-face reality of eternal life in the presence of our God and Christ. We might also say that cancer is one "down payment" on inevitable *death*, giving one bad taste of the reality of our mortality. Cancer is a signpost pointing to something far bigger: the last enemy that you must face. But Christ has defeated this last enemy (1 Corinthians 15). Death is swallowed up in victory. Cancer is merely one of the enemy's scouting parties, out on patrol. It has no final power if you are a child of the resurrection, so you can look it in the eye.

5. You will waste your cancer if you think that "beating" cancer means staying alive rather than cherishing Christ.

John Piper:

Satan's and God's designs in your cancer are not the same. Satan designs to destroy your love for Christ. God designs to deepen your love for Christ. Cancer does not win if you die. It wins if you fail to cherish Christ. God's design is to wean you off the breast of the world and feast you on the sufficiency of Christ. It is meant to help you say and feel, "I count everything as loss because of the surpassing worth of knowing Christ Jesus my Lord." And to know that therefore "To live is Christ, and to die is gain" (Phil. 3:8; 1:21).

David Powlison:

Cherishing Christ expresses the two core activities of faith: dire need and utter joy. Many psalms cry out in a "minor key": we cherish our Savior by needing him to save us from real troubles, real sins, real sufferings, real anguish. Many psalms sing out in a "major key": we cherish our Savior by delighting in him, loving him, thanking him for all his benefits to us, rejoicing that his salvation is the weightiest thing in the world and that he gets last say. And many psalms start out in one key and end up in the other. Cherishing Christ is not monochromatic; you live the whole spectrum of human experience with him. To "beat" cancer is to live knowing how your Father has compassion on his

beloved child, because he knows your frame, that you are but
dust. Jesus Christ is the way, the truth, and the life. To live is to
know him, whom to know is to love.

*6. You will waste your cancer if you spend too much time reading
about cancer and not enough time reading about God.*

John Piper:

It is not wrong to know about cancer. Ignorance is not a virtue.
But the lure to know more and more and the lack of zeal to
know God more and more is symptomatic of unbelief. Cancer
is meant to waken us to the reality of God. It is meant to put
feeling and force behind the command, "Let us know; let us
press on to know the LORD" (Hos. 6:3). It is meant to waken
us to the truth of Daniel 11:32, "The people who know their
God shall stand firm and take action." It is meant to make
unshakable, indestructible oak trees out of us: "His delight is
in the law of the LORD, and on his law he meditates day and
night. He is like a tree planted by streams of water that yields
its fruit in its season, and its leaf does not wither. In all that he
does, he prospers" (Ps. 1:2-3). What a waste of cancer if we
read day and night about cancer and not about God.

David Powlison:

What is so for your reading is also true for your conversations
with others. People will often express their care and concern by
inquiring about your health. That's good, but the conversation
easily gets stuck there. So tell them openly about your sickness,
seeking their prayers and counsel, but then change the direction
of the conversation by telling them what your God is faithfully
doing to sustain you with ten thousand mercies. Robert Murray
McCheyne wisely said, "For every one look at your sins, take
ten looks at Christ." He was countering our tendency to reverse
that 10:1 ratio by brooding over our failings and forgetting the
Lord of mercy. What McCheyne says about our sins we can
also apply to our sufferings. For every one sentence you say to

others about your cancer, say ten sentences about your God, and your hope, and what he is teaching you, and the small blessings of each day. For every hour you spend researching or discussing your cancer, spend ten hours researching and discussing and serving your Lord. Relate all that you are learning about cancer back to him and his purposes, and you won't become obsessed.

7. You will waste your cancer if you let it drive you into solitude instead of deepen your relationships with manifest affection.

John Piper:

When Epaphroditus brought the gifts to Paul sent by the Philippian church, he became ill and almost died. Paul tells the Philippians, "He has been longing for you all and has been distressed because you heard that he was ill" (Phil. 2:26). What an amazing response! It does not say *they* were distressed that he was ill, but that *he* was distressed because they *heard* he was ill. That is the kind of heart God is aiming to create with cancer: a deeply affectionate, caring heart for people. Don't waste your cancer by retreating into yourself.

David Powlison:

Our culture is terrified of facing death. It is obsessed with medicine. It idolizes youth, health, and energy. It tries to hide any signs of weakness or imperfection. You will bring huge blessing to others by living openly, believingly, and lovingly within your weaknesses. Paradoxically, moving out into relationships when you are hurting and weak will actually strengthen others. "One anothering" is a two-way street of generous giving and grateful receiving. Your need gives others an opportunity to love. And since love is always God's highest purpose in you, too, you will learn his finest and most joyous lessons as you find small ways to express concern for others even when you are most weak. A great, life-threatening weakness can prove amazingly freeing.

Nothing is left for you to do except to be loved by God and others, and to love God and others.

8. You will waste your cancer if you grieve as those who have no hope.

John Piper:

Paul used this phrase in relation to those whose loved ones had died: "We do not want you to be uninformed, brothers, about those who are asleep, that you may not grieve as others do who have no hope" (1 Thess. 4:13). There is a grief at death. Even for the believer who dies, there is temporary loss—loss of body, and loss of loved ones here, and loss of earthly ministry. But the grief is different—it is permeated with hope. "We would rather be away from the body and at home with the Lord" (2 Cor. 5:8). Don't waste your cancer grieving as those who don't have this hope.

David Powlison:

Show the world this different way of grieving. Paul said that he would have had "grief upon grief" if his friend Epaphroditus had died (Phil. 2:27). He had been grieving, feeling the painful weight of his friend's illness. He would have doubly grieved if his friend had died. But this loving, honest, God-oriented grief coexisted with "rejoice always" and "the peace of God that passes understanding" and "showing a genuine concern for your welfare" (Phil. 4:4, 7; 2:20). How on earth can heartache coexist with love, joy, peace, and an indestructible sense of life purpose? In the inner logic of faith, this makes perfect sense. In fact, because you have hope, you may feel the sufferings of this life more keenly: grief upon grief. In contrast, the grieving that has no hope often chooses denial or escape or busyness because it can't face reality without becoming distraught. In Christ, you know what's at stake, and so you keenly feel the wrong of this fallen world. You don't take pain and death for granted. You love what is good, and hate what is evil. After all, you follow in the image of "a man of sorrows, acquainted with grief" (Isa.

53:3). But this Jesus chose his cross willingly "for the joy set before him" (Heb. 12:2). He lived and died in hopes that all come true. His pain was not muted by denial or medication, nor was it tainted with despair, fear, or thrashing about for any straw of hope that might change his circumstances. Jesus' final promises overflow with the gladness of solid hope amid sorrows: "My joy will be in you, and your joy will be made full"; "Your grief will be turned to joy"; "No one will take your joy away from you"; "Ask, and you will receive, so that your joy will be made full"; "These things I speak in the world, so that they may have my joy made full in themselves" (selection from John 15–17).

9. You will waste your cancer if you treat sin as casually as before.

John Piper:

Are your besetting sins as attractive as they were before you had cancer? If so, you are wasting your cancer. Cancer is designed to destroy the appetite for sin. Pride, greed, lust, hatred, unforgiveness, impatience, laziness, procrastination—all these are the adversaries that cancer is meant to attack. Don't just think of battling *against* cancer. Also think of battling *with* cancer. All these things are worse enemies than cancer. Don't waste the power of cancer to crush these foes. Let the presence of eternity make the sins of time look as futile as they really are. "What does it profit a man if he gains the whole world and loses or forfeits himself?" (Luke 9:25).

David Powlison:

Suffering really is meant to wean you from sin and strengthen your faith. If you are God-less, then suffering magnifies sin. Will you become increasingly bitter, despairing, addictive, fearful, frenzied, avoidant, sentimental, or godless in how you go about life? Will you pretend it's business as usual? Will you come to terms with death on your terms only? But if you are God's, then suffering in Christ's hands will change you, always slowly, sometimes quickly. You will come to terms with life and death on his terms. He will gentle you, purify you, cleanse you of vanities. He will make you need him and love him. He will rearrange your priorities, so that first things come first more often. He will walk with you. Of course you'll fail at times, perhaps seized by irritability or brooding, escapism or fears. But he will always pick you up when you stumble. Your inner enemy—a moral cancer ten thousand times more deadly than your physical cancer—will be dying as you continue seeking and finding your Savior: "For your name's sake, O LORD, pardon my iniquity, for it is very great. Who is the man who fears the LORD? He will instruct him in the way he should choose" (Ps. 25:11-12).

10. You will waste your cancer if you fail to use it as a means of witness to the truth and glory of Christ.

John Piper:

Christians are never anywhere by divine accident. There are reasons for why we wind up where we do. Consider what Jesus said about painful, unplanned circumstances: "They will lay their hands on you and persecute you, delivering you up to the synagogues and prisons, and you will be brought before kings and governors for my name's sake. This will be your opportunity to bear witness" (Luke 21:12-13). So it is with cancer. This will be an opportunity to bear witness. Christ is infinitely worthy. Here is a golden opportunity to show that he is worth more than life. Don't waste it.

David Powlison:

Jesus is your life. He is the man before whom every knee will bow. He has defeated death once for all. He will finish what he has begun. Let your light so shine as you live in him, by him, through him, for him. One of the church's ancient hymns puts it this way:

Christ be with me, Christ within me,
Christ behind me, Christ before me,
Christ beside me, Christ to win me,
Christ to comfort and restore me.
Christ beneath me, Christ above me,
Christ in quiet, Christ in danger,
Christ in hearts of all that love me,
Christ in mouth of friend and stranger.[1]

In your cancer, you will need your brothers and sisters to witness to the truth and glory of Christ, to walk with you, to live out their faith beside you, to love you. And you can do the same with them and with all others, becoming the heart that loves with the love of Christ, the mouth filled with hope to both friends and strangers.

Remember you are not left alone. You will have the help you need. "My God will supply every need of yours according to his riches in glory in Christ Jesus" (Phil. 4:19).

---

[1] Cecil F. Alexander, "I Bind unto Myself Today" (1889).

An Interview with
John Piper

JOHN PIPER AND JUSTIN TAYLOR

October 7, 2005

The following interview is drawn from the transcript of an interview of John Piper by Justin Taylor, conducted on October 7, 2005.[1] In order to reflect the actual conversation, we have kept our edits to a minimum. All of the questions were unrehearsed and unbeknownst to John ahead of time, except for the question marked with an asterisk, which was added later for the purposes of this book.

Justin Taylor:

> Pastor John, you've become known as a champion of and a celebrator of God's control of all things. But I wonder if you always thought that way. Is it something you grew up thinking? Maybe you could tell us a little bit of your theological journey to get to this place—if you didn't start your journey believing in God's absolute sovereignty.

John Piper:

> No, I didn't start believing that way. The paradox is that my dad, Dr. Bill Piper—an evangelist all my life and still doing a little bit of evangelizing in the Shepherd Care Center where he lives with memory loss in Greenville, South Carolina—lived the sovereignty of God. I can remember his prayers always aimed at the glory of God, depending on the sovereignty of God. And

---

[1] Audio of this interview can be obtained from http://www.desiringGod.org.

he would use those words, and I remember them as a child. The other side of the paradox is that he would never, ever call himself a Calvinist, and to this day he thinks that's a very bad word to use.

The sticking point for my dad is the fact that in the Reformed tradition and understanding of Scripture the act of regeneration by the Holy Spirit precedes and enables faith, which I believe with all my heart is what the Bible teaches. But my dad doesn't. And we still get along well because I think he's totally inconsistent! He thinks it wrecks evangelism. So I grew up not knowing this was a tension, and, therefore, hearing and absorbing a lifestyle of radical dependence upon the sovereignty of God, and hearing, without knowing it, an articulation of theology not in sync with the life. (That's my assessment of what was happening.)

So when I went to college and began to hear people give a framework to this, I revolted against the sovereignty of God. That's not where I was theoretically in my head—though emotionally I think that's the way I would have responded to a tragedy even then. So from 1964 till about halfway through the 1968–69 school year at Fuller Seminary, I would have argued with anybody who believed what I believe today. I would have said, "No way. That cannot be the case with the Bible, and it cannot be the case philosophically."

When I arrived at Fuller Seminary, I took a class on systematic theology with James Morgan, who died of stomach cancer while I was there, and another with Dan Fuller on hermeneutics. And coming from both sides—theology and exegesis—I was feeling myself absolutely cornered by all the evidences of God's sovereignty in the Bible. And I can remember . . . maybe two little anecdotes.

I can remember standing outside the classroom one day, and I got in front of James Morgan. He was a very big man until he got cancer. He was just huge and a really great teacher, about thirty-six years old. And I can remember he had a big black armband, and he'd march in protest to the Vietnam war (this was 1968–69). He said, "I love Jesus, John Piper." He was teaching me all this stuff about the sovereignty of God. And I got in his face one day. I said, "Watch this, Morgan." And I dropped a pencil right in front of his face, and declared: "*I dropped it!*" That was my defense of free will.

The other anecdote occurred at the end of Dan Fuller's class after he had patiently pointed to the Bible and the Holy Spirit. I can remember going home after class. (This was before I was married. Noël and I were married in December 1968, and I took Dan Fuller's class that fall.) I would put my face in my hands in my room, and I would just cry because my world was coming apart. I just couldn't figure anything out. So I'm really patient and tender with people who struggle with this—I hope I am anyway. I give them a lot of space to move gradually to where God is taking them.

But at the end of James Morgan's theology class, I wrote in a blue book (this was back when we used blue books for final exams): "Romans 9 is like a tiger going around devouring free-willers like me." And it did. Romans 9 just held me until 1982 when I wrote *The Justification of God*[2]; I had to come to terms for myself and for my students when I was teaching at Bethel College. *What does Romans 9 really mean?* I had heard all the efforts to escape what seemed to be its plain meaning, and they never commended themselves. Even in scholarly ways they never commended themselves. So I would date my transition from a kind of unsophisticated believer—in terms of my autonomy and my self-determination—to a biblical vision of God's sovereignty over my life in his grace in the fall of '68 and on into '69.

Justin Taylor:

One more personal question before we get to some more theological questions. You and I were chatting on the phone earlier, and you mentioned that today is a very special day in your life. It's your mother's birthday today [October 7]. And if my math is right, she would have been eighty-seven?

---

[2] John Piper, *The Justification of God: An Exegetical and Theological Study of Romans 9:1-23*, 2nd edition (Grand Rapids, Mich.: Baker, 1993).

John Piper:

That's right.

Justin Taylor:

I wonder if you could tell us the significance of your mother and her birthday for this topic of suffering and the sovereignty of God.

John Piper:

The question is relevant because my mother was killed thirty-one years ago, when I was twenty-eight years old, in a bus accident in Israel. I chose not to build it into the message of this book—because I feel like I beat the drum too much sometimes. But it shows you how little I've suffered really. I've really not suffered very much, because this is the biggest loss I've ever had. I was twenty-eight years old and I lost my mother, and it was huge. To this day, if I choose, I can cry. I can choose to cry. I just think about a certain thing and I can cry. And I cried every day for six months when my mother died.

But here's the relevance for this context. I was twenty-eight years old. I was six years into my confidence in the total sovereignty of God. And as that phone call happened—many of you have gotten these phone calls too—it's a brother-in-law this time. And he said, "Johnny, I've got bad news. Are you ready?" "Yes." "Your mother was just killed in a bus wreck in Israel, and your dad may not make it." And I said, "Do you know any more?" He gave me what details he had. And as I hung up, my little two-year-old Karsten is pulling on my pant leg. "Daddy, sad? Daddy, sad?"

And I say to my wife, "Mother's dead, and Daddy may not make it. Just let me be alone for a while." I walked back to the bedroom and kneeled down by the bed and cried for two hours. I just heaved for two hours. And never once did I have any emotional anger at God. Never once did it occur to me I should somehow get upset about God. I simply thought, "If God cannot control the flight of a four-by-four flying through the front of a bus after a van hits it, I can't worship him." How can you worship a God who just fumbles the ball? He can't control a piece of lumber? That's not a God I'm going to worship. It is far easier to me to worship a God who is totally in control and offers me the mysterious hope *this is going to be good for you, for her, for your dad, for the cause of evangelism.* And I could tell you stories if we had time. I could tell you stories from my father of what that did for his ministry. He remarried a year later. I did the wedding. Now he's lost his second wife after twenty-five years. But what God did in his ministry . . .

I can remember riding with my daddy in the ambulance, with my mother in the hearse behind us. We were coming from Atlanta, Georgia to Greenville, South Carolina, and Daddy was crying on and off and saying, "Why was I spared? God must have something for me. God must have something for me." And I just sat and listened, and, oh, did God have something for him!

So I can see little teeny glimpses of what God was up to. I still would love to have my mother know my grandchildren. Believe me. I would *love* to have this woman influencing my children, her great-grandchildren—but that was not to be. I submit under that sovereign hand, and I believe in a God who was in total control and did what was best for her, best for me, best for my dad, even best for my sister, who, when looking into my mother's coffin upon its arrival from Israel ten days later, fainted onto the floor because the embalming situation wasn't so good.

Justin Taylor:

I think when a lot of us think about suffering—if we're not thinking about our personal lives—we're thinking about the persecuted church around the world. I recently read an article that quoted an unnamed underground Chinese church leader. And here's what he said, and I'd like to get your reaction to it. This was his word to us Americans: "Stop praying for persecution in China to end, for it is through persecution that the church has grown. We, in fact, are praying that the American church might taste the same persecution so revival would come to the American church like we have seen in China."[3] So when I read that quote, two questions emerged: (1) Should we *start* praying for persecution here? (2) And should we *stop* praying for persecution to end over there?

John Piper:

When I think of Hebrews 13:3—"Remember those who are in prison, as though you were in prison with them . . . since you also are in the body"—it seems like what the author is trying to say there is that you can imagine what it's like to have your hands tied down or to be tortured or beaten. And the Golden Rule would be *do unto others as you would have them do unto you*. Therefore, certainly go visit them, don't leave them without help, and imagine what you would want. And so I can't help but think that a good heart would long for anyone who is being hurt not to be hurt anymore. In fact, I think our churches should labor to relieve suffering in the world, especially eternal suffering.

It feels a little bit like presumption to me to dictate to God in my prayer the strategy of purification for the church, unless I am praying for a particular command in the Bible. God no doubt uses persecution to purify the church, and he may do that for us here. Here's the way I do it for myself—just for me, not the church: When I get on my knees and think about my struggles with pride or fear or greed or complacency or lack of love, what I say to God is, "Lord" (this is a really dangerous prayer, I think), "whatever it takes. Whatever it takes to break me of pride, of the fear of man, of greed, of cancer . . . if it takes loss of family, ministry—do it. I want to be holy. I want to be conformed to the image of Jesus Christ. Do whatever it takes." That feels biblical to me, whereas to tell him, "today what I

---

[3] Dan Wooding, "Chinese Christians Are Praying That Persecution Comes to the American Church," http://across.co.nz/PrayingforPersecution05.html (accessed March 9, 2006).

need is a car wreck" or "today what I need is more pain"—that seems presumptuous.

Nobody ever says, "I made my greatest advances in holiness on the happiest days of my life." Nobody says that. Everybody says, "I made my greatest advances in holiness on the hardest days of my life." Everybody talks that way. But once you've talked that way long enough and you want to be holy badly enough, then I can see why people would gravitate towards: "Give me some bad days. Give me more bad days." But I don't find it in the Bible, and I do find empathy in the Bible, and the Golden Rule in the Bible, and the danger of presumption in the Bible. And so I'm inclined not to encourage us to pray that way.

So when I think about China, I want to pray, "Cause the Word of God to run and triumph by whatever means you choose. Make the church grow. Same thing here. Whatever you have to do to purify the church, to make the church less oriented on things that are light and frivolous and fun, and more oriented on things that are weighty and glorious and beautiful and powerful, do whatever you have to do to raise up a powerful evangelical church." That feels more "let God be God" than the other.

Justin Taylor:

It seems like we could endure a lot of suffering if we just have the presence of God. But there's a form of suffering, as you know, that entails the seeming absence of God. And I think that's oftentimes the most painful—whether it's a health issue, or a child having cancer, or being stuck in a habitual sin and begging God with tears for repentance and crying day after day after day. What do you do when it seems like God is not near, and no matter what you do, he does not seem to answer? C. S. Lewis, in *A Grief Observed*, described it like this:

A door slammed in your face, and a sound of bolting and double bolting on the inside. After that, silence. You may as well turn away. The longer you wait, the more emphatic the silence will become. There are no lights in the windows. It might be an empty house. Was it ever inhabited? It seemed so once. . . .[4]

How do you counsel people in that sort of situation where it seems so dark and silent?

John Piper

That's a good way to ask the question, I think, because counsel is what's needed there among other things. And when you ask, "How do you counsel them?" I take that to mean "What demeanor should you have and what words should you speak?"

And I think the first demeanor you should have is to come alongside and to be honest about your own struggles and get your arm around them and be a partner and a helper. "I'm with you." "I'm alongside you." "I'm not above pushing you or squashing." "I'm around." That would be a how-to-counsel first, so that they have a sense that they're not alone in that kind of struggle.

Secondly, I would remind them of psalmists who seem to speak out of that kind of *How long, O Lord? How long?* I have retreated to Psalm 40 for myself and for people that I've counseled for years.

I waited patiently for the LORD; he inclined to me and heard my cry. He drew me up from the pit of destruction, out of the miry bog, and set my feet upon a rock, making my steps secure. He put a new song in my mouth, a song of praise to our God. Many will see and fear, and put their trust in the LORD. (vv. 1-3)

But it starts with "I waited," and thankfully it doesn't say a week, a month, a year. It's just open: "I waited patiently for the

---

[4] C. S. Lewis, *A Grief Observed* (New York: Bantam, 1961), 4-5.

LORD." So I would draw the person's attention to the fact that people that we know who are saints of God have walked through dark nights of the soul where they waited for God, meaning they must feel distant here. But instead of throwing in the towel on God, they're waiting. They're waiting.

Thirdly, depending on whether they're emotionally able to take this, I would begin to interpret for them their situation so that they can draw some conclusions other than the absence of God. That's *their* interpretation of what's going on. It's probably wrong. And therefore they are not in an emotional framework, or maybe a theological framework, to get it right. They're seeing a few circumstances—this went bad; this went bad; this went bad; I tried this and it didn't work—and now the conclusion must be that God is gone. That's not necessarily the only conclusion. So you analyze their situation, and then you show them from the Scripture that God wasn't gone in numerous times where people thought he was gone or it looked like he was gone.

One of the most helpful sequences in the Bible for me—and you all know this story and have used it the same way I have because you've walked through things—is Joseph in the Old Testament. I love to graph. One time I graphed the life of Joseph on paper. He's a star, and he's having dreams that he's going to be the king and be bowed down to someday. And he's above his brothers and he's not handling that very well, making enemies among his brothers.

So one day they throw him into a pit. And that's the first little downward spin on the graph. And after a while Reuben comes and pulls him up, and Joseph thinks, "Oh good, it's going to go better." The graph line of his life comes up a little bit, and then they sell him into slavery and there the graph goes down again. And in slavery he gets a job at Potiphar's house and that seems to go well; his boss has confidence, so there's a little upward jog in the graph. And then this woman tries to seduce him and he runs away from her, did what was right, and he goes into prison for it. There he goes down again. And a little while later he gets the confidence of the jailer and that seems hopeful; the graph goes up a bit. But these two people are there to say, "Tell us our dreams." And Joseph tells them their dreams and then he says, "Remember me when you come back to Pharaoh, Mr. Cupbearer." But the cupbearer forgets Joseph for two more years. And that's the bottom of the graph. That's thirteen years.

And you know what happens next. He gets made the vice-president of Egypt and it all turns out for good: "You meant it for evil but God meant it for good" (Gen. 50:20). And I ask people, where are you on your thirteen-year fall? You have been fighting this for thirteen years. Have you been abandoned for thirteen years? And they might have been, but not if they are Christians. Most people can locate themselves one year, two years, three years, four years, five years down this graph. I say, look, even though God had a plan for Joseph in his apparent abandonment, it looked like everything was going wrong. When Joseph tried to do his very best, it went wrong. But God was never against him. Never. As a Christian you're interpreting your situation wrongly if you think that. If you cast yourself on the Lord, if you trust him, if you love him, he's going to work everything together for your good, if it takes thirteen years or twenty-seven years. There are so many stories about how he has done this. And then you tell stories from your own life or people you know, or church history, and you try to help people interpret their life differently.

And the last thing I would say is—and this is true in virtually every counseling situation—ultimately we want to orient people on the cross. We want to get them to Calvary because in the end you can always look at Jesus hanging on the cross and ask, is that infinite worth not sufficient to cover my sin? Is it not sufficient to cover my problem? Is it not sufficient to give evidence that he will help me? Just fall there.

Justin, I know what you would ask me if you were a real skeptic and questioner. You would ask, "What if they say, 'I don't think I'm included'?"—which you should ask.

Justin Taylor:

What if they don't think they're included?

John Piper:

If you're a Calvinist you might ask, am I elect? If you're not a Calvinist you just might ask, is my faith authentic? It's the same kind of problem experienced at the same level. And the bottom-line answer to that is not a simple little "here it says, 'If you believe, you have the Holy Spirit.'" Have you believed? Yes. Where's the Holy Spirit? He's in my heart. That does not work. That simply does not work. That is so superficial, because the issue is, am I really believing? Because the Bible says there are going to be some people in the last day who are stunned when he says, "I never knew you; depart from me" (Matt. 7:23). They're going to think they were believing all the time, but they were not believing. So how do I know if I am believing? That's the kind of terror that will keep you awake at night and make life really hard. The bottom-line answer is: Look to Christ. Look to Christ. Look to Christ. Only in looking to Christ and the cross does Romans 8:16 powerfully happen. "The Spirit bears witness with our spirit that we are the children of God."

I can't give anybody assurance that they're truly saved. I can't give anybody assurance that they're elect. But God can. And it's a miracle. You pray for it and you wait for it, and you don't stand in front of the mirror looking endlessly into your soul with introspection. That comes periodically, but mainly you stand in front of the cross and you keep looking and looking and looking. And in looking you are saved.

Justin Taylor:

Just to add my own anecdote: Last year a farmer gave me an analogy. He told me that when a farmer is plowing his field and wants to make a straight line, he focuses his eyes upon a spot in the distance. The result is that the line is straight. But if he looks down and tries to see where he's going, he'll go off course. To put the cross at the center of our attention is exactly right.

For this next question, I'll tell you what the question is first and then I'll set it up. The question is: where is God? Everybody asks, where is God? Tsunamis come, 9/11 comes, Hurricane Katrina, etc. Personally—and perhaps it's because those are more abstract—I struggle less with the "where is God" question in some big natural catastrophe than I do with the issues like abuse, especially sexual abuse of children. And so I want to ask the "where is God" question, but I want to frame it by reading a quote from *The Brothers Karamazov*, which one person at least has said contains *the* greatest argument against God's existence and the problem of evil. So if you'll allow me here, I just want to read this quote and then ask you: where is God in this situation? This is from chapter 4, where Ivan is talking to Alyosha about Russian children. He says:

There was a little girl of five who was hated by her mother and father. . . .

This poor child of five was subjected to every possible torture by those cultivated parents. They beat her, thrashed her, kicked her for no reason till her body was one bruise. Then, they went to greater refinements of cruelty—shut her up all night in the cold and frost in a privy [outhouse], and because she didn't ask to be taken up at night (as though a child of five sleeping its angelic, sound sleep could be trained to wake and ask), they smeared her face and filled her mouth with excrement, and it was her mother, her mother did this. And that mother could sleep, hearing the poor child's groans!

Can you understand why a little creature, who can't even understand what's done to her, should beat her little aching heart with her tiny fist in the dark in the cold and weep her meek, unresentful tears to dear, kind God to protect her? Do you understand that, friend and brother, you pious and humble novice? Do you understand why this infamy must be and is permitted? Without it, I am told, man could not have existed on earth, for he could not have known good and evil. Why should he know that diabolic good and evil when it costs so much? Why the whole world of knowledge is not worth that child's prayer to dear, kind God![5]

So where is God in a situation of that kind of terrible torture of children and rape of children? Can one maintain idea that God is absolutely sovereign over all things with that kind of evil?

John Piper:

Yes. The question *where* is metaphorical and hardly has an answer. "On the throne of the universe preparing a place for the little girl in heaven that will recompense her ten-thousand-fold for everything she is experiencing." "Preparing hell for her parents so that justice will be done perfectly." And those who look upon both the heaven recompense and the hell recompense will bow in sovereign wonder at the justice of God. Those are possible answers to *where* he is.

But I think the nub of the issue is whether anything sufficiently good could come from a world in which that is ordained. I don't know whether this man is speaking for Dostoevsky or not. I don't remember it well enough. Does the speaker have a vision of God as the supreme value of the universe? It seems that when he says, "the whole world of knowledge is not worth that," he does not put the knowledge of God where the Bible puts the knowledge of God. The knowledge of God and his glory is the highest experience of man. And my own conviction—whether this will be a relief or whether it would be presumptuous to you—my own conviction is that because of the argument of Romans 1:19-22 and John 9 and a few others, all children who are born and die the way that little girl did, or in less horrible ways, are elect and will go to heaven.

You don't have to go to Dostoevsky. All you need to do is read about the dashing of the infants in the Old Testament ordained by God explicitly. I can draw some pictures of what

---

[5] Fyodor Dostoevsky, *The Brothers Karamazo*, chapter 4.

that looks like for some of you, and it would be worse than that. Therefore, this is not an external problem. This is a biblical problem. We have our God ordaining the dashing of infants against the stone. And the solution to that in my mind, to the degree that there is one for finite minds, is that those infants will be repaid ten-thousand-fold for the pain that they endured. The perpetrators will be punished appropriately. And this is likely the one that most of us don't think through enough; namely, the reason that such horrors exist in the physical realm and the moral realm is to display the outrage of sin. The outrage of sin against the holy God.

Let me see if I can help you feel what I'm saying here. When Adam and Eve fell by rebelling against God, God subjected the entire universe to corruption. You might say that's an overreaction. Well, if you bring your brain to the Bible and shape the Bible by your brain, that's what you're going to say. But if you let the Bible describe what's happening and shape your brain by the Bible, the conclusion you should draw is that sin is unfathomably outrageous. To turn your back on the living Creator God and prefer an apple to him is the ultimate outrage. It is infinitely outrageous. It deserves infinite punishment. And what God does in bringing the whole universe into subjection to futility—Romans 8:20—is to create a horrid parable of the outrage of moral evil. So that everywhere I look when I see outrageous physical evil—suffering—I want my response to be, "Oh how infinitely outrageous and repugnant is sin against the holy God." So I understand all the physical horrors of the world as symbolic of the horrors of the moral reality of sin against God.

Let me go a little step further. When Jesus died on the cross, you can come at that in one of two ways. You can say that not only was there Adam and Eve's sin, which was so evil it brought down the entire universe, but there have been in every one of us ten thousand of those sins. And multiply that by the number of people who have lived on the earth, or just take the church and multiply our sins—each one of which is no less grievous than choosing an apple over God—and therefore every sin that is committed should bring down the whole universe on our heads with physical horrors like this. And Jesus Christ hung on the cross and displayed the infinite value of God's worthiness to be treasured, not traded away. And now, stand and wonder at the value of the Son of God, that his suffering could match all of those universe-crushing sins for which he died. Or you could come at it from the side of Christ and see how gloriously supreme he is and how infinitely valuable he is, and then draw the conclusion about how terrible sin is.

What I'm saying in addition to those preliminary things is that every time we see something horrific, some horrible accident, our thoughts should be about the outrage of sin, not the injustice of God. These stories I've heard about people backing over their own children with their car. What would that mean? How would that feel—that bump, and you get out, and everything in you would scream. I knelt beside a man and put my arm around him about three weeks ago whose little girl was in the middle of Eleventh Avenue with a blue tarp over her. She had just walked across the road behind her dad. Hit. Got killed instantly right down the street from our house. And he just sat there staring at her. "I didn't mean to. I didn't mean to," he said. So we've all tasted this. And when we see the horrific things that happen in the world, what should we feel?

I think instead of calling God into question, we should see them as evidences in our lives of the outrage of our sin and the horrific evil and repugnance of sin to a holy God. And God is displaying to us the outrage of our sin in the only way that we can see it, because we don't get upset about our sinning. We only get upset about the hurt. How many of you lose sleep— well, some of you are good saints and you do—over your own fallenness? Most of us get bent out of shape about things that hurt our bodies, but it's our sins that are the ultimate outrage. So I think the kind of repugnance Dostoevsky is talking about is a display of how horrifically terrible our own sin is. And then Christ arrives, bears all that outrage, and by his own suffering undoes suffering. I want to summon people to Christ as the final solution to that problem.

Justin Taylor:

You just ended there talking about sin and our hearts as Christians. And probably the most famous sentence you have written is "God is most glorified in us when we are most satisfied in him." So God gets the glory through our happiness, our satisfaction in him. If that's the case—if God is so passionate about his glory and everything he does is about getting glory for his own name—then why do Christians sin so much? It would seem from a human point of view that at this point in my life, if I was this much holy God would be getting this much glory. I'm only this holy or this holy. So what's the correlation there? And what's the reason, do you think?

John Piper:

You are so right. My sin is my greatest burden. Why? Why? Why is the process of sanctification so slow? And the first answer is because I am so evil. But the comeback is: but God, your God, is sovereign. He can do whatever he wants. And if he's most glorified in us when we're most satisfied in him and he cares about his glory infinitely, why doesn't he advance your satisfaction in him, cut the roots of more sins, and therefore get more glory for himself more quickly? And that is an absolutely crucial question. And I have dealt with more people—I'm not sure if this is true but close—who are ready to give up their Christian faith precisely because of the slowness of their sanctification, rather than because of physical harm that's been brought to them or hurt that's come into their life. They're just tired. "I just can't fight it anymore. I can't succeed. I'm not making any progress. It just can't be real." So that is a horribly real and dangerous situation to be in.

Free will is a zero answer here, because at the last day in the twinkling of an eye at the last trumpet when Christ descends, he will with the snap of his finger make us holy. You will never sin again after the Second Coming, unless you're in hell. You will never sin again after your death, if you're a believer. So God at a point in time can sanctify you instantaneously—the spirits of just men made whole (Heb. 12:23). Therefore, if he wanted to, he could do it now without ruining this so-called free will. If he can do it at the end of your life so that you're perfect for eternity, he can do it now. And he doesn't do it.

This means I have more to learn. I try not to come to this Book, the Bible, now dictating, "That can't be. That's a stupid way to run the world." I try to go under this Book, and my mind just gets blown every day of my life almost. This is a mind-blowing book. You try to get your mind not around but just into this Book. Remember, Chesterton said something like: mad men try to get heaven into their head, and poets try to get their head into the heavens. I try to get my head into the heaven of this Book instead of trying to dictate to this Book how God should sanctify us.

Therefore, I draw this conclusion: "God, if you love your glory infinitely and you are more glorified in me when I am more satisfied in you, and my sin is being manifest by the slowness of my being satisfied in you totally, then it must be that the struggle that I'm having with my own sin will somehow in some way cause me to be more satisfied in you." Someday. And one way to conceive of it is this: I'll look back on my sin when I'm in heaven and say, "How could such grace have carried on with me?" and I'll love his grace more than I ever would have, had I made progress more quickly.

Now, that's a terribly dangerous thing to say because you're all going to go out and sin to beat the band now. You're all going to give up on your quest for holiness. You're all going to give up on trying to be satisfied in God. Don't do that. In other words, that would be again making your brain supreme and trying to tell this Book what to do. You don't bring your brain and say, Okay, I drew that logical inference and now I should live a life of sin that grace may abound. Let us sin that our satisfaction in you would abound in your grace. Paul said of people who think that way, "their condemnation is just" (Rom. 3:8). Therefore, do what the Bible says. Be perfect as your heavenly Father is perfect. And every day that you fail, be on your face giving thanks to the cross of Christ.

Justin Taylor:

So if God is sovereign over everything—from the rising and falling of nations, on the one hand, to the particles of dust in a sunbeam, on the other—then what is the motivation for us to effect change? In other words, if God is sovereign—if his purposes will be accomplished with or without us—then is there any necessity to our involvement?[6]

John Piper:

This is a crucial question for me because I have heard Christians say recently that believing in the sovereignty of God hinders Christians from working hard to eradicate diseases like malaria and tuberculosis and cancer and AIDS. They think the logic goes like this: If God sovereignly wills all things, including malaria, then we would be striving against God to invest millions of dollars to find a way to wipe it out.

That is not the logic the Bible teaches. And it is not what Calvinists have historically believed. In fact, lovers of God's sovereignty have been among the most aggressive scientists who have helped subdue creation and bring it under the dominion of man for his good—just like Psalm 8:6 says: "You have given him [man] dominion over the works of your hands; you have put all things under his feet."

The logic of the Bible says: Act according to God's "will of command," not according to his "will of decree." God's "will of decree" is whatever comes to pass. "If the Lord wills, we will live and do this or that" (James 4:15). God's "will of decree" ordained that his Son be betrayed, ridiculed, mocked, beaten, forsaken, pierced, and killed. But the Bible teaches us plainly that we should *not* betray, ridicule, mock, beat, forsake, pierce, or kill innocent people. That is God's "will of command." We

---

[6] See introductory paragraph.

do not look at the death of Jesus, clearly willed by God, and conclude that killing Jesus is good and that we should join the mockers. No.

In the same way, we do not look at the devastation of malaria or AIDS and conclude that we should join the ranks of the indifferent. No. "Love your neighbor" (Matt. 22:39) is God's will of command. "Do unto others as you would have them do unto you" (Matt. 7:12) is God's will of command. "If your enemy is hungry, feed him" (Rom. 12:20) is God's will of command. The disasters that God ordains are not aimed at paralyzing his people with indifference, but mobilizing them with compassion.

When Paul taught that the creation was subjected to futility (Rom. 8:20), he also taught that this subjection was "in hope that the creation itself will be set free from its bondage to decay and obtain the freedom of the glory of the children of God" (v. 21). There is no reason that Christians should not embrace this futility-lifting calling now. God will complete it in the age to come. But it is a good thing to conquer as much disease and suffering now in the name of Christ as we can.

In fact, I would wave the banner right now and call some of you to enter vocations of research that may be the means of undoing some of the great diseases of the world. This is not fighting against God. God is as much in charge of the research as he is of the disease. You can be an instrument in his hand. This may be the time appointed for the triumph that he wills to bring over the disease that he ordained. Don't try to read the mind of God from his mysterious decrees of calamity. Do what he says. And what he says is: "Do good to everyone" (Gal. 6:10).

Justin Taylor:

I think this will be the final question: What are you doing in your own life to prepare for suffering and death? And how do you counsel all of us here to prepare for suffering and death—whether we're in the final chapters of life or young people not knowing when the Lord will take us or what he will give us? How do you prepare for suffering and death?

John Piper:

I have a funny habit that I've mentioned before, and I've done it for the last three nights so I know the habit is still there: I can only sleep on my left side. I have no idea why. I wish it weren't the case because it gets achy. But if I try to sleep on my right side I just lie awake. So I'm always on the left side. So Noël is behind me, and I face the door. It seems like the manly thing to do! And as I'm lying there with my head on my pillow, I take my wrist and I catch my pulse. I can just see the alarm clock with its big, yellow numbers. And it doesn't have a second hand, so I have to count for a whole minute. And as soon as the six goes to seven—like 10:36 going to 10:37—I start counting: one, two, three, four. I count just to see what my sleeping pulse rate is. And when I'm done before I go to sleep I remind myself: *Anyone of those beats* [finger snap] *stop, and it's finished.* There's no reason this heart should keep beating, absolutely none, except God. If he wanted to, he could say to any one of those beats, "last beat," and I'm done. Will I wake up in heaven or in hell? I ask myself that.

And I walk myself through the gospel and I look at Jesus and I look at the cross, and I try to get as absolutely personal as I can. Nothing formal. Nothing mechanical. No forms. No sermons. Just picturing Jesus if this heart stopped—there I am face to face, either as Judge or Savior. And I say: Jesus, as much as it lies within me, you are my God. You are my Savior. You are my Lord. I renounce all reliance upon myself. I dedicate myself to you. I trust your blood wholly for my salvation. And I now commit myself to you for this night. If I should die before I wake, I pray the Lord my soul to take.

I would commend that as something to wake you up seriously to your mortality. But strategically the answer to your question is: "Be killing sin or it will be killing you" (John Owen). So set your sights to destroy any known sin in your life, lest you fall. "Let him who thinks that he stand take heed lest he fall" (1 Cor. 10:12).

Secondly, be in the Word of God every day seeking to see Christ as your treasure. I'm very intentional about the way I use this Book. I'm reading through the Bible with my typical Bible reading plan that most people have at the church.[7] But I'm on the lookout for God and for Christ, not just moral precepts; I'm on the lookout for God. *Show me your glory that I might be transformed from one degree of glory to the next* (2 Cor. 3:18). It is seeing the glories of Christ in the gospel. That's why I almost never stop my reading unless I catch a little bit of the Gospels, just to see Jesus functioning on planet Earth. So I look at him and I love him. I come away with something almost every day that is just stunning about Jesus that enables me to commune with him in an admiring, personal way because I just saw the way he was in the Bible.

And third, pray that God would preserve you and keep you in all suffering and in your dying hour. I frankly sometimes worry about dying. I've watched a lot of people die over twenty-five years in the pastorate. For some it's been so sweet, and for others it has been horrific. And some of the greatest saints experience the hardest dying. And therefore, I don't know what I'll do. And I assure myself, you get the ticket when you get on the train.

That's the way Corrie ten Boom described how the grace to die well arrives—on time, not before. She wondered, will I be able to endure the torture? And her dad said, "When you take the train do I give you the ticket three weeks ahead or do I give you the ticket when you get on the train?" And she said, "When I get on the train." "Well, God has a grace for you for your torture. He'll give it to you when the torture comes."

And I think that's very biblical because there's a correlation of Matthew 6:34 and Lamentations 3:23. "Sufficient to the day is the evil thereof." "His mercies are new every morning." So

---

[7] "The Discipleship Journal Reading Plan," available at http://www.navpress.com/Magazines/DJ/OriginalBibleReadingPlan.asp?opt=old (accessed March 12, 2006).

every day has its appointed trouble, including the day of your death; and every day has its appointed mercies for those troubles, no more. If you reach forward and bring tomorrow's troubles into today and say, Lord, give me the grace for tomorrow's troubles, he'll say, I will give you the grace for that tomorrow. But you have to have a mighty deep confidence that God's going to come through for you, and that's what faith is, I believe. And that's why we go to the Word.

I could list off a lot more means of grace that God has appointed. I think fasting and elements of voluntary self-denial are wise for American wimpy Christians who never endure any hardship at all and calculate their whole lives to avoid hardship. I think we ought to build into our lives some artificial hardships called fasting, self-denial. Take up your cross daily and follow me; he who denies himself will be my disciple (Luke 9:23). So that's just another means of grace.

The list of ways to prepare ourselves to suffer well goes on and on. Worship corporately with God's people. Be in a small group where you are exhorted regularly to stay close to Jesus. "Take care, brothers, lest there be in any of you an evil, unbelieving heart, leading you to fall away from the living God. But exhort one another every day, as long as it is called 'today,' that none of you may be hardened by the deceitfulness of sin" (Heb. 3:12-13). We are all vulnerable to drifting away from the living Christ if we don't have people in our lives getting in our face to tell us the truth about God when we can't see the truth, especially the truth that's uncomfortable to us. So stay in this Book mainly, because it will give you guidance in all of the preparations for your death and for your suffering that you need.

Justin Taylor:

Thank you very much for taking this hour. And I wonder if you would close in a word of prayer.

John Piper:

Incline our heart, O God, to your testimonies and not to getting gain (Ps. 119:36). And then open our eyes over the page that we may see wonderful things out of your law (Ps. 119:18). And then unite our heart to fear your name (Ps. 86:11). And then satisfy us in the morning with your steadfast love that we may rejoice and be glad in you all our days (Ps. 90:14). And then send us, O God, so satisfied in Christ that we count everything as rubbish compared to the surpassing value of knowing him (Phil. 3:8). And would you sever, O God, the roots of sin in our lives so that we are sold utterly to righteousness and love. And so make this people gathered here, I pray, the most radical risk-taking kinds of Christians in the cause of justice, in the cause of love, in the cause of missions, in the cause of evangelism that they can possibly be. I ask this in Jesus' name. Amen.

Subject Index

Person Index

Scripture Index

desiringGod

If you would like to explore further the vision of God and life presented in this book, we at Desiring God would love to serve you. We have thousands of resources to help you grow in your passion for Jesus Christ and help you spread that passion to others. At our website, www.desiringGod.org, you'll find almost everything John Piper has written and preached, including more than forty books. We've made over thirty years of his sermons available free online for you to read, listen to, download, and in some cases watch.

In addition, you can access hundreds of articles, find out where John Piper is speaking, learn about our conferences, and browse our online store. John Piper receives no royalties from the books he writes and no compensation from Desiring God. The funds are all reinvested into our gospel-spreading efforts. Desiring God also has a whatever-you-can-afford policy, designed for individuals with limited discretionary funds. If you'd like more information about this policy, please contact us at the address or phone number below. We exist to help you treasure Jesus Christ and his gospel above all things because he is most glorified in you when you are most satisfied in him. Let us know how we can serve you!

Desiring God
Post Office Box 2901 Minneapolis, Minnesota 55402
888.346.4700 mail@desiringGod.org